ABROAD

A Miscellany of English Travel Writing, 1700-1914

Books by Alan Wykes

NOVELS
Pursuit till Morning
The Music Sleeping
The Pen Friend
Happyland

LITERATURE
A Concise Survey of American Literature

BIOGRAPHY AND PROFILES
Snake Man
Nimrod Smith
Doctor Cardano
Hitler
Himmler
Goebbels
Heydrich
Lucrezia Borgia
Reading: Biography of a Town

TOPOGRAPHY
An Eye on the Thames

SOCIOLOGY
Gambling: A Definitive Study

HISTORY
1942: The Turning Point
*Air Atlantic: A History of Civil and
    Military Transatlantic Flying*
The Siege of Leningrad
The Nuremberg Rallies
The Royal Hampshire Regiment

ANTHOLOGY
A Sex by Themselves

COLLABORATIONS
The Brabazon Story (with Lord Brabazon of Tara)
Hunter's Tracks (with J. A. Hunter)
Mariner's Tale (with W. H. Scott-Shawe)
The Great Yacht Race (with Denys Rayner)

PLAY
Surrender at Noon

ABROAD

A Miscellany of English Travel Writing, 1700-1914

Compiled by
ALAN WYKES

MACDONALD·LONDON

Introduction and commentary © Alan Wykes, 1973

First published in Great Britain in 1973
by Macdonald & Jane's
St Giles House
49 Poland Street
London W 1

Made and printed in Great Britain by
Tonbridge Printers Ltd
Peach Hall Works, Tonbridge, Kent
ISBN 0 356 04568 4

for
NIKI
Nicola Russell
my god-daughter abroad

CONTENTS

LIST OF ILLUSTRATIONS

The illustrations opposite page 209 are from Archiv Gerstenberg; all
the others are from the Radio Times Hulton Picture Library.

ACKNOWLEDGEMENTS

My thanks to all who have, wittingly or unwittingly, put me on the track of sources that might otherwise have escaped me; also to ʾhe publisher's editor, Richard Johnson, who took boundless trouble with the presentation. The passages by Arnold Bennett and Somerset Maughan are repoduced by kind permission of A. P. Watt and Son.

AUTHOR'S NOTE

The dates given are in every case those of the editions used; likewise the spellings and punctuation, except that the long-tailed 's' has been replaced by the less quaint letter familiar to today's readers.

Introduction

A word about words.

Travel was originally 'travail' and meant – as it still does
with that spelling – 'bodily or mental labour or toil, especially of
a painful or oppressive nature; exertion; trouble; hardship;
suffering'. Nothing about pleasure. And even travel, thus spelt, is
defined bleakly as the 'act of travelling or journeying', or, as a
verb, 'to go round soliciting orders'. Again nothing about the
fulfilment of the spirit, curiosity, the excitement of unfamiliar
surroundings, or the amazement generated by marvels.

'Tour', 'to go in a circle or turn about', is equally old and
equally French. 'Tourist' is much more modern. *The Oxford
Dictionary* cautiously puts its first use at 1800. But the economist
Adam Smith had used it in the 1770s : 'The Grand Tourist,'
he remarked sourly, 'commonly returns home more conceited,
more unprincipled, more dissipated, and more incapable of any
serious application, either to study or to business, than he could
well have become in so short a time had he lived at home.'

Smith's spleen was vented less on travel as such as on the
impression created by the Macaronic dandies, with their ridiculous
wigs and effete manners, who set foot abroad because they
considered 'forreine wenches ached for them lustily' and all
Europe 'awaited their instruction in the courtesies of Englishmen
of position'. Only too often they had no position and few
courtesies.

Some two thousand years earlier, Plato had also expressed
disapproval of travel, though for more philosophic reasons. No

13

one under forty, he laid down, was in any circumstances to travel abroad. The over-forties might go, though only on ambassadorial missions. But even Platonic laws could not stifle the travel urge in people; and the English, being by temperament curious and by location well placed, proved to be explorers and discoverers of no mean accomplishment, as Richard Hakluyt so assiduously recorded in his anthology of exploration *Voyages* in the sixteenth century.

Not until the end of the seventeenth century, however, did travel for the sake of broadening the mind begin to assume such importance in the ordinary Englishman's life. Even that importance was at first largely superficial. The schoolboy translation of *Voici le jeune anglais avec son sang froid habituel* as 'Here comes the young Englishman with his usual bloody cold' had a vein of truth in it. Those who found the spas at Bath or Tunbridge unsuccessful in curing them of their climatic snivels and rheumatism ventured to Germany for more efficacious waters or to Italy for a sunnier aspect. There were fewer who went for the sake of seeing the wonders of the ancient world or the art treasures of the Renaissance.

Fewer, but a growing number. The aristocracy had sent their sons abroad for cultural advancement since the days of Elizabeth I. The Restoration and the Peace of Utrecht in 1713 stabilized political conditions in Europe to an extent that allowed commoners as well as noblemen to travel with less fear of getting caught up in wars and civil disturbances. Consequently, travel could be justified for pleasure as well as health. Catering for the wealthy Englishman and his family, aristocratic or not, became a promising commercial enterprise.

Even with Europe in a state of relative peace the pleasures of travel could be gained only at considerable hazard and expense. The roads were for the most part awful; even those who could afford a private carriage and a courier to make all arrangements found the experience no light matter; while those bound by economic necessity to the public transport of the diligence suffered the roads, the risks of highwaymen, and the foulness of the inns in even less comfort.

Nonetheless the idea of the 'tour' from one foreign city to
another for intellectual stimulation gradually seeped down the
social scale until it became part and parcel of conventional
education for the ordinary well-to-do English family. It was called
the Grand Tour, and by the middle of the eighteenth century had
assumed a tremendous social cachet.

Grand Tourists have left extensive records of their journeyings.
They confirm that many Britons were everlastingly, if
surreptitiously, looking for England – a trait the mainland
Europeans were happy to satisfy by learning the commercial bits
of the English language, calling inns by such encouraging names
as 'Hôtel d'Angleterre', and preparing 'le bifsteak'. Towns where
the *Edinburgh Review* or the *Gentleman's Magazine* could be
found had the edge on places that were indifferent to the
Englishman's nostalgia. Hazlitt said, famously, 'the rule for
travelling abroad is to take our common sense with us and leave
our prejudices behind'; but he was not typical, and in any case
much of his enjoyment of foreign places was dutiful rather than
genuine.

The grand inconveniences of the Grand Tour were by no
means limited to the discomforts of travel. Brigandage was not
the only form of roguery abroad. Couriers familiar with the post
roads and hotels knew their own value and the less honest played
on it accordingly. One of them, Silas Merewether, records the
profitable details of a year as a courier in France and Germany.
He made directly from fees paid by anxious tourists £423; from
hotel keepers to whom he took business £308 17s. 0d.; from
customs officials for tip-offs £12 10s. 3d.; from travellers whose
anxiety to avoid the customs was more valuable than the officials'
anxiety to detect their contraband £80 5s. 5d.; and from
'assembling ladys in the company of gentlemen wishing to know
them, in quiet places where they mayn't be seen, a good pannier
of French and other Forreine coyns'.

Easy money; and apparently easily extracted from those who
could afford to travel the relatively easy way – in spite of the
repeated adjurations of those who had been before 'not to spend

more money than is requisite with Decency and the Character of
an English Man'.

The Grand Tour took in other things besides the art and
architectural treasures of Florence, Milan and Rome. You could
enjoy the gaiety of Paris; shudder at the sinister freak shows of
Nuremburg; learn business methods from the remarkable Jewish
community of Vienna. There were also the great natural beauties:
the Bavarian forests, the Swiss mountains, the vistas of the Rhine.
Some influences were to be avoided: 'St Peter's is in its
proportions much to be admired', wrote a Mrs Bousquet in her
diary of her travels, 'but the Popish arrangements must be
shunned off;' other influences travelled in a circle with the
tourists and arrived back in England: the French composer
Lully's minuet and the South German ländler achieved immense
popularity in English ballrooms; Lord Burlington, one of the
most famous of the Grand Tourists, encouraged the English
architects of whom he was the patron to adopt the Palladian
style; housewives with an eye to cuisine were quick to appreciate
the value of pastas, truffles, globe artichokes.

By and large, though, the English mocked at continental
customs, loftily ignored the languages, and expressed distaste for
the food. But they rarely failed to get what they considered to be
value for their money. Including passport (two guineas), overland
fares at 1s. 6d. a mile (the Channel crossing was half a guinea),
lodging and food, and courier's fees, the Grand Tour, lasting the
best part of a year, cost not much less than £500. Therefore every
'sight' guide-book or recommendation offered must be taken in or
there would be a feeling of having been cheated. Thus, though
the travel of the day was by our reckoning snail-like, the
Englishman gained his reputation for hurry and bustle; also for
the mountains of luggage that might accompany him. Charles
Burney, famous for his *History of Music,* took with him on his
research journey to France and Italy in 1770, *inter alia,* bed
and linen, fine and rough clothes, two pistols, measuring
instruments and compass, palliatives for occasional sickness, an
'iron machine' for use on the inside of bedroom doors lacking

bolts or locks, and a multiplicity of journals and tablets for
recording his impressions.

Burney was a serious traveller with a professional purpose.
Those who toured merely to satisfy the convention might well go
less prepared and have to suffer additional inconvenience
accordingly. French beds were verminous, the food too rich for
English stomachs, robbers might murder one in one's hotel room
if they thought the prey worth while. Once determined to make
the tour for convention's sake, however, there was no denying
the indefatigability of the English. What they really needed was
some kind of honest and reliable courier organization to plan
and act for them in advance, relieving them of practical burdens
and allowing them to concentrate on the pleasurable and
profitable part of tourism. An enterprise to fill exactly those
needs was to come. But first there was a revolution in the
method of travel.

Macaulay (who appears in a less flattering light elsewhere in this
anthology) said he believed 'that of all inventions, the alphabet
and the printing press alone excepted, those inventions which
abridge distances have done most for the civilization of our
species'.

The prototype of the modern railway, the line from Liverpool
to Manchester, was opened in September 1830 and was a
spectacular success. It carried 71,951 passengers and 4,063 tons of
freight in its first three months of existence. By 1846 England
was riddled with 4,540 miles of railway track and the doom of
canal and coach traffic was certain. The doom of passengers
foolish enough to travel by steam train was also gloomily
prophesied : 'The terrifying speeds [30 miles an hour] cannot
but affect delicate lungs'; 'the movement of the trains will produce
apoplexy in those of a sanguinous disposition'; 'to pass through
cuttings and tunnels will occasion catarrhs and multiply agues'.
All the same, it was the passengers who multiplied rather than
the agues, and profits rocketed to heights as fantastic as the speed
of the trains. The Railway Age had begun and its steam

17

transport spread the doctrine of the Industrial Revolution.

The first continental railway was opened in 1835 and ran from Brussels to Malines. Macaulay, having pointed out the civilizing effect of 'abridging' distances, noted also that if the railway penetrated farther into Europe 'the Grand Tour as an object in itself will disappear.' That too was to some extent true. The hustling Englishman was now to have a chance of extending his itinerary at less cost and, as railway travel improved, at considerably less inconvenience. By 1842 the inclusive cost of the rail and cross-Channel journey from London to Paris had fallen to £2 19s. 6d. as against some £8 by diligence. International amity also gained a fillip : Prussia and Belgium were linked by rail in 1843 (representatives of the two countries shook hands across the boundaries to an accompaniment of military bands playing, inexplicably, *Rule, Britannia*); the Mont Cenis railway tunnel to link France and Italy was begun in 1857 and did away with the necessity for crossing the Alps on foot or sedan chair, or circumventing them by taking ship from Marseilles to Livorno. There was now every opportunity for the tourist to hustle more, see more, and cogitate even less than he had before on the philosophic aspects of travel.

It was at this time of potentially expensive tourism that the organizational genius of Thomas Cook entered upon the continental travel scene.

Cook was already known as an organizer of 'excursions' – trips based on a specially low price for a guaranteed number of trippers with a particular objective. His first had been successfully run on 5 July 1841, when he chartered a special train on the Midland Railway to take 570 fervent abstainers (he was one himself) to a temperance meeting at Loughborough, charging them a shilling each for the 24-mile return journey from Leicester. Other excursions to temperance and evangelical meetings followed and the Midland Railway Company quickly chipped in with an offer to make him their excursion agent with a percentage on all tickets sold.

Stern moralist though Cook was, he saw no evil in pleasure as such, particularly if it included 'contemplation of the beauties created by God and the historic works of man'. In these two categories Mount Ruabon and Liverpool respectively were included in a half-guinea round trip organized in 1845. He personally wrote and printed a special guide-book for the tour (he owned a small printing works that published *The Monthly Temperance Messenger*), and, rightly sensing that his unsophisticated tourists would be unfamiliar with the business of arranging their own accommodation, booked their hotel rooms in advance and issued them with coupons that had only to be presented on arrival.

Privately owned beauty spots also fell to the spur of his ceaseless energy. He persuaded both the Duke of Rutland and the Duke of Devonshire to allow him to organize conducted tours over their estates (thus anticipating the Stately Homes business by a century) and was never defeated by rebuffs. (When refused a concession by the Tyne Leith Steamship Company for a tour up the east coast of Scotland, where there were as yet no railways, he switched the route to Fleetwood and up the west coast to Ardrossan.)

By 1851 Cook was considering an organized tour across the Atlantic, where the foundation colonies of the British Dominion of Canada were already established and which thousands of emigrants were now crossing. He had in mind a tourist link with the already widening British Empire, which before the end of the century was to embrace two million square miles. But John Ellis, Chairman of the Midland Railway Company, foresaw a considerable loss of his company's profits if Cook was going to encourage his tourists to spend the bulk of their excursion fares on maritime travel and persuaded his excursion agent to arrange trips to the Great Exhibition instead.

'There, my dear Mr Cook,' he wrote, 'you have, in little, the Wealth and Beauty of all nations, without the need to set foot outside *terra firma*.'

Dissuaded for the time being from extending his activities

outside England, Cook immediately set up excursions to Hyde Park, where the Crystal Palace (so christened by *Punch* in denigration) housed the first international exhibition ever to be held. It was promoted by the Society of Arts and beneficently presided over by the Prince Consort. The Society of Arts' *raison d'être* was 'the union of art and commerce', and judging by the excruciating and perverted taste displayed in the manufacture and decoration of the hundreds of vulgar and useless exhibits it was a union unblessed. No matter : it was an attraction to buyers from all over the world and one of its aims was to be 'A Temple of Peace' (Christian pacificism not having yet been ousted by the Crimean war), which G. M. Trevelyan refers to in his *English Social History* as 'merely a foolish expedition to the Black Sea, made for no sufficient reason, because the English people were bored by peace'. (The exhibits of pacificism included a huge cast-steel gun from Krupps of Essen which gained one of the most substantial prizes 'for originality and purpose'.) Temples of Peace were very much Cook's cup of tea and the idea of Paxton's vast glasshouse with its thousands of examples of the world's manufactures was the cup of tea of multitudes of Britons. Cook shepherded 165,000 of them to Hyde Park during the five months the Great Exhibition was open and was steadily making £150,000 profit.

One of them, a Miss Laura Allardyce, visiting the exhibition with her parents, is enlightening about Cook's methods :

Papa and Mama were *very happy* on the journey, which was tedious in length but as comfortable as may be, for Mr Cook had provided an ingenious arrangement of long metal cylinders filled with hot water to fit along the floor of the coach. These were re-filled at the stops (I think from the locomotive machine) and none of us had to tolerate cold feet. At London we were welcomed by a *Guide* carrying Mr Cook's authority and then given the location of our lodgements. These in our case are of great convenience, for we are in Spring Street, Paddington, a very clean and stylish house with two very obliging and respectful servants who would be models for our Gwyneth to follow. From there to Hyde Park is a pleasing walk and the weather is fine. Crossing sweepers abound and it is scarce necessary to raise the hem of one's dress. We followed our Guide to the Exhibition and were put through the gates without bother, for all was settled beforehand as you know, and we were in an infinitely superior position to those who must wait in a *queue* for admission. One may spend time as one wishes, but one rarely moves far without seeing one of Mr Cook's *guides* who will give all manner of information and one of them calls regularly at all houses and places where visitors stay so that we may all be assembled for the return without mischance.

Cook's concern for the comfort and well-being of his tourists was based on his ability to identify himself with them and his remarkable business acumen in being able to anticipate their needs. His self-identification was perhaps not surprising : he came, after all, from the same respectable class as they; but he had done no travelling himself except as a foot-slogging evangelist, and there is no evidence that he had more than hearsay knowledge of the Grand Tour. Anticipating their problems was perhaps largely a matter of common sense; shaping the practical answers to these problems, however, required a persistence in gaining the attention of others and convincing them of the business possibilities of co-operation that in correspondence and interviews alone must have taken great slices of time from what were still his principal activities – evangelism and temperance. In that, though, he was typically Victorian in being able to find time for everything yet still live at a considerably slower pace than that of the twentieth century. He had the advantage, of course, of living in an era that was stuffed with commercial possibilities on which fortunes were to be founded; and few in that age of widening education and progress towards classless society would look sideways at any promising proposition. All the same, organization in the minutest detail required the same amount of trouble and time that it needs today – and without the benefit of modern mechanical devices.

Cook told his wife Marianne, 'There have been no signal failures in the tour to the Exhibition and therefore it might seem that there is little to be learnt; but there is as much to be learnt from success as from conspicuous failure, for success is *relative* and one cannot know how much *more* successful a thing should have been if one had concerned oneself more in this direction or in that.'

Two years later, in 1853, the Dublin Exhibition – on a very much smaller scale than the grand affair in Hyde Park – gave Cook his chance to set his tourists' feet aboard ship for a brief spell, though not very satisfyingly for him. 'This is but a country where English is understood if not very intelligibly spoken,' he wrote to Marianne. 'It is my desire that something much more should be done for those whose curiosity encloses other nations, other countryside, and such panoramas of architecture as are pleasing or remarkable and those works of art we know only from descriptions or copies.'

Thus Cook entered upon the continental travel scene.

It was yet another Exhibition – Paris 1855 – that afforded him the opportunity. This time he had to face rivalry. The Manchester Society of Arts arranged an excursion at a return fare of 13s. 9d. (the Foreign Office co-operated with the Society by issuing passports free); but Cook's return fare of £1 11s. offered much more comfortable railway accommodation and included the services of a doctor and a series of lectures on 'The Place of Machinery in the Art World', one of which was given during the Channel passage – with, apparently, remarkably sedative effects on the passengers' stomachs.

That first Paris International Exhibition was the foundation of Cook's continental business. People at home were becoming blasé about travel. The railways were getting a great deal of criticism, especially from *Punch* and its ilk. The Railway Joke, like the Mother-in-Law joke, was firmly established. (*Inspecting official to strapping lad of sixteen:* 'Come now, you cannot convince me you are at half fare because you are only twelve years old.' *Strapping lad:* 'Well, I was when the train started.') There was a growing conviction that only those who had crossed the Channel could take their place in society as conversationalists

22

in the drawing-rooms of the 1860s. Those who had experienced
the conducted tours of Mr Cook through France, Italy and
Switzerland – 'superb Switzerland with its scenic glories and
incomparable service', as his advertisements said – found much to
complain of on their return. One carping critic of the New Steyne
Hotel at Brighton told of :

A coffee-room ingeniously designed on the principle of an oven,
the windows not made to open; a dinner of yesterday's pease-soup
and the day before yesterday's cutlets; not an ounce of ice; and all
beverages – wine, water and beer – in exactly the state of the Church
of Laodicea.

Suddenly, too, tourists started ignoring the tunnels that had
been bored through the Alps at great expense for their
convenience and began to spread themselves about the mountains
like flies. Young ladies with the vapours born of ennui were told
gravely by their physicians – the same physicians who up to now
had prescribed nothing but rest and steamed fish – that 'the
mountain air and exercise are extremely beneficial and may be
purchased at the most moderate expense from Mr Cook's offices
in Fleet Street.' (Edward Whymper, though not exactly in the
same category, was set upon his mountaineering career by a
Cook's tour on which he had embarked for the sake of getting
scenic material for his wood engravings.) The English tourist had
become physically as well as spiritually indefatigable.

He was also becoming, like his pseudo-aristocratic ancestor,
the subject of growing criticism for his superficiality, his mania
for exercise, his inability to handle his own travel arrangements,
his gawping attitude to curiosities, his belief that he was being
'educated' by tearing about the continent armed with alpenstocks
and copies of Murray's guide-books. Cook answered such
criticisms in level tones in his magazine *The Tourist* :

Let me ask why anyone's susceptibilities should be outraged or his
refinement trampled on because thirty or forty Englishmen and
Englishwomen find it convenient to travel in the same train, to

coalesce for mutual benefit, to sojourn for a little time in the same cities.

Charles Lever, the British Vice-Consul at Spezia and clearly a man with underlying possibilities of nastiness, said the cities of Italy were 'deluged with these creatures'. He referred to them as 'dowdy, uncouth, tossed, crumpled and facetious'. He also told influential people in Spezia that many of the Cook's tourists were convicts who had been rejected by the Australian colonies and were being dumped in every Italian city. Some Italians seem to have taken this malicious lie seriously, and Cook found his tours impossible to arrange in many places. He tried to convince the Foreign Office of the damaging nature of the attack, but was met with stony indifference.

On a less malicious and more thoughtful – if also more pompous – note there was the theory that tourism was positively damaging to aesthetics and international relationships. This took up a great deal of space in the correspondence columns of *The Times*. Typically :

I say, Sir, that culture is now perishing in a vulgar scamper to the offices of a certain Mr C—, who conducts parties to foreign places under the guise of widening the horizons of their appreciation. My father was one who took the Grand Tour truly to enter into the lives of those other nations, and he enriched his culture by so doing. Today any flippetygibbet maidservant may put her foot outside the bounds of her Homeland and return filled with opinions of grossest error on the conditions of society. She shrieks these abroad in the streets, telling her betters that all Frenchmen are hottentots because their observance of the Sabbath is different from ours; that all Italians are greasy monsters because they use much oil in their cooking; that all Germans are liars; that the Swiss do nothing but yodel and make cuckoo clocks and the Norwegians are all libertines. They have heard of Mr Ruskin and perhaps peeped into one of his books and now scorn any notion about art that is not supported by him. They have met no one but the train guard, the customs official, Mr C—s' guide and the beggars who encumber the fountains of Rome. They know nothing of the peasant or agricultural condi-

tions that make up any of the societies they flit through in abominat-
ing trains. Nor do they absorb any of the intellectual content of
other nations. But they take the audacity to reproach all who have
done so by more studious means simply because they have been 'on
the continent' and believe themselves now to be diplomatic and
artistic judges ready to advise our Ambassadors very readily on what
should be done in any and every field. International relations are, I
say, being ruined by catchpenny methods. And have no doubt about
it, those who follow Mr C—'s vulgar banner will as soon follow the
banner of others who adopt the same principles.

'Pro Bono Publico' (as he naturally signed himself) was of
course saying very much the same as Adam Smith had said of
the members of the Macaroni club a century earlier. But he
missed making a point that had a certain validity : that the
British characteristic of insularity was paradoxically strengthened
by making travel easier. Suddenly the French were 'Froggies'
(not because of anything to do with their culinary arts but because
of the heraldic toad on the armorial shield of Paris), and similar
mildly abusive sobriquets were foisted on other European nations.
The diarists of the Grand Tour, who somewhat pathetically
revealed that what they really sought abroad was England, had
emerged again in a new generation, numerically as well as
umbilically stronger. Chauvinism, if not xenophobia, was to a
considerable extent nourished by tourism. (A century later
English nostalgia is being catered for by the standardized hotels
and the home-from-home encouragement of the 'English cuppa
served here with fish and chips' notices displayed by those
restaurateurs wishing to cash in on it.)
   As for those who broke Cook's monopoly of the tourist trade
and flaunted a similar 'vulgar banner' for proliferating tourists to
rally round, these came thick and fast upon the scene as Cook
proved himself even more successful in handling increasingly
complex arrangements. The Cyclists' Touring Club, Toynbee
Travellers' Club and Polytechnic Institute emphasized the
educational value of travel and backed the emphasis with
preparatory lectures and home study of the places to be visited.

Henry Lunn concentrated on members of the Nonconformist churches and later developed his lecture tours to Greece. There were agencies that specialized in matiness among the tourists and others that offered dignified exclusiveness. ('Ladies and gentlemen of the tour are not called upon to be guided in flocks : individual attention is given.') Indefatigable tourists found equally indefatigable organizers to encourage the increasing craze for travel.

Imperialism too was fostered by tourism. The millions of square miles of the widening British Empire were, until the organized tour, known only to emigrants, members of the armed forces and colonial service, and students of maps that symbolized in red the expanding bounds of Victoria's domain. But in 1886 Cook's son John had conducted the first American tour and this gave tourists their first glimpse across the border into colonial Canada. The English already had a firm foot in Egypt when a new kind of Cook's tour was planned for the Holy Land. It involved a fleet of boats being specially built for travel up the Nile and a portable city of tent accommodation, mules, field kitchens, and flocks of 'romantically attired' Arab servants. Thus the mysterious Orient seeped into the English tourist's portfolio and to his own way of thinking justified him in voicing strong opinions on the British occupation of Egypt when a naval force was sent in ('Damn it, Sir, send a gunboat !') to stop the rebellion in Alexandria in 1882. He could now claim to be a 'travelled' Imperialist who had seen more of the Queen Empress's empire than Victoria herself had seen.

In 1872, when Jules Verne's *Round the World in Eighty Days* was being serialized in a Paris paper, the first round-the-world tour was organized. Needless to say it was Cook who organized it. This circumnavigation was more leisurely than Verne's – it lasted close on a year – and embraced all the continents except Australia. Now Hong Kong, India, Singapore and Ceylon were added to the Imperialist globe-trotter's itinerary. For an inclusive 210 guineas he could be conducted by Thomas Cook personally into all but the farthest corners of the empire and return home bristling with tales about primitive conditions and complete lack of understanding of the British way of life.

'It must be drilled into the natives,' another Pro Bono Publico wrote to the *Morning Post*, 'that if they are to be honoured by British rule they must first attach themselves to us with the strong twine of language.' ('But never the twine shall meet,' *Punch* commented.) There was a great deal in similar tone about hygiene, religious and marital customs, and the dire effects of tropical climate. Something positively Teutonic seemed to emanate from these world tourists as they attempted to regiment 'subdued' nations into some sort of shape pleasing to the empire-builder's concept of empire.

There were also, though, floods of books and lectures on the marvels to be encountered. Rhapsodic descriptions of Indian feudal magnificence were given by speakers at every Literary and Mechanical Institute in the provinces. Teachers of Urdu claimed to be miraculously able to 'give the intending tourist a grounding in all the essential dialects of Her Majesty's Indian subjects within the space of 12 hourly lessons, thus facilitating ease of comprehension'. The newly established Army & Navy Stores had many calls upon their stock of lantern slides of 'oriental and exotic views' for the drawing-room entertainment of those unfortunates upon whom the joys of the tour were to be thrust. Mudie's circulating library reported an unprecedented demand for factual accounts of Empire travel and publishers were far from slow in satisfying it with scores of tenth-rate books by hack writers and memoirs and diaries by tourists anxious to cash in on the market. (Such things were the first to be discarded in selecting the extracts for this anthology.) Christmas cards depicting oddly un-Christian temples were popular among tourists who had chummed up on the voyage and were keeping in touch.

Thomas Cook himself had been commissioned to write a series of descriptive articles for *The Times* and the *Daily Mail* during the round-the-world tour, and these formed a basis for sober evaluation of the state of the Empire. Historians and

economists hastened to advise the government on the pacification
and suppression of the Boers and Zulus. The literal riches of the
earth in diamonds, gold and agricultural land were investigated
by prospectors. The mildest protests of the Indian races were put
down as 'seditious utterances' and dealt with in a manner that
in due course was indeed to lead to sedition. And one bewildered
correspondent asked :

Are we thus to rearrange and meddle simply because a hundred
tourists have touched upon the fringes of the Empire? Should we
not recall Benjamin Franklin's wise remark that 'A great Empire,
like a great cake, is most easily diminished at the edges?' It is
disturbing that a pleasure cruise should prompt so much that is
dangerous.

All such solemnity, however, was restricted to a very small
section of sobersides. The great mass of people had no leaning
towards empire-building or empire-ruling. It was simply a
pell-mell event in which they participated but over which they
had no control.

They continued, however, to 'Follow the Man From Cook's',
as a popular musical-comedy hit was to tell them. And at the turn
of the century there was scarcely a place of any interest that was
not open to them with a minimum of effort. Thomas Cook died in
1892, but his son and three grandsons went on developing the
business into a travel organization that could, and did, arrange
pilgrimages to Mecca, safari tours involving the transportation
of hundreds of elephants across the provinces of Indian princes,
and the immediate erection of veritable 'towns' of hostels in
places where the existing townships were too primitive. There
was a world-wide foreign exchange system which obviated all
the troubles of letters of introduction and bankers' letters of
credit. And the Army & Navy or Civil Service Stores would
supply them with travel equipment to meet every conceivable
need other than the guide-books and tourist accessories sold in
Cook's palatial premises in Ludgate Circus.

There was not in fact a great amount of equipment needed

by the brash tourist of the new century. After all, Cook's – and
by now, of course, the many other travel organizations – had
gone into business to take the load of travel problems off the
tourist's shoulders. As early as the 1850s Cook had included in
the overall price of an excursion 'on request' an 'unspillable ink
bottle' for the benefit of those who wished to send a postcard
from the journey's end terminus announcing safe arrival. And
with his customary thoroughness he tried to anticipate the minor
as well as the major needs of his tourists. (Miss Allardyce's
footwarmer might be said to have been a necessity in those days
of unheated trains.) As photography developed he would arrange
for the conveyance of the photographer's clumsy equipment.
Entomologists hoping for rare specimens were provided with
killing-bottles. When it was advantageous to tourism he bought,
like any modern Texan oil millionaire, whatever would serve his
purpose, however great the price. For example, it was simpler
and cheaper for him to control the continental sleeping-car
system of Wagons-Lit and the Mount Vesuvius Railway by
purchase than by royalty or commission. So he bought them.

The beginning of the twentieth century saw the firm acceptance
by employers of the idea of holidays with pay. The Victorian
notion that a man should be paid well for the time he was at
work and lose time for holidays had come under fire, not from
Working Men's Associations (the early form of trade union) but
from the employers themselves. 'The head of a Bristol firm,'
says J. A. R. Pimlott in *Englishman's Holiday,* 'announcing the
grant of a week's holiday with pay in 1889, expressed the hope
on behalf of the firm that it would materially contribute to the
health and happiness of the workpeople, and there is no reason
to doubt that there was an element of genuine philanthropy in the
new attitude.'

This psychologically sound condition of employment naturally
produced an explosion in the tourist agency business. As the
minor wars of South Africa and the skirmishes on the borders
receded into memory, and the tremendous advances in

steamship travel brought even the remotest corners of the
Antipodes within a six weeks' journey from England, the
temptation to 'see the world' was more than could be resisted.
Such lengthy tours were by their very time scheme beyond the
one-week-with-pay employees; but there was no dearth of
applicants from the retired employing classes.

'I look forward to my retirement and a journey under
the auspices of the excellent Cooks to soothe me for my eternal
rest.' Thus the owner of a profitable Warrington brewery in
1910. He could take his choice, for the £1,000 he wanted to
spend (prices were steadily advancing), of a luxurious world tour
offering him 'contemplation of all the ancient wonders of the
world and an insight into the disposition of the King Emperor's
colonial possessions', or concentrate on the Empire alone 'visiting
every major city in His Majesty's Dominions and seeing for
himself the remarkable development of Australia with its
extensive sheep and cattle farms, the strange contrasts of India,
the primitive loyalties of the Africans and Maoris . . .' *et cetera.*

He could also, if he wanted to be different and rather more
snobbish, visit the new playground of Europe, the Riviera, and
against a background of supposed moral laxity spend his days
in the casinos and his nights in the sumptuous surroundings of
the hotels where the highest grade entertainers would appear
before him – almost certainly including Seymour Hicks and the
song 'Follow the Man From Cook's'.

Nor was there any diminution of interest in the Alpine tour.
An earlier tourist, Frederick Harrison, had warbled with joy
about the Swiss 'elixir of life . . . revelation . . . religion' and had
written, somewhat embarrassingly, that he 'was carried out of
all good sense and self-control by the fascination of this new
transcendant world. I deserted my friends and comrades, I raced
about the crags and rattled down the snow glissades, tramped
through the night, rose to see the dawn in midsummer, and
behaved like a youth in a state of delirium, for to know, to feel, to
understand the Alps is to know, to feel, to understand the entirety
of humanity. The Alps are international, European,

humanitarian.' Up to the time of the First World War something
of this whooping dottiness seems to have infected sufficient tourists
to need 168,625 beds in nearly 2,000 inns; but then suddenly a
new attraction, skiing, put Scandinavia far more firmly on the
tourist map than it had ever been before. The brochures of the
travel agencies coined the phrase 'Land of the Midnight Sun'
and the beautiful, blond Nordic people became a must for the
visitations of the tourist.

Here in his heyday, then, before the lamps went out all over
Europe, the Englishman abroad had become a distinctive type.
He was caricatured and taunted and because he had proliferated
into every stratum of the social scale – the day tripper to
Folkestone was just as much a tourist as the man on the
Mediterranean cruise – there were definite opportunities to mock
his habits. With his loud clothes and demands for attention he
faintly echoed the Macaroni. But now it was not a superior
being who was mocking him. His own words – thousands of
them written across more than two centuries, plus the words of
other nationalities who encouraged him to their shores – stood in
evidence. There was the Englishman abroad – warts, graces and
all. I hope the selection of such recorded evidence that I have
made here adds up to a recognizable portrait.

1. *Blandishments*

In the matter of language it is always best to go to a little more trouble and learn the exact equivalent if possible. 'I am an Englishman and require instant attention to the damage done to my solar topee' is far better than any equivocation that may be meant well but will gain little respect.

Guide to the Native Languages of Africa
by 'A Gentleman of Experience', 1890

Français and Anglais both spoken in this restaurant. Choose the side of the menu that is your native tongue.
Deep Apple Pie   Tarte aux pommes Profondes

Menu in a Quebec restaurant circa 1912

An attenuation is often understood better than a circumlocution.
Exempli gratia:
'Why is there no marmalade available?' is better understood in the form 'Quelle marmalade non?' 'Bring marmalade' may be simply rendered as 'Marmalade demandez' always remembering that the z is silent as in 'deman*day*'. The little English joke about jam may be easily translated if one wishes to amuse the proprietor: 'Hier, marmalade; demain, marmalade; mais jamais marmalade de jour.' Such little pleasantries are often appreciated.

French for the English by 'A Gentleman of
Quality', 1894

The blandishments presented to potential tourists were numerous
and varied – as indeed they still are. They came from official
handbooks sponsored by the progenitors of government tourist
bureaux, from hoteliers and shopkeepers, and of course from
other travellers who reported on what they'd seen and enjoyed.
The examples here carry their own alluring messages; but
it is as well to point out that, odd though it may seem, the
flat-footed statistics and solemn revelations of the *Guide to the
Great Siberian Railway* were intended to encourage the English.
The *Guide* was published in 1900 and translated by a Miss
L. Kúkol-Yasnopólsky to gain the attention of tourists and
businessmen who had hitherto, perhaps understandably,
neglected the enchantments of the Siberian steppes.

More obviously encouraging attractions such as flushing
lavatories, wholesome air, and courtesy in customs offices were
set forth in many books and written of in countless letters to
friends and relations at home; and the Victorians no doubt found
much to look forward to in such promised philosophical pleasure
as contemplating the contemplation of happiness in the benevolent
institutions of Charles Dickens's Massachusetts. Also, since
familiar things were in themselves an encouragement to venture
abroad, many advertisers in the guide-books offered reassurance
on the ready availability of patent medicines and cosmetics.
People had been put off before by the thought that their favourite
placebos might be unobtainable across the Channel.

However misguided some of them may seem, then – like the
bleak mention of the swamps of Chórnaya, or the reference to
the liability of Russian villages to have bells left in them
overnight – there is an allurement about these extracts that at
worst aroused interest and at best yearning – as in Ford's
panegyric on the climate of southern Spain, and the romantic
picture of Tahiti evoked by Dumas and used by a French
shipping line in a brochure to encourage English tourists to visit
Polynesia. For it was believed, not without reason, that those
insular English needed encouragement.

*   *   *

HE TALKED with an uncommon animation of travelling into distant countries; that the mind was enlarged by it, and that an acquisition of dignity of character was derived from it. He expressed a particular enthusiasm with respect to visiting the wall of China. I caught it for the moment, and said I really believe I should go and see the wall of China, had I not children, of whom it was my duty to take care. 'Sir,' said he, 'by doing so, you would do what would be of importance in raising your children to eminence. There would be a lustre reflected upon them from your spirit and curiosity. They would be at all times regarded as the children of a man who had gone to view the wall of China – I am serious, Sir.'

JAMES BOSWELL, *Tour to the Hebrides*, 1785

*

THE SUPERIORITY of the climate of the South of Spain over all other regions of Europe, which was pointed out in our former editions, is now ratified in the able and practical treatise of Dr Francis, the 'Clark of Spain', and the first to grapple professionally, after much personal experience and examination, with this hygienic subject. Fair Italy, with her classical prestige, her Catholic associations, her infinite civilization, and ready access, has long been the land of promise to our travellers expatriated in search of health. But the steam and rail of England have now annihilated time and space, and her pen has pioneered the path to distant Spain, and dissipated the delusions and dangers of banditti and garlic. Independently of a more southern latitude, the geometrical configuration of Spain is superior; while the *Apennines,* the backbone of Italy, stretching N. to S., offer no barrier to northern cold, the *sierras* of Spain, running E. and W., afford complete shelter to the littoral strips. Again, where the skiey influences of Italy are enervating and depressing, the climate of the Peninsula is bracing and exhilarating. Free as a whole from malaria, *dryness* is the emphatic quality of the climate. *Malaga* justly may be pronounced the most favoured winter residence in Europe, and claims to be the real Elysian fields – *pace* those of Paris and Naples.

As Spain itself is a conglomeration of elevated mountains, the treeless, denuded interior, scorching and calcined in summer, keen, cold and wind-blown in winter, is prejudicial to the invalid; the hygienic characteristics of the maritime coasts to the W. from Vigo to San-Sebastian, are soothing and sedative – a relaxing influence prevailing as the French frontier is approached; the strip to the E., from Barcelona to Cadiz, is more bracing and exhilarating; midway, in Murcia, occur the driest regions in Europe, with Malaga for the happy medium.

The benefits derived by well-timed change of climate in cases of consumption, dyspepsia, bronchitis, and chronic complaints, the climacteric failure of *vis vitæ*, and the vivifying influence on the health of mind and body – reoxygenated, as it were – are matters of fact. The stimulus of glowing light, and the effect of warm and constant sunshine on surfaces chilled by the wet blanket of fog and cloud, works wonders. The insensible transpiration proceeds constantly; the skin then does its work to the relief of the internal organs. The water drunk in Spain, where – in the warmer portions – diabetes and dropsy are little known, is deliciously pure. The wines of the south especially – Malaga and Manzanilla – are dry, cheap, and wholesome. The *cuisine*, in a country where people eat to live, not live to eat, will indeed keep body and soul together, but will tempt no weak and wearied '*stomach*' to repletion. The peptic benefits of climate on the natives are evident by the way they digest an oil, vinegar, and vegetable diet, and survive chocolate, sweetmeats, and bile-creating compounds. The *sustaining* effect is proved by the untiring activity of the very under-fed masses, where many seem to live on air, like chamelions. How strong are Spanish lungs – *teste* their songs – and how few are their winter-coughs – *teste* their churches! – The *brain*, again, in a land of *No se sabe*, and where there is no reading public, no hourly penny-post or *Times*, is left in comparative rest – rare boons these for the two organs that have the least holiday under the mental and physical toil entailed by our over-refined civilization. The very dullness of Malaga – prose is the tutelar of Spanish towns – benefits the invalid. There are no wearying aesthetic lions to be encountered – no Madame Starké to be *'done'* – no marble-floored and peopled Vaticans to be slidden through – no cold Coliseums to be sketched – no Fountains-of-Egeria picnics – no 'season' dinnerings and late balls, to excite, fever and freeze by turns; at Malaga the invalid leads a quiet life, calm as the climate, and, blessed with an otiose oriental real *dolce-far-niente* existence, can leave nature to her full *vis medicatrix*. To be always able to bask in the open air, to throw physic to the dogs, to watch the sun, the country, and the people, with the satisfaction of every day getting better, are consolations and occupations sufficient.

RICHARD FORD, *Handbook for Travellers in Spain*, 1855

*

THE AIR of *Padua* is very wholesome, the water good, and there is plenty of every thing from the adjacent country. The streets are narrow and the buildings lofty, which renders the lower rooms very dark. Most of the streets have piazzas, which shelter the people from rain and sun, but contribute to the narrowness and obscurity of the streets. There are a great many magnificent palaces inhabited by a numerous, but half ruined nobility, occasioned, as 'tis said, by pursuing their revenge from generation to generation; these quarrels and feuds might have been easily suppressed by the republic, did they not find their account in the confiscations arising from murders which happen on those occasions; not to mention that they are less apprehensive of a revolt, while the nobility of the conquered provinces continue at variance. For these very reasons the *Venetians* are said to encourage the scholars of the university to insult and abuse the townsmen, and even to murder them in the streets, assembling in companies between the pillars of the porches, crying out *Qui va li! Who goes there?* True it is that the university having lost its reputation by these disorders, and the number of scholars consequently decreasing, the streets are not so dangerous in the evening as formerly.

THOMAS NUGENT, *The Grand Tour,* 1749

*

THE WEATHER set in fine, and at 6 o'clock when we quitted Geneva, the Mountains of Gex were very beautifully covered with white clouds lying close one to the other as I have seen 'em only before in an opera scene. They remained still several hours and at length their highnesses got up with great state and mounted the sky very slowly on their aerial journey. Today I saw several of these clouds begin to form themselves on the sides of the hills I passed, and found that what I took for snow was often these thin clouds, but tonight there is no doubt left of the snow in our neighbourhood.

But to go back to Geneva I must just make a remark or two concerning hasty conclusions in a strange country. At the *Ballance* in Geneva where we lodged and boarded and were very well entertained, an excellent table, good company, good wine and cleanliness, which we all agreed was comparatively better than anything we had met with since Paris and indeed superior to the general entertainment in that place. But I find there is no judging of the provisions of a country or the manner of serving it, by what entertainment one meets with at inns or hotels – for all these good things we had met with at the Ballance in Geneva were so much surpassed by those of what was looked on as a *plain* supper in a private family to which I was invited with my companions, that it set me a reflecting that at Passy chez M. Billon, at Paris with M. Suard and at Lyons with M. Rigaud etc., the same thing had happened. The soup so much better, the boullie, better meat and better dressed – the ragouts, fricandeaux, entremets etc., etc., all so much better than at the best inns or hotels, that it is the highest injustice to say how the French families in general live from what these tables afford.

CHARLES BURNEY, *Men, Music and Manners*, 1773

*

I NOW find Utrecht to be the same agreeable place which my friend Dalrymple found it fifteen years ago. We have brilliant assemblies twice a week and private parties almost every evening. La Comtesse de Nassau Beverweerd has taken me under her protection. She is the finest woman on earth. She has shown me the greatest civility, and has introduced me upon the very best footing into the gay world of this city. I begin to make acquaintance with the people of fashion, and hope to be agreeable to them. There are so many beautiful and amiable ladies in our circle that a quire of paper could not contain their praises, though written by a man of much cooler fancy and a much smaller handwriting than myself.

JAMES BOSWELL, *Boswell in Holland*, 1763–4

*

NORWAY IS rapidly becoming the most popular holiday resort in Europe. Nature has lavishly endowed the country with a rich store of wonders; its attractions are not only strikingly grand, but so varied and numerous as to make a tour in Norway a constant transformation scene. It is the Land of the Midnight Sun, the Land of the Fjord, Foss, and Fell, relieved by lovely valleys and fertile plains, whilst the graceful birch and hardy ash intermingle with fine forests of towering pine. It offers a field of attraction for all, to the traveller for pleasure, to the archaeologist, the geologist, the botanist, the angler, the sportsman, and the mountaineer. The endless pinewoods of east Norway give rest to the eye; along the southern coast one can enjoy the fertile vegetation of leafy trees. The silent and solemn nature of the mountains draws the pedestrian towards the heights where the eye looks over a world of stones, snow and ice, while the mountain peaks tower up as reminders of nature's revolutions in former periods of the earth. The fjords of the west coast, which cannot be surpassed by any in Europe, afford scenery which cannot but make lasting impressions, and he who travels along the coasts of Nordland and Finmarken in between the mountainous islands will, under the light of the Midnight Sun, feel himself carried into a light beaming fairy world. The people are proverbially upright, courteous, and hospitable, and the accommodation and food throughout the country are all that can be wished for. In many cases the hotels vie with the best Continental establishments. The means of conveyance are numerous and comfortable, and the roads excellent, so that there is on the whole nothing to deter the most delicate person from visiting Norway. Indeed, to those wishing to re-establish their health, or requiring relaxation from work, the pure, invigorating highland air of a Norwegian summer would probably prove a most beneficial and pleasant medicine.

T. BENNETT, *Norway,* 1913

*

AT THE present time, Siberia is the collective name for all the Asiatic dominions of the Russian Empire, exclusive of Transcaucasia, Transcaspia and Turkestán; the Urál and Turgái steppe territories, stretching beyond the river Urál and far into the interior of Central Asia do not belong to Siberia, their administrative centres being situated in European Russia. There have been frequent discussions among philologists as to the meaning of the word 'Siberia': some suppose that it is a local word of the Zyriáns and Ostiáks, but common to all the Urál races and adopted by the Nogáis. In connexion with some archaeological researches among the remains of prehistoric civilization, students of the East of Asia suppose that the word Siberia may be identified with the name of the Huns or Savirs.

At present Siberia proper includes the following regions:

1) Western Siberia comprising the governments of Tobólsk and Tomsk in the basin of the Ob, subject to the general system of administration adopted in the governments of European Russia.

	sq. miles.	sq. versts.
Tobólsk gov.	26,749.9	1,295,758.0
Tomsk gov.	15,572.5	749,819.3
Total	42,322.4	2,045,577.3

2) Eastern Siberia, comprising the governments of Yeniséisk and Irkútsk in the basin of the Yeniséi, and the territory of Yakútsk in the basin of the Léna, Yána, Indigírka and Kolymá, under a governor-general resident at Irkútsk.

	sq. miles.	sq. versts.
Yeniséisk gov.	46,699.8	2,259,562.3
Irkútsk gov.	14,542.8	703,650.3
Yakútsk ter.	71,358.3	3,452,655.3
	132,600.9	6,415,867.9

3) The north-western part of the Asiatic steppes, comprising two territories under the authority of the governor-general of the Steppe country.

	sq. miles.	sq. versts.
Akmolínsk ter.	9,903.0	479,200.2
Semipalánsk ter.	8,856.7	428,527.8
	18,759.7	907,728.0

4) The Amúr Littoral region comprising three territories and the Island of Sakhalín, united under the governor-general of the Amúr region, including the Russian part of the Amúr basin and the Littoral belonging to the basin of the Pacific Ocean, together with the peninsula of Kamchátka and the Island of Sakhalín.

	sq. miles.	sq. versts.
Transbaikál	11,325.2	547,965.6
Amúr ter.	8,128.1	393,366.6
Littoral ter.	32,125.0	1,562,662.0
Sakhalín	1,379.0	66,762.0
	52,957.3	2,570,756.2

Thus, Siberia embraces an immense superficial area of 246,640.3 square geographical miles, within 45° and 77° of N. latitude and 60° and 190° E. longitude.

Bounded on the north by the Arctic, and on the east by the Pacific Ocean, Siberia extends towards the south to the Chinese Empire, and is bounded on the west by the Urál range.

In size, the area of Siberia represents the 1/13 part of the continental surface of the globe, and is about $1\frac{1}{2}$ times as large as

Europe, $2\frac{1}{3}$ times as large as the surface of European Russia, and 25 times as large as Germany.

Guide to the Great Siberian Railway, translated by
Miss L. Kúkol-Yasnopólsky, 1900

*

AT THE Hankö Sea Baths the physician, Dr Herman Börsum, treats ailments as follows: Rheumatism and Neuralgia, Neurosis, Cardial Affections, Catarrhal conditions, Cutaneous diseases, Scrofula, Mild Anaemia and Chlorosis, Debility, Abdominal affections, Convalescence. The Curative Media are sulphurous gytje baths, sea weed lye baths, hot sea baths, pine-needle baths, steam baths, carbonic acid baths, sea bathing on open beach, etc.

T. BENNETT, *Norway,* 1913

*

UNDER ROYAL PATRONAGE
Perfect freedom from Coughs in Ten Minutes, and instant relief and a rapid cure of Asthma and Consumption, Coughs, Colds and all Disorders of the Breath and Lungs, are insured by

DR LOCOCK'S PULMONIC WAFERS

Cures of Consumption in Newcastle   Dec. 5, 1845
Gentlemen, – I can myself speak of your Wafers with the greatest confidence, having recommended them in many cases of pulmonary consumption, and they have always afforded relief when everything else has failed; and the patients, having been surfeited with medicine, are delighted to meet with so efficient a remedy, having such an agreeable taste.

J. MAWSON
13, Moseley Street, Newcastle-on-Tyne.

Cure of 29 Years' Asthmatic Cough. Middleton, near Manchester. Sir, – I am now 44 years of age, and I have been afflicted with an asthmatic cough since I was a boy of fifteen years of age; during that time I have resorted to every means in my power to remove it, but in vain, until last Sunday, when I sent for a small box of

Dr Locock's Wafers. I have taken two boxes since, and from the effects they have had upon me I feel no doubt of a speedy recovery.

G. STRINGER

Witness, M. Lynch, Chemist, Market-street.

DR LOCOCK'S COSMETIC

A delightfully fragrant preparation for improving and beautifying the complexion; Rendering the Skin clear, soft, and transparent; removing all Eruptions, Freckles, Sunburn, Tan, Pimples, and Roughness; curing Gnat Bites, and the Stings of Insects. In the process of Shaving, it allays all smarting, and renders the Skin soft and smooth.

Sold in Bottles, at 1s. 1½d., 2s. 9d., and 4s. 6d. each. Beware of Counterfeits. Observe the words, 'DR LOCOCK'S COSMETIC,' on the Government Stamp outside the Wrapper.

SOLD BY ALL RESPECTABLE CHEMISTS

THROUGHOUT ITALY

MURRAY'S *Handbook to Southern Italy*, 1855

＊

VENICE, *Sept.* 1765

SIR,

We came from *Padua* to *Venice,* by the river *Brenta,* in a private boat. There are boats which set out every day to and from *Padua,* like our stagecoaches, and carry passengers for about a shilling; but it is usual for people of a certain rank, to take a vessel to themselves. It is larger than a *Gravesend* boat, and is provided with a room built in the middle, and covered in, big enough to hold twenty persons at least; every expence included, it costs an *English* company about thirty-five shillings. The river *Brenta* is famous for the beauty of the country houses built on its banks, which here, as through all *Italy,* bear the name of palaces. We did not disembark, to visit the gardens of these palaces, and, therefore, cannot give our judgment upon the subject; but they

42

are much celebrated by the people of the country. When you arrive within four or five miles of *Venice,* at a place called *Fusina,* where the river opens into the *Laguna,* (lake) on which the city and adjacent islands are situated, you hire gondolas. Here a wonderful scene opens to every stranger, when he first casts his eye on this enchanting prospect. There are few Gentlemen who are not, in some degree, apprized of what they are to expect from the views they have seen of this place, painted by *Canaletti*; nevertheless, the real object exceeds, in beauty, what the imagination is led to conceive from these draughts; which, however, seldom happens, as the representation of buildings in pictures is generally more gaudy and flattering than the life itself. Here the fuel, being wood, there is no dirty smoak to deface the heavens, the water, and the buildings. There are no dirty barges, nor dirty men; for the Barcaroles (Gondaliers) have most of them an elegant waterman's livery, and the others, who are not in Gentlemens service, being a sober body of men, are not in rags, like the lower sort of people in *England,* who spend all they can get in porter, or spirituous liquors.

In *Venice* there is one large canal, which runs through the middle of the city, in this form, and which receives into it a prodigious number of smaller canals. Almost every house has one door communicating with a street, and another opening immediately upon a canal. There are a few canals from which you land into a narrow street, betwixt the house and the canal. The houses, the gondolas, and the canals, were there no other curiosity, would be very amusing; but the delights of this place are the views of the islands in the neighbourhood. South of the city is another range of buildings and canals, called *Giudecca*; they are divided by a canal, of the breadth of the *Thames* at *London*; and here an airing upon the water, is the diversion of the *Sunday* evening, and festivals, an hour before dark. The ladies, with their *Cavalieri Servanti,* (called *Cicesbei* in other parts of *Italy*) row backwards and forwards near the bank of the *Giudecca,* as, in former days, our gentry in *England* frequented the ring in *Hyde-Park.*

In the way to the *Lazaretto,* the island where quarantine is performed, you pass in sight of several islands, where the churches, convents, &c. furnish an abundant entertainment to the Virtuosi, who have a taste for *Palladio, Titian, Paul Veronese, &c.* One of the most curious sights we saw amongst these curiosities, was the famous Mr——, who was performing quarantine at the *Lazaretto.* All the *English* made a point of paying him their compliments in that place, and he seemed not a little pleased with their attention. It may be supposed that visitors are not suffered to approach the person of any who is performing quarantine. They are divided by a passage of about seven or eight feet wide. Mr—— was just arrived from the East; he had travelled through the *Holy Land, Egypt, Armenia, &c.* with the Old and New-Testament in his hands for his direction, which he told us have proved unerring guides. He had particularly taken the road of the *Israelites* through the wilderness, and had observed that part of the *Red Sea* which they passed through. He had visited *Mount Sinai,* and flattered himself he had been on the very part of the Rock where *Moses* spake face to face with God Almighty. His beard reached down to his breast, being of two years and a half growth; and dress of his head was *Armenian.* He was in the most enthusiastic raptures with *Arabia,* and the *Arabs;* like theirs, his bed was the ground, his food rice, his beverage water, his luxury a pipe and coffee. His purpose was to return once more amongst that virtuous people, whose morals and hospitality he said are such, that, were you to drop your cloak in the highway, you would find it there six months afterwards, an *Arab* being too honest a man to pick up what he knows belongs to another; and were you to offer money for the provision you meet with, he would ask you with concern, why you had so mean an opinion of his benevolence, to suppose him capable of accepting a gratification. Therefore money, said he, in that country, is of very little use, as it is only necessary for the purchase of garments, which, in so warm a climate, are very few, and of very little value. He distinguishes, however, betwixt the wild and the civilized *Arab,* and proposes to publish an account of all that I have written.

I should do an injustice to our resident, Mr *Murray*, did I not mention the politeness with which he receives us, and all his countrymen. I do not doubt, but that from a man of his understanding, and communicative disposition, I shall learn all a traveller would wish to know.

I am, Sir, &c.

SAMUEL SHARP, *Letters from Italy*, 1767

*

AT CHRISTMAS we had a month of vacation. I then went to The Hague, where I passed three weeks in the most brilliant gaiety. The style of living there is much in the manner of Paris. I found my relations there to be people of the first rank, and was treated by them with the utmost civility. I had recommendations to a variety of people. I was presented to the Prince of Orange and the other princes there, to all the foreign ambassadors – in short, to everybody. I passed a couple of days at Leyden, where I supped twice with the young prince of Strelitz, our Queen's brother, once at his own house, once at the house of Mr Gordon, Lord Aberdeen's brother; and now I am returned to the seat of the dutch muses and have resumed my studious regularity with much satisfaction.

JAMES BOSWELL, *Boswell in Holland*, 1763–4

*

IN ALL the public establishments of America, the utmost courtesy prevails. Most of our Departments are susceptible of considerable improvement in this respect, but the Customhouse above all others would do well to take example from the United States and render itself somewhat less odious and offensive to foreigners. The servile rapacity of the French officials is sufficiently contemptible; but there is a surly boorish incivility about our men, alike disgusting to all persons who fall into their hands, and discreditable to the nation that keeps such ill-conditioned curs snarling about its gates.

When I landed in America, I could not help being strongly impressed with the contrast their Custom-house presented, and the attention, politeness and good humour with which its officers discharged their duty.

CHARLES DICKENS, *American Notes,* 1842

*

CHERNORÉCHENSKAYA. IV class station (586 v. from Krivoshchékovo, 1918 v. from Cheliábinsk). The village of Chernoréchenskoe of the Achinsk district close by, on the small river Chórnaya, lies in a swampy and wooded country along the Siberian highway; it has a population of 1,406. This settlement was founded in the XVIII century and contains a church built in 1834 in honour of the Archangel Michael; some documents preserved in the church testify that previous to its construction, in the winter of 1833, a bell weighing 42 puds was brought in the night to the village and left there by an unknown individual. There is a parish school.

Guide to the Great Siberian Railway, 1900

*

The Tahitian woman rises with the sun, that is, at six o'clock in the morning. In Tahiti the day has just twelve hours. The sun rises at six o'clock in the morning and sets at six o'clock in the evening. At these two times of the day it is possible to set a watch without fear of inaccuracy. In fact, a watch is unnecessary, God having given everyone the large timepiece called the sun. So at six o'clock in the morning the Tahitian woman rises with the sun. Upon awakening, she runs to the river, wrapped in the garment in which she has slept. Having reached the edge of the stream where there is rarely more than a foot and a half or two feet of water, she removes her wrap and crouches on her heels; she then unfastens her hair, letting it fall like a veil, and through every pore of her skin finds a voluptuous delight in the invigorating freshness of the water. As all the women have the same habit, they congregate in the river between six and eight o'clock in the morning. This river is their club where they chat, or rather gossip – the only word that can describe their incessant chatter. They might be termed a flock of fresh water birds who warble in emulation of one another.

At eight o'clock the aquatic sequence terminates; each woman has exhausted what she has to say, and is refreshed for a few hours; her appetite has returned, and she goes back to her house. The Tahitian woman in her food instincts is a true child of nature; like the Arab she eats heartily if there is much to eat; little if there is little. Her breakfast, frugal or abundant, is suspended near her hut from the branch of a tree in a basket. Usually the basket contains figs, a slice of breadfruit, and a piece of fish cooked in ashes, like the suckling pigs of the New Zealander, and wrapped in the leaves in which it was grilled. She begins with the fish, which she dips in a bowl of salt water and then drains before eating, just as we handle green walnuts. Finally she nibbles the fish; after the fish she has dessert, accompanying it with two or three glasses of excellent water brought from a neighbouring spring. In this manner she breakfasts. When she has finished – the act of eating usually takes place inside her hut – she takes her mat, the small pillow on which she rests her head, and her Bible.

Then, carrying this load, she goes out, selects some tree – guava, coconut, pandanus, or orange – places her mat in the shade, lays her cushion at the tip of the mat, lies down on the mat, rests her elbow on the pillow, her head on her hand, with the other hand holding the Bible, and reads. Either from lack of interest in a tale that is always the same, or from drowsiness, gradually her head drops on its support, the Bible falls from her hand, her head seeks the pillow in anticipation of what might occur, the eyes close, and the reader falls asleep. Thus she rests for two or three hours, moving but slightly from the position taken for sleeping, or assumed when sleeping.

At noon or one o'clock she awakes. Still drowsy she runs again to the river. This time she wears her dressing-gown and her *paser*; as in the morning she quickly drops all her garments and kneels among her companions. Then the chatter begins again, but less rapidly than in the morning; it is warm and everyone is tired, even of talking. After one or two hours of bathing she returns to her hut; but since the road burns the soles of her feet, she now walks on the grass and flowers which adorn both sides of the road. Returning home about two o'clock she arranges her costume, braids her hair, places fresh flowers behind her ears, and goes out to pay visits in the village.

To whom? To the officers! The officers stroll, or smoke at their windows.

The Tahitian woman is fond of little drinks, cigars, and pieces of sugar. If she desires a little drink, she stops near the officer from whom she expects this gift, gives him her brightest smile and says: '*Ma namou iti*' – a little brandy for me.

If a piece of sugar, the smile remains the same; the phrase alone varies. '*Ma tiota iti*', says the collector. This means: a little piece of sugar for me.

If she has an urge to smoke a cigar, the same smile, but a slight change in the formula. '*Ma ava ava iti*', she says – a little smoke for me.

The officer gives her his cigar, the woman takes two rapid puffs which she soon exhales, then a third, which she makes as long as possible.

Thereupon, she coquettishly salutes the officer, returns him his cigar, and departs, her head turned back, making rings with the smoke which she throws vertically into the air. All this is accompanied with little flirtations full of grace. She then returns home by the longest route; it is four o'clock, the officers are about to dine at Marius's or Bremont's.

She has procured a supply of flowers in the officers' garden; she has two hours before her; it is now time for her, too, to dine and arrange her crown. The crown arranged, she dons her finest robe, a silk robe if she has one, then listens to see whether she can hear music in the government garden. At the first sound of the brass instruments, the Tahitian woman leaves her hut and walks toward the garden. She meets a friend and takes her by the little finger; thus they arrive, two by two, holding themselves like recruits on parade. Having entered the government garden, they

It has really become quite impossible to hold one's place in Society unless one has travelled . . .

. . . or to hold on to one's wit, one's food, one's hat or one's balance for that matter.

What crowds! What excitement! How quaint to see the pantechnicon inscribed SERVICE DES BAGAGES! How completely French!

But damn it, you can tell by the cut of their jib that the people are FOREIGN, damn it!

The horses are unreliable and the drivers inexpressibly coarse. Besides the French have graven images along the roadside. It is all most unfortunate.

Why are all these foreign persons clambering aboard? Are we to have no privacy?

Is this the Notre Dame of which Mr Hugo wrote so eerily? Where are the gargoyles?

I wouldn't exactly say that we'd had a pleasant journey, Lucy. How insecure the sea is!

squat on their heels, retaining with admirable equilibrium their balance during long hours.

Their numbers are soon so great, and they are crowded so closely together, that a pin thrown in the air would not find room to alight on the ground, and a variegated carpet appears to extend completely over the government court. At first immobile, and apparently interested only in listening to the music, they finally end by gradually moving heads, arms, then the whole body in unison. All this time, at least ostensibly, they do not appear to dance, but retire into remote corners where they can be seen keeping time while the carpet moves at the corners like a wave.

The officers promenade in the small openings that the Tahitians save for this purpose much as gallants strolling through the Tuileries, the Champs Élysées, or Grand Boulevard pass between the interstices of chairs. They speak a few words of Tahitian to their acquaintances; needless to say the Frenchman speaks Tahitian as he speaks all other languages, that is, badly. They know only two phrases in our language, which they speak with a charming accent, suitable for a language entirely of vowels.

Here is the first phrase: *'Farani, allé tiné. il e tatra'*.

But is this French?

Certainly; only it is Tahitian French. This actually means: Frenchmen, come to dinner; it is four o'clock.

Here is the second: *'Tantinet fanata tatou!'* Do you understand? No.

'Sentinel, be on your guard!'

Because of the fact that when we were at war with the natives the sentinels, according to their custom, called from time to time to one another: 'Sentinel, be on your guard!'

Remembering this nocturnal cry that attracted them, they repeat it without knowing what it means. About seven o'clock the music ceases. Then the Tahitians return to the shore. As they had rested for an hour, they now promenade in groups, the connoisseurs finding in the movement of their hips a rest from the governmental music.

They stop before verandahs, where officers are smoking and sipping their coffee. Then the *ma namou iti,* the *ma tiota iti,* and the *ma ava ava iti* begin once more. Each one has her small glass, eats her piece of sugar, smokes three puffs from her tiny cigar. Then, this triple gourmandizing satisfied, they remain and crouch as usual on their heels, attempting to play on their eminently French instruments variations of the music they have just heard. In this way a blissful hour is spent. It is the intoxicating moment of the day. The trade winds cease; the laden breeze rises, bringing the aromatic perfume of the mountains; the sea is calm; the sun sets behind the island of Moorea, filling the west with fire, against which stands out in silhouette the blue mass of the mountains. Finally, taps, played by the bands on the ships at anchor, is heard from afar in the harbour. The final signal of retreat will be a cannon shot. But an instant before this cannon shot resounds, the entire group of Tahitian women, like a flock of vari-coloured birds with flapping wings, disappears.

The cannon shot is the warning that they must keep off the streets. The day of the Tahitian woman is now over and night begins. The majority of these charming doves enter a foreign dovecote. Everywhere the officers hold soirées. They play cards and a Tahitian game that resembles beggar-my-neighbour. The French, invariably gallant, have carried politeness to the extreme. They have learned this game as they have learned the language, at the same time and by the same method.

The soldiers who do not play, chat together; and with those who do not care to play, chat together, talking of friends who are absent on expeditions in the island, or who have left permanently to return to the sterile land, as they call our land, la belle France.

The conversation runs as follows: Do you recall such and such a man, the first day we saw him on the river? *Avoi!* What would you say if he were here! He spoke Tahitian so well! *Avoi.* We shall never see him again! He is dead, *avoi!* He is married, *avoi, avoi!* Then they weep repeating *avoi, avoi,* until the hour to depart arrives, when they take their leave. Some, perhaps, do not depart. If they remain, they do not pass their time in idleness! There is no infringement of the regulations if they do not leave until day dawns. If anyone leaves, the officer must escort his departing guest or one who is entering, in order to protect the beautiful belated Tahitians from the sentinels.

At six o'clock in the morning, another day like the previous one commences; the next day is the same, and thus the hours pass indefinitely between bathing, flowers, music, gambling, love.

ALEXANDRE DUMAS, *père, The Journal of Madame Giovanni,*
translated from the French edition of 1856 by
Marguerite E. Wilbur, 1944

*

A QUIET refined hotel may be thought of in Froknerne Bye's private hospice, where is near the House of Parliament. Here it is highly patronised and recommended by all nobilities of both England, German and Americans. There is flushing lavatory arrangements on the English model and great conveniences may be had for Kr.2.50–8.00 per diem.

T. BENNETT, *Norway,* 1913

*

I SINCERELY believe that the public institutions and charities of this capital of Massachusetts are as nearly perfect, as the most considerate wisdom, benevolence, and humanity, can make them. I never in my life was more affected by the contemplation of happiness, under circumstances of privation and bereavement, than in my visits to these establishments.

CHARLES DICKENS, *American Notes,* 1842

*

IN PATIALA I slept in a bed plated with gold. My apartment consisted of five rooms for my sole use. There were fifteen dining-rooms in the palace. As many different dinners were served each day. The old Maharajah kept 500 horses for his own use. There were, when I was there, 143 cooks, scullions and other kitchen helpers, of whom seventeen cooked only curries. In the armoury I was shown the famous Patiala emeralds, each as large as a dessert spoon, and a necklace which, when I tried it on, covered half my person with streams and lakes of diamonds. It was set by Cartier and contained pink, yellow, greenish and what I should call pale brown diamonds all as large as my thumb-nails.

Still in the armoury of Jodhpur, handling now a snake-headed anklet encrusted with emeralds and now an ear-ring like an inverted pagoda, each storey built of rubies and hung with infinitesimal bells, I exchanged tales of palace India with the surprising Mr Allen. His fingers were as accurate and delicate as the instruments they used. They never fumbled or hesitated. They never made a mistake. I remember telling, while we looked at a jewelled bridle that must have been very uncomfortable to handle, how, in a Southern Indian palace, I saw the ruling Maharani in full dress. The weight of her jewels was so great that she could not stand without the support of two attendants. Her anklets of gold, studded with emeralds, weighed 100 ounces each and were valued at £1,400. Over her slender feet she wore flat strips of gold attached by chains to jewelled toe rings. The same precious metal covered the backs of her hands and was held in place by diamond links attached to her rings and bracelets. She could not bend her elbows because her arms were covered solidly from wrist to shoulder with wide bracelets of precious stones. Diamonds blazed upon her breast and hung in a multitude of chains far below her waist. Her throat was stiffened by collars of emeralds and rubies.

Down the full length of her plaited hair, from the crown of her head to her knees, hung a sort of fishtail of gold set with jewels. It was about three inches wide at the top and it tapered to the point where a pear-shaped diamond hung. I calculated that the eighteen-year-old queen was wearing more than her own slight weight in treasure and the value of at least a quarter of a million sterling.

Anon., A Jubilee Handbook to India, 1897

*

AT THE Christiana Missionshotel, 5 Kirkegaden, four languages are spoken at all times and electric alarm bells ring throughout the hotel.

T. BENNETT, *Norway,* 1913

*

A JOURNEY to Italy was still in his thoughts. He said, 'A man who has not been in Italy is always conscious of an inferiority, from his not having seen what it is expected a man should see. The grand object of travelling is to see the shores of the Mediterranean. On those shores were the four great Empires of the world – the Assyrian, the Persian, the Grecian and the Roman. All our religion, almost all our law, almost all our arts, almost all that sets us above savages, has come to us from the shores of the Mediterranean.'

JAMES BOSWELL, *Tour to the Hebrides,* 1785

2. Advisers, Informants, and Admirable Crichtons

Your servant must be told the size of the drink you wish him to bring you. 'Chota peg' is small and is usually associated with the memsahib; 'Burra peg' is large and is confined to the officer class.

Manual of Social Instruction for Her Majesty's Indian Army, 1888

As a general rule it should be observed that English is always understood if it is spoken clearly and accompanied by appropriate gestures or mime. His Majesty the King Emperor is personified in every Englishman abroad and orders must be given in a suitably imperious manner. Shout if necessary, but never dissemble. God is your authority.

Preface to *Experiences of a Missionary on the Dark Continent*, 1908

The most intimate details of the anatomy are required in dealing with foreign physicians. 'Please, a tisane to relieve the pain caused by falling upon my coccyx' would be *de trop* in Tunbridge Wells but *de rigueur* in the Holy Land.

Cook's *Tourist Guide to the Nile*, 1899

54

The classic piece of travel advice was given to an American
missionary preparing to go to Darkest Africa : 'Make sure you
take with you a bottle of Gin, a bottle of French vermouth, and
a cocktail shaker.' Horrified, he protested that he was a teetotaller
and could have no possible use for these implements of Satan.
'Don't you believe it,' he was told. 'These implements of the
devil, as you call them, are a permanent guard against being
lost. For though you may well be in the heart of the African
jungle, lost beyond recall and in despairing solitude, you have
only to mix a Dry Martini for the immediate magical appearance
of at least eight people who will tell you you are mixing it wrong.'

Advisers have abounded in the field of travel as in other walks
of life. I wish only that more of their bounty could have been
spread through these pages. Only Mr Punch is cynical in his
Small Change for Persons Going on the Continent. The rest are
in solemn earnest – exemplarily, Richard Ford as he nudges us
to 'hoist British colours everywhere' and 'avoid all semi-bandit,
fancy-ball extravagances in dress'. Chauvinistic it may be, but
it was in keeping with the times, as was Dr Chambers' gargantuan
hamper 'to stay the appetites' between meals.

As for informants, it could be argued that there is but little
distinction between informants and guides; and indeed some of
them appear in both sections. But there is a subtle difference.
Here the tone is more unbuttoned, we are being told things less
for the money we've paid for our cicerones' services than for
the chummy reason that they think we'd like to hear what they
have to say. We are invited to share the reverence attending the
Grand Duke's filling of the wheelbarrow or nod sagely on hearing
of the Estramadurans' carbuncles. It is all intended to widen
our knowledge of the world.

Admirable Crichtons have existed since long before the first to
be thus named – who, incidentally, wasn't Barrie's castaway butler
but James Crichton the sixteenth-century philosopher who was
killed in a street brawl while visiting Mantua. They are the
people who always know where the can-opener is and how to
make a comfortable bed with thistles. James was nicknamed

55

'admirable' for his learning rather than his practicality, but Francis Galton, many of whose pages in *The Art of Travel* have been plundered for this anthology, was of the Barrie mould. He knew all about survival and comfort and how to combat mosquitoes – which, being non-British, were to be treated with contempt. He would have known exactly how to send a letter from Santiago during a Small Earthquake in Chile. He never faltered in his instructions on how to make cake from gnats or convert motion into heat. He must have been a great chap to have around, at home or abroad.

*   *   *

THE OBSERVANCE of a few rules in a country where 'manners maketh man' will render the traveller's path one of peace and pleasantness. First and foremost, never forget that the Spaniard is of a very high caste, and a gentleman by innate aristocracy; proud as Lucifer and combustible as his matches, he is punctilious and touchy on the point of honour; make therefore the first advances, or at least meet him a little more than half way; treat him, be his class what it may, as a *Caballero*, a gentleman, and an old and well-born Christian one, *Cristiano viejo y rancio*, and therefore as your equal. When his self-esteem and personal sensitiveness are thus once conciliated, he is quick to return the compliment, and to pay every deference to the judicious stranger by whom he is put in his proper place; all attempts to bully and browbeat is loss of time, as this stiff-necked, obstinate people may be turned by the straw of courtesy, but are not to be driven by a rod of iron, still less if wielded by a foreigner, to despise whom is the essense of nationality or *Españolismo*. It need scarcely be said, in a land so imbued with Orientalisms, that the greatest respect is to be paid to the fair sex for its own sake, whatever be a woman's age, condition, or appearance – nor will love's labour be lost. On landing at Calais, the sooner Mayfair is wiped out of the tablets of memory the better, nor can any one, once in Spain, too constantly remember to forget England. How few there, or indeed anywhere on the Continent, sympathise with our wants and habits, or understand our love of truth and cold water; our simple manly tastes; our contempt for outward show compared to real comfort; our love of exercise, adventure, and alternate quiet, and of all that can only be learnt at our public schools. Your foreigner has no Winchester or Eton.

Civil words and keeping out of mischief's way are everywhere the best defence. Never grudge wearing out a hat or two by touching it or taking it off; this is hoisting the signal of truce, peace, and good will; the sensitive Spaniard stiffens when hats are not off, and bristles up like a porcupine against the suspicion of a *desaire*. Be especially polite to officials, from the odious custom-house upwards; it is no use kicking against the powers that be; if you ruffle them they can worry you by a relentless doing of their duty : these nuisances are better palliated by honey than vinegar; and many of the detentions and difficulties of our unwise travellers are provoked by uncourteous demeanour, and growlings in a tongue as unknown to the natives as the Englishman was to Portia – 'He understands not me, nor I him.' Dismiss the nonsense of robbers from your head, avoiding, however, all indiscreet exhibition of tempting baits, or chattering about your plans and movements. By common preparation mere footpads are baffled : to attempt resistance against an organised band is sheer folly : do not mix yourself with Spanish politics or civil wars – leave them to exterminate each other to their liking, like Kilkenny cats. Avoid logomachies, or trying to convince the natives against their will; it is arguing against a north-east wind, and a sheer loss of time, too; for, in a fine, indolent climate, where there is little to do – no liberty of press or circulating libraries – the otiose twaddlers spin Castilian nonsense by the yard. Mind your own business, and avoid things that do not concern you, taking especial care not to intermeddle.

In the large towns the costume of an English gentleman is the best; avoid all semi-bandit, fancy-ball extravagances in dress; hoist, indeed, British colours there as everywhere. Thin cashmere or *cubica* is far preferable to cloth, which is intolerable in the hot weather. Pay daily visits to Figaro, and carefully eschew the

57

Brutus beards, and generally, everything which might lead the bulk of Spaniards to do you the grievous injury of mistaking your native country. A *capa* or cloak used to be absolutely essential, and is so out of Madrid, *paletots* notwithstanding; and how much in appearance and in health have those Spaniards lost, who, like the Turks, ape the externals of foreign civilization; how skimpy and pigmy and common-place they look stripped of their ample folds: let your cloak be of plain blue colour, faced with black velvet. Remember to get it made in Spain, or it will not be cut full enough to be able to be worn as the natives do: take particular care that it has a cape, *dengue, esclavina,* unless you wish to be an object of universal attention and ridicule; and mind to let your tailor give you a few lessons how to put it on like a Spaniard, and to show you the different modes of muffling up the face, a precaution necessary in the Castiles, where the cold airs, if inhaled, bring on sudden and dangerous *pulmonia.* This artificial *respirator* keeps out both the assassin breath of cold, and the salitrose dust. No English-made *capa* can be properly *embozada,* that is, have its right fold thrown over the mouth and left shoulder, descending neatly half-way down the back. Our cloaks are much too scanty, *no tienen bastante vuelo.* In the conduct of cloaks, remember, when you meet any one, being yourself *embozado* or muffled up, to remove the folds before you address him, as not to do so is a great incivility: again, when strangers continue to speak to you thus cloaked, and as it were disguised, be on your guard.

Take great care, when actually travelling, to get the passport *refrendado y corriente* in time, and to secure long beforehand places in the public conveyance. Carry the least possible luggage you can, never forgetting that none is so heavy and useless in Spain as preconceived prejudices and conventional foregone conclusions, although of genuine London or Paris manufacture. When you do arrive at the place of your destination, if you wish to do or see anything out of the common way, call on the *jefe politico,* or *comandante de armas,* or chief authority, to state frankly your object, and request his permission. For travelling, especially on riding tours and in all out-of-the-way districts, adopt the national costume of the road; to wit, the peaked hat, *Sombrero gacho, calañes,* the jacket of fur, the *Zamarra,* or the one of cloth, the *Marselles*; the grand object is to pass incog. in the crowd, or if noticed, to be taken for a native. You will thus avoid being observed of all observers, and a thousand other petty annoyances which destroy privacy and ruffle temper. You may possibly thus escape the beggars, which are the plague of Spain, and have a knack of finding out a stranger, and of worrying and bleeding him as effectually as the mosquitoes. The regular form of uncharitable rejection is as follows: *Perdone V. (Usted) por Dios, Hermano?* – My brother, will you excuse me, for God's sake? If this request be gravely said, the mendicant gives up hope of coppers. Any other answer except this specific one, only encourages importunity, as the beggars either do not believe in the reality of the refusal, or see at once that you are *not* a Spaniard, and therefore never leave off, until in despair you give them hush-money to silence their whine, thus bribing them to relieve you from the pleasure of their company.

Ladies will do well to adopt the national and most becoming *mantilla,* although in large towns the hideous bonnet is creeping in. They must also remember that females are not admitted into churches except in veils; black also used to be the correct colour for dress. Spanish women generally seat themselves on the pavement when at prayers; it is against all ecclesiastical propriety for a lady and gentleman, even man and wife, to walk about arm in arm in a church. Spaniards, on passing the high altar, always bow; beware of talking during mass, when the ringing of a little bell indicates the elevation of the Host, and the actual presence of the incarnate Deity. It is usual to take off hats and kneel when the consecrated wafer is carried by in the streets; and those Protestants who object, should get out of the way, and not offend the weaker brethren by a rude contempt of their most impressive ceremonial.

Protestants should observe some reserve in questions of creed, and never play tricks with the faith or the eye; *con el ojo y la fe,*

59

nunca me burlare. There is no sort of religious toleration in Spain, where their belief is called *la Fe,* and is thought to be *the* faith, and the only true one. You may smile, as Spaniards do, at a corpulent canon, and criticise what he practises, but take care to respect what he preaches. You will often be asked if you are a Christian, meaning a Roman Catholic; the best answer is, *Crisiano, si, Romano Catolico, no.* Distributors of Protestant tracts will labour in vain, and find that to try to convert a Spaniard is but waste of time. The influence of the Voltaire school with the propagandism of revolution and atheism, has sapped much, both of the loyalty and religion, of the old Castilian; but however the cause of the Vatican may be injured, that of Protestantism is little advanced : for there is no via media, no Bible in Spain; Deism and infidelity are the only alternatives, and they are on the increase. The English are thought to have no faith at all – to believe neither in the Pope or Mahomet, but in gold and cotton alone; nor is this to be wondered at in Spain, where they have no ostensible religion; no churches or churchyards; no Sundays or service, except as a rare chance at a seaport in some consul's parlour. Being rich, however, and strong, they escape the contumely poured out in Spain on poor and weak heretics, and their cash is respected as eminently catholic.

Conform, as nearly as you can, to the hours and habits of the natives, get up early, which is usual throughout Spain; dine or rest in the middle of the day, for when everybody is either at table or the *siesta,* it is no use to be running about sight-seeing when you are the only person awake. *On all occasions pay with both hands;* most locks in Spain are to be picked with a silver key, and almost every difficulty is smoothed by a properly administered bribe, and how small an additional percentage on the general expenditure of a tour through Spain is added by such trifling outlays! Never therefore, cross the Pyrenees to wage a *guerrilla* warfare about shillings and half-crowns. N.B. Have always plenty of small silver coins, for which great is the amount of peace, good will, and having your own way, to be purchased in Spain, where *backshish,* as in the East, is the universal infallible '*open sesamé*' and most unanswerable argument. A Spanish proverb judiciously introduced always gives pleasure, nor need you ever fear offering your cigar case, *petaca,* to any Spaniard, still less if your tobacco be of the legitimate Havana; for next to *pesetas,* rank cigars, as popular instruments of waxing in the favour of Iberian man, and making him your obedient servant.

When on a riding journey, *attend to the provend;* take a *mosquitero* or mosquito net, and some *solution of ammonia,* the best antidote to their stings; avoid all resistance to robbers when overmatched; keep your plans and movements secret; never rub your eyes except with your elbows, *los ojos con los codos,* but use hot water to them frequently, or a lotion of calomel and rosewater; never exercise them in prying about barracks, arsenals, and citadels, and still less in sketching anything connected with military and national defences, which are after all generally but beggarly shows of empty boxes.

Letters of *Introduction* are desirable. In cities, where a lengthened stay is contemplated, their utility is obvious. They may be procured and taken on tours and excursions, but need not always be presented. Of service in cases of difficulties, they involve otherwise much loss of precious time in visits and in formal intercourse with strangers, whom one never saw before and may never meet again; and for your life avoid being carried off from the *posada* to a hospitable native's house, if freedom and taking 'ease in mine own inn' have any charms.

In choice of lodgings, especially in winter, secure upper floors which have a *southern* aspect. The sun is the fire-place of Spain, and where his vivifying rays enter, the doctor goes out; and, dear reader, if you value your life, avoid the sangrados of Spain, who wield the shears of the fatal sisters. Fly also from the *brasero,* the pan of heated charcoal, the parent of headache and asphixia; trust rather to additional clothing than to charcoal, especially to flannel; keep your feet warm and the head cool, by avoiding exposure to midday sun and midnight bottle: above all things, carry not the gastronomics of the cold north into the hot south. Live as the natives do, consuming little meat and less wine; sleep the mid-day siesta as they do, and avoid rash exposure to the delicious cool night breezes. Sleep high, avoiding the ground floor, as the poisonous Malarias of fine climates creep on earth, and more so by night when they are condensed, than by day; throw physic to the dogs, avoiding constipation and trusting to diet and quiet; a blue or a rhubarb dinner pill generally will suffice. Cod liver oil may as well be taken out by consumptive travellers, as it is dear, indifferent, and rare in Spain.

Next to the Spanish bandit and doctors, with whom your purse or life are in danger, avoid investments in Spanish insecurities. Nothing a 'shop-keeper nation' justly dislikes more than a fraudu-lent bankrupt or a stock exchange repudiator; it is safer to buy our Three per Cent Reduced at 100, than Spanish Five per Cents. at 35.

When you have letters of introduction to any Spaniards, both ladies and gentlemen should be very particular in being well dressed on the first visit of etiquette : black is the correct colour of ceremony. Call yourself with your credentials. Ladies should come in a carriage, as *venido en coche* is a mark of respect. If the parties called upon be out, leave your credentials and card, writing on the corner of the latter E. P., which means *en persona*. When you ring at the door, probably an unseen person will exclaim, *'Quien es?'* 'Who's there?' The correct counter-sign is, *'Gente de paz,'* 'Persons of Peace.' As the first visit is always formal, ob-serve how you are treated, and practise the same behaviour exactly when the call is returned. You will be conducted to the best room, the *sala de estrado,* and then led up to the sofa, and placed on the right hand. Very great care will be paid, or in our time used to be paid, to your hat – type of grandeeship – which a well-bred Spaniard seizes and seats on a chair as if it were a person : be careful to pay this compliment always to your visiting friend's beaver. When you get up to take leave, if of a lady, you should say, *'A los pies de V. (usted), Señora,'* 'My lady, I place myself at your feet;' to which she will reply, *'Beso á V. la mano, Cabal-lero,'* 'I kiss your hand, Sir Knight :' *'Vaya V. con Dios, que V.*

lo pase bien,' 'May you depart with God, and continue well;' to which you must reply, *'Quede V. con Dios y la Virgen,'* 'May you remain with God and the Virgin.' Ladies seldom rise in Spain to receive male visitors; they welcome female ones with kisses both at coming and going. A gentleman must beware how he offers to shake a Spanish lady's hand, as it is never done, except when the hand is offered for better or worse; it disarranges her mantilla; nor should he give her his arm when out walking. On leaving a Spaniard's house, observe if he thus addresses you, *'Esta casa está muy á la disposicion de V. cuando guste favorecerla,'* 'This house is entirely at your disposal, whenever you please to favour it.' Once thus invited, you become a friend of the family, *uno de nosotros, de la familia.* If the compliment be omitted, it is clear that the owner never wishes to see you again, and is equivalent to an affront. When a lady makes a visit, a well-bred host hands her down stairs to the door of her carriage, taking her by the hand; but properly no pressure is admissible, although such things have occurred. Remember always to pay a visit of ceremony to your male and female friends on their birth-days, or *el dia de su santo,* and to attend to your costume and put on your best black : on New Year's day bring some small gift with you, as an *estreña.* If, when you call, you are admitted, and a Spanish lady happens to be alone, you should not shut the door, as according to the laws of all social propriety it must be left open, or at least ajar. In walking with a Spaniard, if you wish to show him respect, take care to let him be inside of the two, *tu comes exterior* : the same nicety of relative position should be observed in seating him on a sofa or in a carriage. A well-bred man always when he meets a lady makes way for her, passing outside; although the strict rule in street-walking, which, from their narrowness and the nice point of honour of touchy passengers, has been well defined, is that whoever has the wall on his or her right hand is entitled to keep it.

On passing soldiers on duty, remember that the challenge of a Spanish sentry is *'Quien vive?'* The answer is *'España.'* Then follows *'Que gente?'* The answer is *'Paisano.'* The sooner and clearer strangers answer the better, as silence rouses suspicion; and in Spain a shot often precedes any explanation.

When you meet your Spanish friends, stop, uncloak, uncover, and attend carefully to the whole process of greetings in the market-place. These things are not done there in our curt and off-hand How are you? way. You must inquire after the gentleman's own health, that of his wife (*como está mi Señora la esposa de V.*), his children, et cetera, and then you will be thought to be a *homre tan formal y cumplido como nosotros,* that is, as well-bred as a Spaniard. If when walking with a Spaniard you pass your own house, do not fail to ask him whether he will not step in and untire himself a little, '*No quiere V. entrar en esta su casa, y descansarse un ratito?*' You beg him to come into *his*, not your house, for thus you offer it to him.

This offering obtains throughout. If a Spaniard admire anything belonging to another, his friend instantly places it at his disposal, *está muy á la disposicion de V.* The proper reply is a bow, and some sort of speech like this: '*Gracias, está muy bien empleado*', or '*Gracias, no puede mejorarse de dueño*'. 'Thanks, it is already in excellent hands; it cannot better its master by any change.' In like manner, and especially when outside cities, if any Spaniards pass by when you are lunching, picnicking, or eating, never fail to invite them to share your meal, by saying, '*Gusten ustedes comer?*' 'Will your graces be pleased to dine?' To omit this invitation is a flagrant breach of the laws of hospitality; nor is it always a mere compliment on their part, for every class of Spaniard is flattered if you will partake of their fare. However, it is safer to decline with the set speech, '*Muchas gracias, buen provecho le haga á ustedes*'. Never at all events, in this or on other occasions, omit these titular compliments. Phrases and forms of address are exponents of national character, and how superb is the pomp and circumstance of national character, and how superb is the pomp and circumstance of these swelling semi-Orientals; here every beggar addresses a brother mendicant as *Señor, Don,* and *Caballero,* as a lord or knight. As all are peers, all are '*Vuestra Merced,*' 'Your Grace,' which, when not expressed in words, is understood and implied by the very grammar, as the mode of addressing in the third person, instead of in our curt second 'you', has reference to an implied title. In towns there is scarcely any dinner society, and luckily; nor is such an invitation the usual compliment paid to a stranger, as with us. Spaniards, however, although they seldom *bid* a foreigner, will accept *his* bidding. It is necessary, however, to 'press them greatly;' for the correct national custom is to decline. Remember also to apply a gentle violence to your guest, to induce him to eat, and if you are dining with him, let your stomach stretch a point; for unless you over-eat yourself, he will fancy that you do not like his fare. He will assuredly heap up your mess most profusely, for, as in the East, where dinners are scarce, quantity is the delicate mark of attention. It was in our time by no means unusual for strangers, after eating ices or taking coffee at a public café, to find, when they went to pay, that the bill had already been discharged by some unknown Spaniard. Accordingly, if you see friends of yours thus refreshing themselves, pretty ladies for instance with whom you wish to stand well, you may privately tell the waiter that you will be answerable for their account. It is very easy afterwards, when you meet with your fair friends, to let them infer who was their unknown benefactor. It was sometimes rather dangerous to accompany an extravagant *Andaluza* out shopping, *á las tiendas,* as a well-bred man of the old Spanish school was bound never to allow her to pay for anything. This custom, however, has got somewhat obsolete since the French invasion, good money and manners having become considerably scarcer in consequence of that visitation.

RICHARD FORD, *Handbook for Travellers in Spain,* 1855

*

A MAN advances but a little way into the mountainous country, before he perceives many of the natives, of both sexes, labouring under that species of swelled throat, which the common people call the *Deer's Neck,* and the medical people a *Bronchocele.* I was apprised, before I went into *Savoy,* that in what place soever the

C

inhabitants drink snow water, they are subject to this distemper; but I had not the least idea of such an universality; for, as you approach towards Mount *Cenis,* you find very few exempt from it; and many of those swellings are so enormous, and of so loathsome an appearance, especially in ugly, ragged, half starved old women, that the very sight of them turns the stomach. I do not learn, upon enquiry, that the malady is ever mortal; not but that sometimes the tumour compresses the windpipe so much, as to render respiration very difficult, which, at the long run, though insensibly, may affect life. I was curious in my examination, whether any children were born with this malady upon them : I did not know but that the blood of the mother, imbued with snow water, might operate this effect upon the foetus before birth; however, I was informed, to my satisfaction, that there is no such instance, and even that the swelling never begins to form, till towards two years of age, some examples of which I myself saw.

SAMUEL SHARP, *Letters From Italy,* 1767

*

THE RIVER *Po* gives a Name to the chief Street of *Turin,* which fronts the Duke's Palace, and, when finish'd, will be one of the noblest in *Italy* for its length. There is one Convenience in this City that I never observed in any other, and which makes some amends for the Badness of the Pavement. By the help of a River, that runs on the upper Side of the Town, they can convey a little Stream of Water through all the most considerable Streets, which serves to cleanse the Gutters, and carries away all the Filth that is swept into it. The Manager opens his Sluce every Night, and distributes the Water into what Quarters of the Town he pleases. Besides the ordinary Convenience that arises from it, it is of great use when a Fire chances to break out, for at a few Minutes warning they have a little River running by the very Walls of the House that is Burning. The Court of *Turin* is reckoned the most splendid and Polite of any in *Italy;* but by reason of its being in Mourning, I could not see it in its Magnificence. The common People of this State are more exasperated against the *French* than even the rest of the *Italians*. For the great Mischiefs they have suffered from them are still fresh upon their Memories, and notwithstanding this Interval of Peace, one may easily trace out the several Marches which the *French* Armies have made through their Country, by the Ruin and Desolation they have left behind them. I passed through *Piemont* and *Savoy*, at a time when the Duke was forced, by the Necessity of his Affairs, to be in Alliance with the *French*.

I came directly from *Turin* to *Geneva*, and had a very easie Journey over Mount *Cennis*, though about the Beginning of *December*, the Snows having not yet fallen. On the Top of this high Mountain is a large Plain, and in the midst of the Plain a beautiful Lake, which would be very extraordinary were there not several Mountains in the Neighbourhood rising over it. The inhabitants thereabout pretend that it is unfathomable, and I question not but the Waters of it fill up a deep Valley, before they come to a Level with the Surface of the Plain. It is well stocked with Trouts, though they say it is covered with Ice Three Quarters of the Year.

There is nothing in the natural Face of *Italy* that is more delightful to a Traveller, than the several Lakes which are dispersed up and down among the many Breaks and Hollows of the *Alps* and *Appennines*. For as these vast Heaps of Mountains are thrown together with so much Irregularity and Confusion, they form a great Variety of hollow Bottoms, that often lye in the Figure of so many artificial Basins; where, if any Fountains chance to rise, they naturally spread themselves into Lakes before they can find any Issue for their Waters. The ancient *Romans* took a great deal of Pains to hew out a Passage for these Lakes to discharge themselves into some neighbouring River, for the bettering of the Air, or the recovering of the Soil that lay underneath them. The Draining of the *Fucinus* by the Emperor *Claudius*, with the prodigious Multitude of Spectators who attended it, and the Famous *Naumachia* and splendid Entertainment which were made upon it before the Sluces were opened, is a known Piece of History. In all our Journey through the *Alps*, as well when we

climbed as when we descended them, we had still a River running along with the Road, that probably at first occasioned the
Discovery of this Passage.

JOSEPH ADDISON, Remarks on Italy, 1718

*

THE INHABITANTS of *Leipsic* are generally very rich, as may
well be expected from so great a trade; and live in a splendid
manner. The women dress vastly gay, and very sumptuous in
respect to gold and silver lace, with which they adorn their caps
and gowns. There is a great number of chariots in the town,
which belong to physicians, professors, or merchants; for the
nobility are not allowed to have houses of their own in this city.
They are expensive in their gardens, and especially in their
orangeries, their orange-trees being sent them from *Tunis,* by the
way of *Hamburg.* All round about the town are neighbouring
villages, where the inhabitants unbend themselves with drinking
and dancing, on *Sundays* and festivals; and most of the public
houses are provided with good agreeable wenches for the con-
veniency of the students, whose flames, 'tis thought, would be
more pernicious in town, were they not quenched in this manner.
In one of the suburbs there is a large churchyard, where every
burgher can raise what monument or tomb-stone he please, and
some of them are remarkable for the odd epitaphs upon them. The
following is a specimen of one of those epitaphs upon a merchant's
tomb-stone. On one side there was an account drawn up in a mer-
cantile way thus:

T. A. Blechschmidt	*Creditor for the merit*
debtor for sins com-	*of the blood of* Jesus
mitted 1000000.	Christ 1000000.

On the other side of the stone there was a bill of exchange,
drawn by *Jesus Christ* on God the Father, in the following terms:

1669, the 7th of April at the hour of death.

To T. A. Blechschmidt Stimper *at the day of his death, I* Jesus

Christ *promise to pay by this my letter of exchange, eternal life,*
which I have acquired and merited for him, being satisfied
with his faith and good life.
>   JESUS CHRIST.
>   THOMAS NUGENT, *The Grand Tour,* 1749

*

IMPORTANCE OF COMFORT. Let the traveller, when out in trying weather, work hard at making his sleeping-place perfectly
dry and comfortable; he should not cease until he is convinced
that it will withstand the chill of the early morning, when the heat
of the yesterday's sun is exhausted, and that of the coming sun
has not begun to be felt. It is wretched beyond expression for a
man to lie shivering beneath a scanty covering and to feel the
night air become hourly more raw, while his life-blood has less
power to withstand it; and to think, self-reproachfully, how different would have been his situation if he had simply had forethought and energy enough to cut and draw twice the quantity of
firewood, and to spend an extra half-hour in labouring to make
himself a snugger berth. The omission once made becomes ir-
reparable; for in the cold of a pitiless night he has hardly sufficient
stamina to rise and face the weather, and the darkness makes him
unable to cope with his difficulties.
>   FRANCIS GALTON, *The Art of Travel,* 1872

*

THE PUBLIC coaches or *diligencias* are based, in form and system,
on the French diligence, from whence the name is taken; these
copies are preferable to their originals, inasmuch as the company
who travel by them, from the difficulties of travelling with post-
horses, is of a superior order to those who go by the dilly in
France, and the Spaniard is essentially much higher bred than his
neighbour, and especially as regards the fair sex. The Spanish
diligences go pretty fast, but the stoppages, delays, and 'behind
time' are terrible.

Travelling in the *diligencia,* odious in itself, is subject to the

usual continental drags, *billetes,* and etceteras previously to starting; the prices are moderate, and vary according to the places, the
rotonda, the *interior,* the *berlina,* and the coupé; very little luggage is allowed, and a heavy charge made for all extra. Be very
careful as to directions on your luggage, avoiding the '*Esq.*' and
have it all registered; and take your place in time too, as the
diligencias fill very much, especially during summer; the passengers
are under the charge of a conductor, the *mayoral;* meals are
provided at the coaches' own baiting inns or *paradores,* which
are sufficient in quantity, endurable in cookery, and reasonable in
charges.

On those roads where there are no diligences, recourse must be
had to the original and national modes of travelling. You can hire
a *coche de colleras,* a huge sort of lord mayor's coach, which is
drawn by half-a-dozen or more mules, and which performs journeys from thirty to thirty-five miles a-day, like an Italian vetturino;
this is at once a slow and expensive mode of travel, but not un-
amusing, from the peculiar manner in which cattle and carriage
are driven. This picturesque turn-out, like our 'coach-and-six' in
Pope's time, is fast disappearing. Those natives who cannot afford
this luxury resort to the *galera,* a sort of covered waggon without
springs, which, being of most classical discomfort, is to be sedul-
ously avoided, *que diable allait il faire dans cette galère.* Smaller
vehicles, such as *calesas* and *tartanas,* are also to be occasionally
hired for smaller distances. So much for wheels.

RICHARD FORD, *Handbook for Travellers in Spain,* 1855

*

THE OPEN cars of the American lines afford facilities of contact, and meet the necessities of long journeys far better than the
sectional and boxed-up system of English carriages. Conductors
have thorough command of trains and can meet any emergencies
of travellers without difficulty. Passengers, too, are provided with
many conveniences which cannot be afforded under the English
system . . .

The speed of trains is not equal to that of the English lines.

The Pacific express of the Union and Central Pacific lines, in connexion with the fastest trains east of Chicago, only attains an average of about 19 miles per hour between New York and San Francisco, including short stoppages of 20 or 25 minutes three time a day for refreshments, and longer delays at the junction of lines. It takes about 170 hours to go 3,300 miles, and that includes seven nights in succession in the sleeping car . . .

On the Erie line we travelled from New York to Buffalo in a really pleasant drawing-room car, beautifully carpeted and furnished with elbow chairs, mounted on columns, and capable of being turned about in any direction. This was our pleasantest ride in the 3,300 miles, for which we paid extra $2.50 each passenger.

THOMAS COOK, reporting to the *Daily Mail* his first world tourist trip in 1872

*

AN ADMONITION
to Gentlemen who pass the Alps, *and make the Tour of* Italy.

At *Lyons,* or *Geneva,* the Voiturins, (men who furnish horses for the journey over the *Alps,*) make their demands according to the number of travellers who are on the spot, or (as they hear) are on the road. If there be but few, they are sometimes very reasonable; if there be many, they rise in their demands, and even confederate not to take less than a certain exorbitant sum, stipulated amongst themselves. When there are but few travellers going on, he who takes a passenger has a very good chance upon his arrival at *Turin,* to find customers back again, and, therefore, will agree on very moderate terms. The price of a voiturin and pair of horses is, generally, from eight to ten or eleven louis (guineas,) besides the present of a louis, or at least half a louis, at the end of the journey; however, without accidents to enhance the price, one may expect a pair of horses for eight or nine louis.

Some travellers have not a chaise of their own, but pass the *Alps* in the voiturin's chaise, in which case, the voiturin will sometimes take a man still a louis cheaper, because, when he arrives

71

at *Turin,* he, by this means, has a double chance of bringing back a traveller; for, if the traveller have no chaise himself, the voiturin has one ready for him; and, if he have a chaise, the voiturin leaves his at *Turin* till an opportunity offer of returning it.

In going from *Geneva* to *Turin,* I paid thirty-one louis for six horses and three voiturins; viz. four horses for my coach, and two for my chaise; but then both the coach and the chaise were very heavy. On my return to *Turin,* a voiturin offered to bring me to *Lyons,* the day after my arrival, for twenty-eight louis, but as I chose to make some stay there, this voiturin went off with other Gentlemen, and several travellers happening to come in, none of the voiturins would take me unless I hired six horses to the coach, and paid thirty-six louis, which I was obliged to submit to; and, had I deferred it one day longer, I must have paid forty, as I afterwards learnt from one who set out the following day with the same equipage as mine. It seems the voiturins prefer chaises to coaches, as they demand usually in a higher proportion for a coach and four, than for a chaise and two.

The voiturins, for this sum, defray your charges on the road; they pay for your dinner, supper, and lodging; so that the seven days journey from *Geneva* or *Lyons,* to *Turin,* costs little more than what you contract for with them, the extraordinaries being only the small presents made to the servants, and the expence of breakfasting. The voiturins are generally obliging and busy in providing the best eatables the country affords, because they pay the same ordinary, whether the inn-keepers give you good or bad provisions; besides, they are all ambitious of character, which procures them recommendations from one traveller to another. The voiturin is likewise at the whole expence of carrying you and your equipage over Mount *Cenis,* except a little gratuity which every Gentleman gives to the poor chairmen, perhaps sixpence to each, and a little drink at the resting place, or half way house. As the voiturins are obliged to hire a number of mules, in proportion to the quantity of luggage, and the weight of the chaise, or coach, this consideration, besides the draught for their horses, makes them raise their demands when the equipage is heavy. I would advise no Gentleman to hire horses by the day, and pay for his diet, lodging, and passage over Mount *Cenis,* as he will be much imposed on in many of these articles; but, if he be so inclined, the voiturins will furnish horses at four *Savoy* livres a day each, allowing seven days for going, and seven days for returning, that is, for a chaise and a pair, fourteen times eight livres, about five pounds eighteen shillings; but this, as I have intimated, turns out a dearer method of travelling; and is never to be practised.

The trouble and expence of taking a carriage to pieces, and transporting it over the mountain, lying entirely on the voiturin, except a small present to the coach-maker, it is only to satisfy curiosity that I here give the particular rates, charged by an ordinance of his *Sardinian* Majesty, to prevent disputes and impositions.

Every person who is carried over Mount *Cenis* in a chair, is obliged to employ six chairmen, or, if he be lusty, eight; or extremely corpulent, ten; of which, and indeed, of all disputable matters, the Syndica are appointed by his Majesty absolute judges. The Syndics are magistrates, living the one at *Lanneburg,* on this side of the mountain, and the other at *Novaleze,* which is situated at the other foot of the mountain, on the side towards *Turin;* they are poor men, and not above accepting a small present for drink, but are invested with sufficient power to compel both the muleteers and the chairmen to attend, when any traveller arrives. I had an opportunity, when I went into *Italy,* of seeing this power exerted; for the chairmen were in the midst of their harvest, gathering in the produce of their own little farms, and would gladly have been excused. The Syndic, therefore, rung the alarum-bell, which summons was immediately obeyed, and a sufficient number of them were selected to transport me and my company the next morning.

The pay to each chairman is fifty sous of *Savoy,* that is, two shillings and seven-pence halfpenny. The pay for a mule to carry over a servant is forty sous, about two shillings and a penny. The pay for each mule which carries the baggage is fifty sous, two shillings and seven-pence halfpenny.

A mule is not obliged, by the ordinance, to carry above three hundred and fifty pounds, therefore, if the body of the coach, or chaise, or any parcel of luggage weigh more, it is in the breast of the muleteers to demand what sum they please; a privilege they seldom neglect to avail themselves of, and, sometimes, with great extortion, to the amount of many guineas; therefore, above all men, the *English,* who are reputed rich, should contract with the voiturins to defray this expence. Some *Italians,* who pass often over the mountains, build the body of their coach as light as possible, and of such a structure that it may be separated into two parts, by which contrivance they transport it on the cheapest terms. *Englishmen,* who take their own coaches, should provide such a carriage as may be taken to pieces, which those with a perch do not admit of.

A man may travel post, if he pleases, through the *Alps,* but it is attended with some trouble; and, as I would not advise any one to drive fast on the edges of those precipices, I shall forbear to enter into any detail on that subject.

When you arrive in *Piedmont,* you travel either by the *Post,* or the *Cambiatura.* A foreigner is surprised at the distinction, when he finds there is no difference betwixt the two, except the price; the payment for the post being considerably higher than for the Cambiatura; but the post-horses are the same, and the speed in travelling is the same. It may therefore be concluded, that every body chuses the Cambiatura. I should, however, to be minute, mention that there is one difference, though I have said there is none; for if a man travel in the night, he is obliged to pay the price of the post. I believe I do not exactly know the history of the Cambiatura, but whatever was originally the design, and the practice, every man now easily procures an order for it. The same thing happens with regard to the *Bolletino* in the state of *Venice,* which answers to the Cambiatura in *Lombardy.* Both the Cambiatura and the Bolletino, are orders to the post-masters to furnish horses at the low price; but I was never called upon to shew them at any of the post-houses.

Through all *Italy,* the posts are, upon an average, eight or nine miles, and, perhaps, in *Piedmont,* a little more.

In the *Venetian* state, if a man travel by the post, he must pay sixteen livres and a half for his horses, three livres to the postilion, and half a livre to the hostler, making in all twenty livres, about ten shillings; but as no gentleman travels without a Bolletino, the expence is, eleven livres for the horses, three to the postilions, and half a livre to the hostler, in all about seven shillings and three pence per post.

In the Ecclesiastical State, there is no distinction betwixt the Post and the Cambiatura; and the Post is cheaper than in the other states of Italy. Every post there, is but eight pauls and a half, three pauls to the postilion, and half a paul to the hostler. A paul is about sixpence. It may be remarked, that the Italian Princes give only two pauls to the postilions; but, so much is expected from insults, it is adviseable to pay them three pauls. I knew a nobleman, who, from his princely disposition, gave the postilions five shillings a post, though even that sum did not content them; but such instances of generosity render it very disagreeable to future *English* travellers, who are all supposed to be Lords, and are expected by the postilions to follow the most extravagant examples. No *Englishman* should, therefore, pay more than three pauls, which is a greater reward than a postilion in *England* receives, where other wages are higher, and the necessaries of life dearer than in *Italy.*

Through *Piedmont* and the *Milanese,* post-horses are dearer than in the other parts of *Italy,* the payment together with the eighteen pence given to the postilion, and something to the hostler, amounting to about ten shillings per post.

From *Rome* to *Naples* you may travel post, but the road is so bad, in some places, that I would rather advise the moderate rate of travelling with a voiturin. The most eligible method is, to leave your own carriage at *Rome,* and to go in the chaise belonging to the voiturin; he will carry you (I always suppose two persons) for about four pounds sterling, and pay for your supper and lodging; however, the accommodation is so wretched on the

Neapolitan road, that every gentleman should furnish himself with such cold provision and wine, as will subsist him four or five days.

I would not advise any gentleman to travel with voiturins in the other parts of *Italy*, unless it be necessary for the state of his finances, to take the cheapest method. In point of economy it certainly is preferable; but it is extremely tedious, as they seldom go above two miles and three-quarters in an hour, and what is equally uncomfortable, carry you to the dirtiest and most noisome inns on the road.

SAMUEL SHARP, Letters from Italy, 1767

*

DESCRIPTION OF a Carriole. The *Carriole* is the national vehicle of Norway, but is now seldom met with. It is a two-wheeled vehicle holding one person; the seat is placed well in front of the axle-tree, and fixed by cross-trees to the shafts, which run the whole length of the carriole, the ends projecting behind the axle-tree where they are connected by a board. To this board the traveller's portmanteau is fastened, and the postboy sits on the top of it. Immediately outside and below the trough, close to the splashboard, pieces of iron are fixed whereon to rest the feet. By changing the position of the feet from the trough of the carriole to the irons outside, the legs do not feel cramped, even after a long drive.

T. BENNETT, Norway, 1913

*

WHEN ACTUALLY on a carriage or railway journey it is unwise to make large meals. They are sure to be swallowed in a hurried manner, and in a state of heat and excitement very unfavourable to digestion. The best way is to make no meal at all until the journey is over, but to carry a supply of cold provisions, bread, eggs, chickens, game, sandwiches, Cornish pasties, almonds, oranges, captain's biscuits, water, and sound red wine or cold tea, sufficient to stay the appetites of the party and let a small quantity be taken every two hours.

If this plan be adopted, not only is activity of mind and body preserved, but that heat and swelling of the legs which so often concludes a long day's journey is avoided. Attention to the matter is particularly necessary when the journey continues all night, and for several days in succession, since varicose veins and permanent thickening of the ankles have sometimes resulted from this exertion being combined with too long fasts and hurried repletion at protracted intervals.

THOMAS CHAMBERS, *A Manual of Diet in Health and Disease,* 1875

*

THERE ARE four ways in which travellers who are thrown upon their own resources may house themselves. They may bivouac, that is to say, they may erect a temporary shelter of a makeshift character, partly from materials found on the spot, and partly from the cloths they may happen to possess; they may build a substantial hut, which of course takes a good deal of labour to complete; they may use sleeping-bags; or they may pitch a regular tent. I will speak of these four methods of encamping, – the bivouac, the hut, the sleeping-bag, and the tent, in that order.

General Remarks. – Bivouacking is miserable work in a wet or unhealthy climate; but in a dry and healthy one, there is no question of its superiority over tenting. Men who sleep habitually in the open, breathe fresher air and are far more imbued with the spirit of wild life, than those who pass the night within the stuffy enclosure of a tent. It is an endless pleasure to lie half awake watching the stars above, and the picturesque groupings of the encampment round about, and to hear on all sides the stirrings of animal life. And later in the night, when the fire is low, and servants and cattle are asleep, and there is no sound but of the wind and an occasional plaintive cry of wild animals, the traveller finds himself in that close communion with nature which is the true charm of wild travel. Now all this pleasure is lost by sleeping in a tent. Tent life is semi-civilization, and perpetuates its habits. This may be illustrated by a simple trait; a man who has lived much in bivouacs, if there be a night alarm, runs naturally into the dark for safety, just as a wild animal would; but a man who travels with tents becomes frightened when away from its lights, or from the fancied security of its walls.

In a dangerous country there can be no comparison between the hazard of a tent and that of a bivouac. In the former a man's sleep is heavy; he cannot hear nearly so well; he can see nothing; his cattle may all decamp; while marauders know exactly where he is lying, and may make their plans accordingly. They may creep up unobserved and spear him through the canvas. The first Napoleon had a great opinion of the advantages of bivouacking over those of tenting. He said it was the healthier of the two for soldiers.

Shelter from the Wind. – Study the *form* of a hare! In the flattest and most unpromising of fields, the creature will have availed herself of some little hollow to the lee of an insignificant tuft of grass, and there she will have nestled and fidgeted about till she has made a smooth, round, grassy bed, compact and fitted to her shape, where she may curl herself snugly up, and cower down below the level of the cutting night wind. Follow her example. A man, as he lies upon his mother earth, is an object so small and low that a screen of eighteen inches high will guard him securely from the strength of a storm. A common mistake of a novice lies in selecting a tree for his camping-place, which spreads out nobly above, but affords no other shelter from the wind than that of its bare stem below. It may be, that as he walks about in search of shelter, a mass of foliage at the level of his eye, with its broad shadow, attracts him, and as he *stands* to the leeward of it it seems snug, and, therefore, without further reflection, he orders his bed to be spread at the foot of some tree. But as soon as he lies down on the ground the tree proves worthless as a screen against the wind; it is a roof, but it is not a wall. The real want in blowy weather is a dense low screen, perfectly wind-tight, as high as the knee above the ground. Thus, if a traveller has to encamp on a bare turf plain, he need only turn up a sod seven feet long by two feet wide, and if he succeeds in propping it on its edge, it will form a sufficient shield against the wind.

In heavy gales, the neighbourhood of a solitary tree is a positive nuisance. It creates a violent eddy of wind, that leaves palpable evidence of its existence. Thus, in corn-fields, it is a common result of a storm to batter the corn quite flat in circles round each tree that stands in the field, while elsewhere no injury takes place. This very morning that I am writing these remarks, November 15, 1858, I was forcibly struck by the appearance of Kensington Gardens, after last night's gale, which had covered the ground with an extraordinary amount of dead leaves. They lay in a remarkably uniform layer, of from three to five inches in depth, except that round each and every tree the ground was absolutely bare of leaves for a radius of about a yard. The effect was as though circular discs had been cut out, leaving the edges of the layer of leaves perfectly sharp and vertical. It would have been a dangerous mistake to have slept that night at the foot of any one of those trees.

Again, in selecting a place for bivouac, we must bear in mind that a gale never blows in level currents, but in all kinds of curls and eddies, as the driving of a dust-storm, or the vagaries of bits of straw caught up by the wind, unmistakably show us. Little hillocks or undulations, combined with the general lay of the ground, are a chief cause of these eddies; they entirely divert the current of the wind from particular spots. Such spots should be looked for; they are discovered by watching the grass or the sand that lies on the ground. If the surface be quiet in one place, while all around it is agitated by the wind, we shall not be far wrong in selecting that place for our bed, however unprotected it may seem in other respects. It is constantly remarked, that a very slight mound or ridge will shelter the ground for many feet behind it; and an old campaigner will accept such shelter gladly, notwithstanding the apparent insignificance of its cause.

Shelter from the Sky. – The shelter of a *wall* is only sufficient against wind or driving rain; we require a *roof* to shield us against vertical rain, and against dew, or what is much the same thing, against the cold of a clear blue sky on a still night. The temperature of the heavens is known pretty accurately, by more than one method of calculation: it is −239° Fahr.; the greatest cold felt in the Arctic regions being about −40° Fahr. If the night be cloudy, each cloud is a roof to keep off the cold; if it be clear, we are exposed to the full chill of the blue sky, with only such alleviation as the warming and the non-conducting powers of the atmosphere may afford. The effect is greater than most people would credit. The uppermost layer of the earth, or whatever may be lying exposed upon it, is called upon to part with a great quantity of heat. If it so happen that the uppermost layer is of a non-conducting nature, the heat abstracted from it will be poorly resupplied by communication from the lower ones. Again, if the night be a very calm one, there will be no supply of warmth from fresh currents of air falling down upon it. Hence, in the treble event of a clear blue sky, a non-conducting soil, and a perfectly still night, we are liable to have great cold on the surface of the ground. This is shared by a thin layer of air that immediately rests upon it; while at each successive inch in height, the air becomes more nearly of its proper temperature. A vast number of experiments have been made by Mr Glaisher on this subject ('Phil. Trans.' 1847), the upshot of which is that a thermometer laid on *grass,* under a blue sky on a calm night, marks on an average 8° Fahr. colder than one 4 feet above it; 1 inch above grass, $5\frac{1}{2}°$; 1 foot, 1°; 4 feet, $\frac{1}{2}°$; on gravel and sand the differences are only about one-third as much. Sheep have a practical knowledge of these differences. Often, in an early walk on dewy mornings, I see all the sheep in Hyde Park bivouacked on the gravel walks or Rotten Row. The above figures are the results of experiments made in England, where the air is always moist, and the formation of dew, while it testifies to the cold of the night, assists largely to moderate it. In arid climates the chill would be far greater; such would also be the case at high elevations. One of Mr Glaisher's experiments showed a difference of no less than 28° between the cold on the ground and that at 8 feet high. This might often be rivalled in an elevated desert, as in

George, I'm confused with counting; but I'm of the opinion that one of the smaller trunks is missing.

Certainly I have a passport. I have had a passport for the last twenty-seven inspections and I have it still. Englishmen do not lose passports.

I will fetch the doctor, Sir. I agree the omnibuses are exceedingly high. But Sir's legs are exceedingly low. It is a contretemps.

If this is the bordello quarter it seems peculiarly populous.

I regret to say that at the customs our baggage was searched without regard for even the most intimate apparel. I intend to complain to the proper authorities.

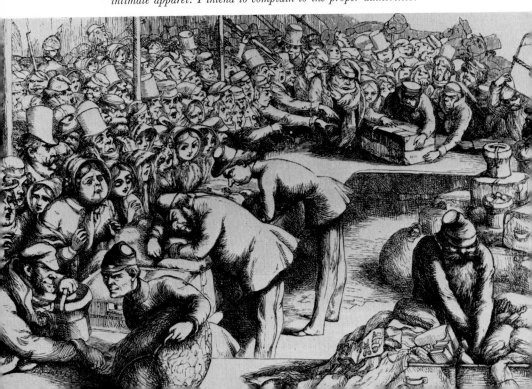

It is not surprising that Mr Farina invented Eau de Cologne.

How very inconvenient! I seem to have lost my purse.

We had an absolutely fearless driver all the way down the Alp.

Is it wise to mix grape and grain?

that of Mongolia. Hence the value of the protection of a roof and a raised sleeping-place, to a man sleeping under a blue sky in still weather, admits of easy interpretation.

Various Methods of Bivouacking. – *Unprotected*. – Mr Shaw, the traveller in Thibet, says : 'My companion and I walked on to keep ourselves warm, but halting at sunset, had to sit and freeze several hours before the things came up. The best way of keeping warm on such an occasion, is to squat down, kneeling against a bank, resting your head on the bank, and nearly between your knees. Then tuck your overcoat in, all round you, over head and all; and if you are lucky, and there is not too much wind, you will make a little atmosphere of your own inside the covering, which will be snug in comparison with the outside air. Your feet suffer chiefly, but you learn to tie yourself into a kind of knot, bringing as many surfaces of your body together as possible. I have passed whole nights in this kneeling position, and slept well; whereas I should not have got a wink had I been stretched at full length with such a scanty covering as a great-coat.'

Bushes. – I have shown that the main object before sleeping out at night is to secure a long wind-tight wall, and that the next is to obtain a roof. Both these objects may be attained by pleaching two or three small neighbouring bushes into one; or branches may be torn off elsewhere and interwoven between the bushes. A few leafy boughs, cut and stuck into the ground, with their tops leaning over the bed, and secured in that position by other boughs, wattled-in horizontally, give great protection. Long grass, &c., should be plucked and strewn against them to make them as wind-tight as possible.

Walls. – A pile of saddle-bags and other travelling gear may be made into a good screen against the wind; and travellers usually arrange them with that intention. Walls of stone may be built as a support to cloths, whose office it is to render the walls wind-tight, and also by lapping over their top, to form a partial roof. We have already spoken of a broad sod of turf propped up on edge.

'The Thibetan traveller cares for no roof overhead if he can shelter himself from the wind behind a three-foot wall. Hence the numerous little enclosures clustered together like cells of a honeycomb at every halting-place, with one side always raised against the prevailing wind.' (*Shaw*). These walls are built round shallow pits, each with its rough fireplace in the middle.

FRANCIS GALTON, *The Art of Travel*, 1872

*

THE SOONER all who start on riding tours can speak Spanish themselves the better, as polyglott travelling servants are apt to be rogues; a retired cavalry soldier is a good man to take, as he understands horses, and knows how to forage in districts where rations are rare. Few soldiers are more sober, patient, and enduring of fatigue than the Spanish; six reals a day, food, lodging, and some dress, with a tip at the end, will be ample pay. He must be treated with civility, and abusive speech avoided.

RICHARD FORD, *Handbook for Travellers in Spain*, 1855

*

DRESS. As various degrees of temperature are frequently passed through during the same day – hot in the valley, sharp and cold on the top of the Fjeld – it is necessary to be provided with clothing which is both light and warm. Extra wraps are very essential on board steamers, especially on the North Cape voyage. A rug or thick plaid is useful as a cushion when driving, and for an extra blanket at night.

For gentlemen the tweed suit is well adapted for the climate, if stout and strong and supplemented by a mackintosh, a dust coat, and warm overcoat; stout shoes should be worn and good warm woollen gloves.

For ladies the travelling dress should be of a strong, light woollen fabric, with a dust cloak, waterproof cloak large enough to cover the dress entirely, and waterproof hood or hat cover, together with additional wraps, in the shape of a wadded jacket and a warm cloak, but garments that confine the arms should be avoided.

Ladies' gloves should have gauntlets to protect the wrists from mosquitoes; and both ladies and gentlemen will find a mosquito veil a very valuable article when fishing.

T. BENNETT, *Norway,* 1913

*

SMALL CHANGE *for Persons Going on the Continent*
Persons of importance being in the habit, at this season of the year, of rushing to the Continent, we have drawn up the following rules, after six trips up and down the Danube and the Rhine, to enable travellers to support the character of Englishmen with that degree of pride and gentlemanly spirit for which they are noted abroad.

1. Write your name in large letters, with date and address, wherever you go. For this purpose, you had better carry about with you a bottle of WARREN'S blacking and a large brush, and you can then lay it on as thick as you please.

2. If you go into a cathedral when service is going on, never mind talking, or staring, or pointing, as much as you like; for it stands to reason, if the people are really as intent on their devotions as they pretend to be, they cannot hear or see you. The best way to test this, is to walk down the aisles with your hat on.

3. Always suspect you are being imposed upon. It is well known that the innumerable small foreign coins were expressly invented to puzzle the English. To guard against giving too much, bargain for everything you have, and try to beat down every item in your bill. Recollect it is the notion of foreigners that every Englishman is stuffed full of money. The sooner you disabuse them of this notion the better.

4. Laugh at everything you do not understand, and never fail to ridicule anything that appears strange to you. The habits of the lower class will afford you abundant entertainment, if you have the proper talent to mimic them. Their religious ceremonies you will also find to be an endless source of amusement.

5. Never mind what damage you do, as long as you can afford to pay for it. Your brothers and sisters will naturally expect some

remembrance of your *tour,* so do not scruple to carry off a *souvenir* of every monument you visit. A saint's finger, or a collection of king's noses, if cleverly taken from the statues, or a whole statue itself taken during the night from its consecrated niche in some lonely street, will convince your relations you have not forgotten them, besides affording you capital sport and healthy excitement in making the collection.

6. Recollect very few people talk English on the Continent, so you may be perfectly at your ease in abusing foreigners before their faces, and talking any modest nonsense you like, in the presence of ladies, at a *table d'hôte.* Do not care what you say about the government of any particular state you may be visiting, and show your national spirit by boasting, on every possible occasion, of the superiority of England and everything English.

7. If you go to a theatre and do not know a word of the language of the pieces, do not hesitate to talk as loudly as you can, or to laugh preposterously at the gibberish, which it is a marvel to you anybody can understand.

8. If foreign states will have foolish laws about passports, it is not to be expected that you, as a free-born Englishman, will tamely submit to them, so always move about as independently as if you were in your own country. If, by a stretch of despotism, you are taken up or sent back, you have your redress by complaining to the British ambassador, or else by sending your case to be laid before Parliament as a *casus belli,* to any distinguished member of the opposition of the time being.

9. Be particular about your diet. Avoid foreign dishes; be sure that the wines are poison; and grumble at everything you get. Recollect that beefsteaks and bottled porter are always kept in the smallest villages for the use of the English.

10. Swear, if you have a mind for it, at the smallest provocation; and, if a fellow is insolent, thrash him, and if anyone interferes, thrash him also. Recollect you can indulge in any violence you please, as long as you have the means to pay for it.

11. Be sure to take English servants with you. They are useful in speaking the language, settling the bills, and taking you to see

the most remarkable sights of the country . . .

12. Buy something at every place you stop at. The foreign articles are not only so much cheaper and better than any you can get in England, but there is also the pleasure of looking at them, and the pride of displaying them before other people, every time your boxes are examined at a custom-house. If you are asked to pay anything extra for them, on the ground of duty, sooner allow every article to be confiscated, than submit to the imposition.

13. Take all your wardrobe with you. Extra luggage is never charged for on the continent, and it would be very foolish to miss an important ceremony, or a royal invitation, for the want of a proper gown, coat, bonnet, cocked hat, pelisse, or regimentals . . .

14. Be sure to cultivate your moustachios the very day you start for the continent, and allow your hair to grow down your back. Buy a dialogue-book, and, if you study it attentively all the way up the Rhine, and at all the places you visit, you will be able, by the time you reach London, to ask 'Which is the nearest way to Cologne?' in no less than eight different languages.

Attend most scrupulously to the above golden rules, and you will never find any difficulty in getting on with the small change with which we have provided you for the trip. Disburse it liberally wherever you go, and you will certainly succeed in making the name of an Englishman respected and beloved all over the continent, and will impress foreigners with the belief that England is without a doubt – what you must always be boasting she is – the most civilized country in the world.

PUNCH, 1845

*

HOLY DAYS

For the benefit of the English it is announced that on Ascension Day the elevators will not be working and on the day of the Feast of the Immaculate Conception there will be no garbage collection in the city.

Public notice in the *Montreal Star*, Quebec edition, c. 1913

WHEN YOU join a party, you must put your right hand on your heart, and say 'Peace be unto you!' You are then told you are welcome; and when you depart, you repeat the ceremony, and are again told you are welcome. On the road a traveller salutes you with, 'May you not be fatigued!' To which you reply, 'May you live long!' If acquainted the salutations become more numerous. Are you strong? Are you well? Are you free from misfortunes? &c. &c.; to all of which you must answer, 'Thanks be to God!' On parting, your friend will tell you that your journey is not a tedious one, and consign you to God's keeping. If invited to dinner, you must reply to the civility, 'May your house be peopled!'; and if you be complimented on any occasion, you must answer that 'I am not worthy of you; it is your greatness'. Every person, high or low, you must address by the title Khan or Agha, to gain his good graces. If he is a moollah or priest, you must call him Akhoond or teacher, if a moollah's son, Akhoonzada. A secretary is called Meerza; which is, however, a cognomen for all nondescript characters, in which class we were numbered. Intimate acquaintances call each other 'lalu' or brother.

ALEXANDER BURNES, *Travels into Bokhara,* 1834

*

THE IMPERIAL Rescript addressed to His Imperial Highness the Grand Duke Tsesarévich on the 17th March 1891, finally and irrevocably decided the question of the construction of the Great Siberian Railroad.

This memorable document was made known by His Imperial Highness upon his again treading Russian soil at Vladivostók, on the 14th May 1891, on his way back from the Far East.

Your Imperial Highness!

'Having given the order to build a continuous line of railway across Siberia, which is to unite the rich Siberian provinces with the railway system of the Interior, I entrust you to declare My will, upon your entering the Russian dominions after your inspection of the foreign countries of the East. At the same time,

I desire you to lay the first stone at Vladivostók for the construction of the Ussúri line, forming part of the Siberian Railway, which is to be carried out at the cost of the State and under direction of the Government. Your participation in the achievement of this work will be a testimony to My ardent desire to facilitate the communications between Siberia and the other countries of the Empire, and to manifest my extreme anxiety to secure the peaceful prosperity of this Country'.

I remain your sincerely loving

ALEXANDER.

The question of the construction of the Great Siberian Railway, which for a third of a century had occupied the attention of the Government and society, was now settled, representing the most important event of the century, not only in our country, but in the whole world.

On the 19th May, at Vladivostók, His Imperial Highness the Grand Duke Tsesarévich, with his own hands filled a wheelbarrow with earth and emptied it on the embankment of the future Ussúri line, and then laid the first stone for the construction of the Great Siberian Railway.

Guide to the Great Siberian Railway, 1900

*

THE EXPENSES OF TRAVELLING IN NORWAY

should be reckoned in a round sum at £1 1s. a head per diem, but, if travelling quietly, without going over too much country, and halting occasionally, the expenses need not exceed 18s. 6d. per diem, and can even be reduced in some districts to 15s., especially if *stolkjærrer* (spring carts) instead of the more costly *caleche* carriages are used.

Pedestrians and Cyclists can average their daily expenditure at 12s. a head, and still less when the trip does not include much travelling by steamer or railway.

For board and lodging (exclusive of wine or beer) the charges are 6 to 9 Kroner per diem, varying according to the pretensions of the station and the district in which the traveller is. The cheapest districts are the Gudbrandsdal, Romsdal, Nordmöre, and the north of Norway, the dearest Hardanger, Voss and Sogn; but then the hotels in the latter districts are of a very superior class, and the living at many excellent.

In the large towns the price per diem at a first class hotel is from 12 to 18 Kroner; but of course more if very expensive rooms are taken.

Many of the country hotels receive boarders at from 5s. to 8s. per diem, if a stay of at least a week is made.

Travellers so often ask what *gratuities* it is customary to give to hotel servants, that it has been thought advisable to give the following scale as a guide to those who wish to remunerate any special civility and attention.

At small hotels and stations 25 to 50 øre a day to the chamber-maid, 25 to 50 øre to the woman who waits upon you, and 25 to 50 øre to the man who attends to the luggage. If only one meal is partaken of 25 øre to the waitress only. At big hotels 50 øre to 1 Krone to the chambermaid, 1 Krone to the head waiter, 1 to 2 Kroner to the portiér, and 1 to 2 Kroner to the man who conveys the baggage to and from the railway station or steamer pier. The above scale is given for one or two persons in the same party; for three or four double the amounts should be paid. If more than a day is spent at an hotel the gratuities are increased proportionately. At some hotels, instead of gratuities, 10 per cent is added to the bill.

T. BENNETT, Norway, 1913

*

THE TRAVELLER on foreign shores, where English is scarcely understood, let alone spoken, unless the speaker raise his voice to inconvenient volume, is advised to carry with him, for his delectation, the Quarterly volume of THE MUSEUM. Volume XXVI, published today, contains devotions to the Fine Arts, Literature, Science and Philosophy, Men and Manners, Poetry and Poesy, Facietiae &c. &c. &c. In particular, the peripatetic gentleman will find of the utmost interest an article on the life of Ali Pacha, of Janina, Vizier of Epirus; Arnott's Account of the Last Illness, Decease, and Post Mortem of Napoleon Buonaparte; and Lawrence's Lectures on Physiology, Zoology, and the Natural History of Man. THE MUSEUM is to be obtained of all newsmen, booksellers, Postmasters and Clerks of the Roads, price *6s. 8d.* sewed.

Advertisement in The Times, 19 October 1822

*

I. – PASSPORTS

Before the traveller is allowed to enter the kingdom of the Two Sicilies, his passport must bear the visa of a Neapolitan minister or consul. If he arrive by sea, it must be signed by the Neapolitan consul resident in the port of embarkation. This regulation applies even to travellers who may be on their way to Malta or the Levant, and who may wish to land at Naples during the few hours which the steamer may stay on her passage. If the traveller arrive by land from Rome, his passport must not only have been signed by the Neapolitan ambassador in that capital, and distinctly *specify the route* intended to be taken, but, if the traveller intend to visit any places which are not on his direct route to Naples, such as Isola, Arpino, &c., *the names of those places must be inserted in the passport,* or he will not be allowed to proceed to them. The frontier station, where the passport is demanded and viséed, is frequently at a distance from the Dogana, particularly in the provinces away from the great lines of road. In such cases the traveller will be sent in charge of a gendarme direct to the Dogana, without being allowed to visit any place by the way. These frontier dogane are under the direction of the *Giudice di Circondario,* who is subject to the immediate control of the *Sottintendente* of the district. Any instance of incivility or of excessive authority on the part of the Giudice should be immediately reported to the Sottintendente at the chief town of the district, and, if necessary, to the Intendente or Governor of the province, who resides always in the principal city. These officers are men of education and intelligence, and are always ready to redress any grievance to which the traveller may be exposed by the petty officers of the Dogana.

The traveller who enters Naples by land, or by the railway from Capua, is required to give up his passport at the barrier of the city or the railway station, and to name the hotel at which he intends to lodge. In exchange for his passport he will receive a *biglietto* or printed receipt, which must be presented at the police office within 48 hours. The simplest plan is to place it in the hands of the landlord of the hotel, who will make the necessary arrangements.

If he arrive by sea, he must present himself to the police of the port on landing, and take the usual receipt for his passport. No stranger is allowed to remain in Naples longer than a week who does not provide himself with a permission to reside (*Carta di Sicurezza*), which is granted for two months. It is personal, and is consequently necessary to each individual of a party. The landlord usually arranges this in two days, charging 6 carlini per head, of which 41 grani are paid to the police and 19 to the *commission-naire*. Before leaving Naples for a foreign state, the passport must have the visa of the minister or consul of the country to which the bearer belongs. No fee is charged at the British legation, but American citizens have hitherto paid 2 dollars to the United States Consul. To go from Naples to Rome, after the signature of the British minister the visa of the Papal nuncio is required; that of the police is then necessary; and, lastly, the signature of the minister of foreign affairs.

A *lascia-passare* for Terracina and for the gate of San Giovanni at Rome ought to be obtained through their banker in the latter city by persons travelling in their own carriage. On leaving Naples by sea, it is desirable to have, in addition to the visa of the police and the minister, the signatures of the consuls of those countries at whose ports the vessel will touch on her passage. These signatures must be obtained before the Neapolitan minister will grant his visa. The charges upon passports when travelling by steam from Naples to Marseilles, touching at the intermediate ports, are :

British minister, o; Police, 6 carl; Papal Nuncio, 6 carl; Tuscan consul, 6 carl.; Sardinian consul, 4 francs, except to passports issued by the British Secretary of State, on which no charge is made; French consul, 3 francs; minister of foreign affairs, 1 piastre. The passport must be left at the office of the steamer the day before its departure, in order that the captain may fulfil all the necessary formalities at the Board of Health. From Naples to Sicily a guarantee is required from the banker of the traveller before the police will grant their signature, which costs 6 carlini; the passport must then be signed by the British minister; and if it be intended to go on to Malta, this is to be specified in the visa of the latter, and the passport must have also the signature of the minister of foreign affairs. The same rule applies to citizens of the United States. Even an excursion to Pæstum cannot be undertaken without a special passport from the prefecture of police, at the usual cost of 6 carlini. Travellers by post to any part of the kingdom must be furnished with an order for post-horses from the postmaster-general, which is never granted until the passport be regularly signed for departure, *buono per partenza*.

2. – FRONTIER AND CUSTOM-HOUSES

Travellers are liable to four custom-house examinations between the frontier and Naples, at every one of which a timely fee of a few carlini will save the traveller much inconvenience.

By a decree of 1852, which removed the prohibition formerly existing, foreign horses are now allowed to be imported by the payment of a small duty at the frontier, with the exception of a peculiar breed from Dalmatia.

Carriages arriving by sea are liable to a heavy duty, in the form of a deposit, but not when arriving by land. Should the carriage remain in the kingdom one year, the traveller must pay 10 ducats more, and when it is exported the fact must be certified to, or the banker who has guaranteed the duty on its arrival will be liable . . .

3. – INNS

In addition to the information respecting inns given in detail in our accounts of the different towns, we may here observe, as a general rule, that travellers should make their bargain with the landlords on their first arrival. All foreigners make it a rule to adopt this precaution, and for this reason they not only pay about a third less than English travellers, but escape the annoyances and delays of disputed bills. The principal hotels in the capital rank among the best and the dearest in Italy. Within the last few years the landlords have lessened one source of cost, by the introduction of tables-d'hôte and coffee-rooms; but we are convinced that they will still further consult their own interests by adopting in every branch of their establishments, and especially in the charges for apartments, a scale of prices which will put an end to the reproach that they have the dearest inns in Italy. The third-rate inns of Naples have not the pretensions or the comforts to justify high prices; and for this reason they are usually frequented by foreigners, who are less dependent than Englishmen on comfortable quarters for the enjoyment of travelling. There is perhaps no city in Italy which offers in itself more inducements than Naples to prolong a residence; and we trust that the respectable landlords of the hotels will in future insure the lengthened sojourn of English travellers, by arranging a fixed scale of charges consistent with the known expenses of life at Naples.

In the provinces, the towns, and even the cities, are very unequally provided. In some the inns are not inferior to those of the second class in the capital; in others, they are scarcely worthy of the name. In the remote districts the *osterie* are as bad and comfortless as they were in the time of Montaigne, except that the wooden shutters have mostly been replaced by glazed panels. The cookery in such places is on a par with the accommodation.

MURRAY'S *Handbook to Southern Italy,* 1855

*

THE QUANTITIES of *Chorizo* and *Pimentesco* eaten in Estremadura produce carbuncles. The Spaniards, however, although tremendous consumers of the pig, whether in the salted form or from the skin, have to the full the abhorrence to the unclean animal in the *abstract*. In delicate parlance he never was named except with an excuse, *con perdon sea dicho*. *Muy puerco* (like the Moslem *Haluf*) is their last expression for all that is most dirty, or disgusting. *Muy cochina* never is forgiven, if applied to woman. It is equivalent to *vacca* or cow of the Italians, or to the canine feminine compliment bandied among our fair sex at Billingsgate, nor does the epithet imply moral purity or chastity.

RICHARD FORD, *Handbook for Travellers in Spain,* 1855

*

A SHOOTING excursion into the primeval forest of British Guiana is one to be undertaken in all seriousness; for of vehicles, horses, or interior roads there are none, and all locomotion is accomplished by water.

The proper period of the year, too, has to be studied, and the plan of campaign has to be thought out. Tent-boats, Indian paddlers, and negro servants must be hired in advance, guns, ammunition, and fishing tackle carefully selected – to say nothing of ordinary impedimenta, including the indispensable grass-hammock, both for sleeping in at night and for the purpose of a midday siesta. Tins of pressed food, bags of flour, jars of salt butter, bottles of brandy and Schiedam, with the latter's usual accompaniment, Angostura bitters with swizzle-sticks, have to be stowed away in the smallest compass – viz., in the useful Indian baskets made by the 'Bucks' for travelling in the bushy interior. A spare suit of tweed or flannel, thick as well as thin, socks, strong shooting-boots and moccasins, complete the inventory. The list may be amplified *ad infinitum;* but these are necessities. It is to be remembered that the excursion is made into the interior of a mighty forest-covered continent, where Indian *benabs* are the only representatives of civilized caravansaries; where the sparse population retire before your advance, unwilling to entertain or receive you within their gates; where neither doctors nor apothecaries can minister to your ailments – in fact, you become for the nonce a child of the forest, and must learn, if ignorant before, to 'paddle your own canoe.'

But in this respect I am slightly wrong, for it is possible, and even requisite, to engage the services of an experienced bushman, Indian or Creole, to 'boss the show'. This man is literally a fac-totum. He is cook, butler, gamekeeper, and boatman. Sitting either in the bow or stern of the frail *courial* or canoe, he guides its passage with unerring skill through rocks and shallows. Marching in advance of the party, he cuts a path through the thickest bush. In presence of game, his keen eye notes every paw-print; he scents the peccary; he listens, with ear to the ground, to the dis-appearing patter of frightened deer, or enjoins silence to catch the distant growl of the jaguar, or the low bellow of the cruel cayman; he vents his deadly spleen against the ubiquitous monkey, which too often heralds the approach of the shooting-party; and he treats with disdain the chattering macaw, or the startled ibis. Story, or song, or jest, from any of the party on the war-path would be an unendurable insult.

Lt.-Col. E. Rogers, *Advice to the Traveller in British Guiana,*
1897

*

Occasional Means of Quenching Thirst. – *A Shower of Rain* will yield a good supply. The clothes may be stripped off and spread out, and the rain-water sucked from them. Or, when a storm is approaching, a cloth or blanket may be made fast by its four corners, and a quantity of bullets thrown in the middle of it; they will cause the water that it receives, to drain to one point and trickle through the cloth, into a cup or bucket set below. A reversed umbrella will catch water; but the first drippings from it, or from clothes that have been long unwashed, as from a macintosh cloak, are intolerably nauseous and very unwhole-some. It must be remembered, that thirst is greatly relieved by the skin being wetted, and therefore it is well for a man suffering from thirst, to strip to the rain. Rain-water is lodged for some days in the huge pitcher-like corollas of many tropical flowers.

94

Sea-water. – Lives of sailors have more than once been saved when turned adrift in a boat, by bathing frequently and keeping their clothes damp with salt-water. However, after some days, the nauseous taste of the salt-water is very perceptible in the saliva, and at last becomes unbearable; such, at least, was the experience of the surgeon of the wrecked 'Pandora'.

Dew-water is abundant near the sea-shore, and may be collected in the same way as rain-water. The storehouse at Angra Pequeña, in S.W. Africa, in 1850, was entirely supplied by the dew-water deposited on its roof. The Australians who live near the sea, go among the wet bushes with a great piece of bark, and brush into it the dew-drops from the leaves with a wisp of grass; collecting in this way large quantities of water. Eyre used a sponge for the same purpose, and appears to have saved his life by its use.

Animal Fluids are resorted to in emergencies; such as the contents of the paunch of an animal that has been shot; its taste is like sweetwort. Mr Darwin writes of people who, catching turtles, drank the water that was found in their pericardia; it was pure and sweet. Blood will stand in the stead of solid food, but it is of no avail in the stead of water, on account of its saline qualities.

Vegetable Fluids. – Many roots exist, from which both natives and animals obtain a sufficiency of sap and pulp, to take the place of water. The traveller should inquire of the natives, and otherwise acquaint himself with those peculiar to the country that he visits; such as the roots which the eland eats, the bitter water-melon, &c.

To purify water that is muddy or putrid. – With muddy water, the remedy is to filter, and to use alum, if you have it. With putrid, to boil, to mix with charcoal, or expose to the sun and air; or what is best, to use all three methods at the same time. When the water is salt or brackish, nothing avails but distillation.

To filter Muddy Water. – When, at the watering-place, there is little else but a mess of mud and filth, take a good handful of grass or rushes, and tie it roughly together in the form of a cone, 6 or 8 inches long; then dipping the broad end into the puddle, and turning it up, a streamlet of fluid will trickle down through the small end. This excellent plan is used by the Northern Bushmen – at their wells quantities of these bundles are found lying about. (Andersson.) Otherwise suck water through your handkerchief by putting it over the mouth of your mug, or by throwing it on the gritty mess as it lies in the puddle. For obtaining a copious supply, the most perfect plan, if you have means, is to bore a cask full of auger-holes, and put another small one, that has had the bottom knocked out, inside it; and then to fill the space between the two, with grass, moss, &c. Sink the whole in the midst of the pond; the water will run through the auger-holes, filter through the moss, and rise in the inner cask clear of weeds and sand. If you have only a single cask, holes may be bored in the lower part of its sides, and alternate layers of sand and grass thrown in, till they cover the holes; through these layers, the water will strain. Or any coarse bag, kept open with hoops made on the spot, may be moored in the mud, by placing a heavy stone inside; it will act on the same principle, but less efficiently than the casks. Sand, charcoal, sponge, and wool, are the substances most commonly used in properly constructed filters: peat charcoal is excellent. Charcoal acts not only as a mechanical filter for solid impurities, but it has the further advantage of absorbing putrid gases. Snow is also used as a filter in the Arctic regions. Dr Rae used to lay it on the water, until it was considerably higher than its level, and then to suck the water through the snow.

Alum. – Turbid water is also, in some way as yet insufficiently explained, made clear by the Indian plan of putting a piece of alum into it. The alum appears to unite with the mud, and to form a clayey deposit. Independently of this action, it has an astringent effect upon organic matters: it hardens them, and they subside to the bottom of the vessel, instead of being diffused in a glairy, viscous state, throughout the water. No taste of alum remains in the water, unless it has been used in great excess. Three thimblefuls of alum will clarify a bucketful of turbid water.

Putrid Water should always be purified by boiling it together with charcoal or charred sticks, as low fevers and dysenteries too often are the consequences of drinking it. The mere addition of charcoal largely disinfects it. Bitter herbs, if steeped in putrid water, or even rubbed well about the cup, are said to render it less unwholesome. The Indians plunge hot iron into putrid water.

Thirst, to relieve. – Thirst is a fever of the palate, which may be somewhat relieved by other means than drinking fluids.

By exciting Saliva. – The mouth is kept moist, and thirst is mitigated, by exciting the saliva to flow. This can be done by chewing something, as a leaf; or by keeping in the mouth a bullet, or a smooth, non-absorbent stone, such as a quartz pebble.

By Fat or Butter. – In Australia, Africa, and N. America, it is a frequent custom to carry a small quantity of fat or butter, and to eat a spoonful at a time, when the thirst is severe. These act on the irritated membranes of the mouth and throat, just as cold cream upon chapped hands.

By Salt Water. – People may live long without drinking, if they have the means of keeping their skin constantly wet with water, even though it be salt or otherwise undrinkable. A traveller may tie a handkerchief wetted with salt water round his neck.

By checking Evaporation. – The Arabs keep their mouths covered with a cloth, in order to prevent the sense of thirst caused by the lips being parched.

By Diet. – Drink well before starting, and make a habit of drinking only at long intervals, and then, plenty at a time.

On giving Water to Persons nearly dead from Thirst. – Give a little at a time, let them take it in spoonfuls; for the large draughts that their disordered instincts suggest, disarrange the weakened stomach : they do serious harm, and no corresponding good. Keep the whole body wet.

Francis Galton, The Art of Travel, 1872

*

Holland enjoys the greatest foreign trade of any country in the world; and in respect to strength and riches, is equal to the other six of the *United Provinces*. 'Tis remarkable, that tho' this country does not produce enough corn for the hundredth part of the inhabitants, yet it is justly considered as the granary of *Europe* : Tho' it has no vineyards, yet it has more wine, and more sorts of wine, than any other part of the world. Tho' it has no woods, yet there are more joiners and carpenters here than in any other part; and more ships, barks, boats and all manner of vessels belonging to it than perhaps all the rest of *Christendom*. In fine, tho' it has scarce any native commodities, or product of its own, yet they import every thing from abroad, and have as great a variety of manufactures, and merchandize, as any nation whatever. It is a magazine, or general store-house, where the product of every country is lodged, bought in very cheap, and often sold out very dear, even to the very country sometimes from whence it is brought.

THOMAS NUGENT, The Grand Tour, 1749

*

THE BULL-FIGHTS at Madrid are first-rate, as becomes the capital of Tauromachia; they begin in April and continue until November; they generally take place on St. Mondays, and in the afternoon; however, ample notice is given by placards. The *aficionado* will, of course, ride out the previous morning to *el Arroyo de Abroñigal,* and see what the *Ganado* is like; he will also secure a ticket on the *shady* side of the *Plaza,* and be sure to be early in the Calle de Alcalá to see the mob, and to reach the *Plaza* half an hour before opening the doors, to see the arrival of the company : how striking the winding street filled with a fierce mob hastening to bloodshed like a parti-coloured snake darting on its prey ! what a circulation of life in this Aorta of the Only Court ! what a din and dust, what costumes and *calesas,* what wild drivers running outside, what picturesque *manolos* and *manolas* inside ! Now indeed, in this pulvere olimpico, we are in Spain, and no mistake, no civilisation of the coat now : but real Spain, and his Majesty of the many, is better to be studied in the streets than the saloons. The dazzling glare and fierce African sun calcining the heavens and the earth, fires up man and beast to madness; now in a raging thirst for blood, seen in flashing eyes and the irritable ready knife, the passion of the Arab triumphs over the coldness of the Goth: how different is the crowd and noisy hurry from the ordinary still life and monotony of these localities. The horrid excitement fascinates the many, like the tragedy of an execution, for, as a lively Frenchman observes, '*La réalité atroce* is the recreation of the savage, and the sublime of common-place souls.' Even quadrupeds seem mad as the bipeds, the poor horses excepted, who are worse *baited* than the bulls.

The *toros* for this *plaza* generally come from the pastures of the Jarama: and that breed was famous even among the Moors; but every *aficionado* will read the splendid description of one of this race in *Gazul's* ballad, '*Estando toda la Corte*'. These verses were evidently written by a practical *torero,* and on the spot: they sparkle with daylight and local colour like a Velazquez, and are as minutely correct as a Paul Potter, while Byron's 'Bull-fight' is the invention of a foreign poet, and full of slight inaccuracies.

The bull-fights at Madrid are first-rate, nothing is economised except the horses: this is the national spectacle, and the high salaries paid at 'Court' naturally attract the most distinguished artists, as they do to our opera in the Haymarket.

Opposite are the gardens of the *Buen Retiro,* and their gate is *la Glorieta.* Returning to the Prado, the view is very striking. The *Prado,* a name familiar to all, is the *Prater,* the Hyde-park of Madrid; here, on the winter days from three to five, and summer evenings from eight to twelve, all the rank, beauty, and fashion appear.

The *Prado,* 'the meadow', was in the time of Philip IV a wooded dip renowned for murder and intrigue political and amatory. It was levelled and planted by the Conde de Aranda, under Charles III, and laid out by José Hermonsilla in the garden walks: the length, from the Atocha convent to the Portillo de Recoletos, is about 9650 feet; the most frequented portion, '*el Salon*', extends from the Calle de Alcalá to the Calle de San Jeronimo, and is 1450 feet long by 200 wide. The *Salon* terminates with the fountain of Neptune, sculptured by one Juan de Mena. Of the seven other fountains those of Apollo and Cybele are

99

most admired; but these stony things count as nothing, when compared to the living groups of all age, colour, and costume which walk and talk, ogle and nod, or sit and smoke. The *Prado*, a truly Spanish thing and scene, is unique; and as there is nothing like it in Europe, and oh, wonder! as there are no London Cockneys on it, it fascinates all who pass the Pyrenees. It is the place to study costume and manner, and was in our time the very 'Rotten Row' of the Only Court. Here one went to look at antediluvian carriages with ridiculous coachmen and grotesque footmen to match, caricatures which amongst us would be put into the British Museum. These lumbering vehicles drove round and round, a routine dull as the Spaniard's and Oriental's monotonous life, where today is the reflection of yesterday, and the anticipation of tomorrow. The exceptions were the equipages of the foreign ministers, and of the few grandees and rich up-starts who managed to purchase those of a departing ambassador, or of those who invested their honest gains on the *Bolsa* in a spick-and-span jingling Parisian *equipage*. Now, these dear old slow coaches are worn out, and have given place to the neat and uninteresting turn-outs from Longacre and the Boulevards. The eternal sameness of the Prado is lost to the guest who tarries but a week, while to the native, custom does not stale, nay this very sameness has a charm among a people who hate innovations, and who, like children and Orientals, prefer an old and the same game to a new one. Where artificial amusements are rare and intellectual pursuits not abundant, when the sun scorches, the shade and a gentle stroll suffice, during which love and love-making becomes an obvious resource and occupation to the young of both sexes; and the appetite for this business grows on what it feeds, until mathematics and political economy seem dry and uninviting pastimes : as the parties get older, their life of love is varied with some devotion, a little stabling, and much tobacco.

Again, it is quite refreshing on the *Prado* to see how united and what good friends all Spaniards *seem* to be. There is no end to compliments and Judas kissings, but deep and deadly are the jealousies and hatreds which lurk beneath; and double-edged are the ideal knives grasped by the murders of the wish, for *muchos beasn á manos, que quiaren ver cortadas:* arsenic mixed in honey is not more deadly sweet.

RICHARD FORD, *Handbook for Travellers in Spain,* 1855

*

CHAPTER XII : *Concerning Owls in Iceland*
There are no owls of any kind in the whole island.

TH. HORREBOW, *Iceland,* 1758

*

MANAGEMENT OF SAVAGES

General Remarks. – A frank, joking, but determined manner, joined with an air of showing more confidence in the good faith of the natives than you really feel, is the best. It is observed, that a sea-captain generally succeeds in making an excellent impression on savages: they thoroughly appreciate common sense, truth, and uprightness; and are not half such fools as strangers usually account them. If a savage does mischief, look on him as you would on a kicking mule, or a wild animal, whose nature is to be unruly and vicious, and keep your temper quite unruffled. Evade the mischief, if you can: if you cannot, endure it; and do not trouble yourself overmuch about your dignity, or about retaliating on the man, except it be on the grounds of expediency. There are even times when any assumption of dignity becomes ludicrous, and the traveller must, as Mungo Park had once to do, 'lay it down as a rule to make himself as useless and as insignificant as possible, as the only means of recovering his liberty'.

Bush Law. – It is impossible but that a traveller must often take the law into his own hands. Some countries, no doubt, are governed with a strong arm by a savage despot; to whom or to whose subordinates appeals must of course be made; but, for the most part, the system of life among savages is–

'The simple rule, the good old plan, –
That they should take, who have the power;
And they should keep, who can.'

Where there is no civil law, or any kind of substitute for it, each man is, as it were, a nation in himself; and then the traveller ought to be guided in his actions by the motives that influence nations, whether to make war or to abstain from it, rather than by the criminal code of civilised countries. The traveller must settle in his own mind what his scale of punishments should be; and it will be found a convenient principle that a culprit should be punished in proportion to the quantity of harm that he has done, rather than according to the presumed wickedness of the offence. Thus, if two men were caught, one of whom had stolen an ox, and the other a sheep, it would be best to flog the first much more heavily than the second; it is a measure of punishment more intelligible to savages than ours. The principle of double or treble restitution, to which they are well used, is of the same nature. If all theft be punished, your administration will be a reign of terror; for every savage, even your best friends, will pilfer little things from you, whenever they have a good opportunity. Be very severe if any of your own party steal trifles from natives: order double or treble restitution, if the man does not know better; and, if he does, a flogging besides, and not in place of it.

Seizing Food. – On arriving at an encampment, the natives commonly run away in fright. If you are hungry, or in serious need of anything that they have, go boldly into their huts, take just what you want, and leave fully adequate payment. It is absurd to be over-scrupulous in these cases.

Feast-Days. – Interrupt the monotony of travel, by marked days, on which you give extra tobacco and sugar to the servants. Avoid constant good feeding, but rather have frequent slight fasts to ensure occasional good feasts; and let those occasions when marked stages of your journey have been reached, be great gala-days. Recollect that a savage cannot endure the steady labour that we Anglo-Saxons have been bred to support. His nature is adapted to alternations of laziness and of severe exertion. Promote merriment, singing, fiddling, and so forth, with all your power. Autolycus says, in 'A Winter's Tale', –

'Jog on, jog on, the foot-path way,
　Merrily bent the stile-a;
A merry heart goes all the day,
　Your sad tires in a mile-a'.

Flogging. – Different tribes have very different customs in the matter of corporal punishment; there are some who fancy it a disgrace and a serious insult. A young traveller must therefore be discriminating and cautious in the licence he allows to his stick, or he may fall into sad trouble.

FRANCIS GALTON, *The Art of Travel,* 1872

3. *Scenes and People*

IT WAS with some trepidation that I ventured to express myself in the native tongue; and I was misguided to do so. 'Me voici, un gentilhomme Anglais' is everywhere understood and curiosity is expressed.

CHARLES W. WILSON, *From Korti to Khartoum*, 1885

THE LANGUAGE everywhere causes confusion. There is the TOWN El Obeyed and the SKEIKH El Obeyed; there is the Haloman of Cairo and the Haloman of Khartoum. I became irritable and said I would write to *The Times* about it.

GENERAL GORDON, *Despatches*, 1884

VOULEZ VOUS *promenade avec moi ce soir?* should be followed, if the reply is in the affiirmative (*oui*) with the additional query *combien?* The transaction is then on a business footing.

Tommies' Guide to Colloquial French, 1914

IT SHOULD be beneath the dignity of any English person to haggle over the price of anything. If the question *Est-ce assez?* is met with denial an attitude of lofty indifference should be affected. Any further importunity, *au pis aller*, should result in an invocation of the name of the Sovereign. Nothing is so alarming to foreigners as an implied call upon the Queen Emperor.

Memorials of a Member of the Aristocracy, 1891

Charles Dickens appears several times in this section, as he does
elsewhere in the book. That should astonish no one. He was no
tourist by nature, but it was his business to observe and record,
which he did voluminously in his *American Notes* and *Pictures
From Italy,* and his sketches of guides, sacristans, cicerones *et al*
are clearly the notes of a novelist subconsciously recording
characters for possible future use while simultaneously reporting
for the benefit of his immediate readers in the *News Chronicle*
what he saw on his travels.

Englishmen other than professional writers – who after all
have a vested interest in delineating people and scenes – are not
generally good at verbal sketches. They are too self-centred. It
does not often occur to them that other people have sensibilities
that are revealed by words, gestures and expressions worth
recording. Thomas Babington Macaulay, travelling from Rome
to Naples in 1839, bribed the customs official at the frontier to
let his luggage through unexamined. The man then attempted
politely to prolong his conversation with the distinguished
Englishman, whereupon he was mercilessly snubbed. 'To think,'
Macaulay commented, 'that a public functionary to whom a
little silver is a bribe is fit society for an English gentleman!'
Macaulay too was a writer of course; but a far more egotistical
and ponderous one than Dickens, and far more typical of the
Englishman abroad with his arrogant superiority.

Here, then, are vignettes and scenes; here are people revealing
themselves – Johnson and Boswell arguing, Robert Falcon
Scott in the simplicity of his diary entry – or being illuminated
by the bright beam of the professional eye, the incisive etching of
the professional pen of the Englishman abroad.

* * *

THE BIRDS were astir, the cicadas had begun their music, and the
Urania Leilus, a strange and beautiful tailed and gilded moth,
whose habits are those of a butterfly, commenced to fly in flocks
over the tree-tops. Raimundo exclaimed 'Clareia o dia!' – 'The
day brightens!' The change was rapid : the sky in the east assumed

suddenly the loveliest azure colour, across which streaks of thin white clouds were painted. It is at such moments as this that one feels how beautiful our world truly is! The channel on whose waters our little boat was floating was about two hundred yards wide; others branched off right and left, surrounding the group of lonely islands which terminate the land of Carnopijó. The forest on all sides formed a lofty hedge without a break : below, it was fringed with mangrove bushes, whose small foliage contrasted with the large glossy leaves of the taller trees, or the feather-and fan-shaped fronds of palms.

Being now arrived at our destination, Raimundo turned up his trousers and shirt-sleeves, took his long hunting-knife, and leapt ashore with the dogs. He had to cut a gap in order to enter the forest. We expected to find Pacas and Cutías; and the method employed to secure them was this : at the present early hour they would be seen feeding on fallen fruits, but would quickly, on hearing a noise, betake themselves to their burrows; Raimundo was then to turn them out by means of the dogs, and Joaquim and I were to remain in the boat with our guns, ready to shoot all that came to the edge of the stream – the habits of both animals, when hard-pressed, being to take to the water. We had not long to wait. The first arrival was a Paca, a reddish, nearly tailless Rodent, spotted with white on the sides, and intermediate in size and appearance between a hog and a hare. My first shot did not take effect; the animal dived into the water and did not reappear. A second was brought down by my companion as it was rambling about under the mangrove bushes. A Cutía next appeared : this is also a Rodent, about one third the size of the Paca : it swims, but does not dive, and I was fortunate enough to shoot it. We obtained in this way two more Pacas and another Cutía. All the time the dogs were yelping in the forest. Shortly afterwards Raimundo made his appearance, and told us to paddle to the other side of the island. Arrived there, we landed and prepared for breakfast. It was a pretty spot – a clean, white, sandy beach beneath the shade of wide-spreading trees. Joaquim made a fire. He first scraped fine shavings from the midrib of a Bacaba palm-leaf; these he piled into a little heap in a dry place, and then struck a light in his bamboo tinderbox with a piece of old file and a flint, the tinder being a felt-like substance manufactured by an ant (Polyrhachis bispinosus). By gentle blowing, the shavings ignited, dry sticks were piled on them, and a good fire soon resulted. He then singed and prepared the cutía, finishing by running a spit through the body and fixing one end in the ground in a slanting position over the fire. We had brought with us a bag of farinha and a cup containing a lemon, a dozen or two of fiery red peppers, and a few spoonsful of salt. We breakfasted heartily when our cutía was roasted, and washed the meal down with a calabash full of the pure water of the river.

After breakfast, the dogs found another cutía, which was hidden in its burrow two or three feet beneath the roots of a large tree, and took Raimundo nearly an hour to disinter it. Soon afterwards we left this place, crossed the channel, and, paddling past two islands, obtained a glimpse of the broad river between them with a long sandy spit, on which stood several scarlet ibises and snow-white egrets . . .

About one o'clock we again stopped at the mouth of a little creek. It was now intensely hot. Raimundo said deer were to be found here; so he borrowed my gun, as being a more effective weapon than the wretched arms called Lazarinos which he, in common with all the native hunters, used, and which sell at Pará for seven or eight shillings apiece. Raimundo and Joaquim now stripped themselves quite naked, and started off in different directions through the forest, going naked in order to move with less noise over the carpet of dead leaves, amongst which they stepped so stealthily that not the slightest rustle could be heard. The dogs remained in the canoe, in the neighbourhood of which I employed myself two hours entomologizing. At the end of that time my two companions returned, having met no game whatever.

We now embarked on our return voyage. Raimundo cut two slender poles, one for a mast and the other for a sprit; to these he rigged a sail we had brought in the boat, for we were to return by the open river, and expected a good wind to carry us to

Caripí. As soon as we got out of the channel we began to feel the wind – the sea-breeze, which here makes a clean sweep from the Atlantic. Our boat was very small and heavily laden; and when, after rounding a point, I saw the great breadth we had to traverse (seven miles), I thought the attempt to cross in such a slight vessel foolhardy in the extreme. The waves ran very high : there was no rudder; Raimundo steered with a paddle, and all we had to rely upon to save us from falling into the trough of the sea and being instantly swamped were his nerve and skill. There was just room in the boat for our three selves, the dogs, and the game we had killed, and when between the swelling ridges of waves in so frail a craft, our destruction seemed inevitable; as it was, we shipped a little water now and then. Joaquim assisted with his paddle to steady the boat : my time was occupied in baling out the water and watching the dogs, which were crowded together in the prow, yelling with fear; one or other of them occasionally falling over the side and causing great commotion in scrambling in again. Off the point was a ridge of rocks, over which the surge raged furiously. Raimundo sat in the stern, rigid and silent; his eye steadily watching the prow of the boat. It was almost worth the risk and discomfort of the passage to witness the seamanlike ability displayed by the Indians on the water. The little boat rode beautifully, rising well with each wave, and in the course of an hour and a half we arrived at Caripí, thoroughly tired and wet through to the skin.

HENRY WALTER BATES, *The Naturalist on the River Amazon,* 1863

*

NOW FATHER, I think this [Australia] is the Promised Land, but there are faults in it, the water is bad, most of it tastes salt. Adelaide is a very drunken place. Trade is very good here; they get 7s. a day for plastering. The natives are black, some are almost naked. They get a very good living with begging about Adelaide. We have a beautiful cottage in a gentleman's garden. Wood and water, vegetables and cottage to live in, and I have 20s. a week. I am under gardener. We call it Paradise, for we have all the richest fruits and vegetables that's grown; we have melons and every sort of pumpkins; we have the tree of knowledge, peaches, oranges, lemons, grape vines, the tobacco plant. Provisions are very cheap: flour, 2d. per lb.; mutton, 2d. per lb.; legs, 3d. per lb.; beef, 3d. per lb.; sugar, 3d. per lb.; best tea 2s. 6d. per lb.; tobacco 3s. for 4lbs.; drapery goods are as cheap as in London; furniture, pots, iron pans, using things are very dear. They think nothing of money here. Ale is 10d. a pot, spirits are very dear, Cape wine is 1s. a bottle. The colony is in a very prosperous state. I often think of my poor father and mother and brothers and sisters dragged very near to death for half a bellyful of meat, while we have plenty of everything and to spare. We ofttimes talk about the poor white slaves of England, the woolcombers, that said they would not transport themselves to the land of full and plenty. I hope you will let the gentlemen read this letter that gave the money to me, to help me to the promised land.

Emigrant's letter in the *Bradford Observer*, 7 December 1848

*

I SHALL never forget the one-fourth serious and three-fourths comical astonishment, with which, on the morning of the third of January eighteen-hundred-and-forty-two, I opened the door of, and put my head into, a 'state-room' on board the 'Britannia' steam-packet, twelve hundred tons burthen per register, bound for Halifax and Boston, and carrying Her Majesty's mails.

That this state-room had been specially engaged for 'Charles Dickens, Esquire, and Lady,' was rendered sufficiently clear even to my scared intellect by a very small manuscript, announcing the fact, which was pinned on a very flat quilt, covering a very thin mattress, spread like a surgical plaster on a most inaccessible shelf. But that this was the state-room concerning which Charles Dickens, Esquire, and Lady, had held daily and nightly conferences for at least four months preceding: that this could by any possibility be that small snug chamber of the imagination, which Charles Dickens, Esquire, with the spirit of prophecy strong upon him, had always foretold would contain at least one little sofa, and which his lady, with a modest yet most magnificent sense of its limited dimensions, had from the first opined would not hold more than two enormous portmanteaus in some odd corner out of sight (portmanteaus which could now no more be got in at the door, not to say stowed away, than a giraffe could be persuaded or forced into a flower-pot): that this utterly impracticable, thoroughly hopeless, and profoundly preposterous box, had the remotest reference to, or connexion with, those chaste and pretty, not to say gorgeous little bowers, sketched by a masterly hand, in the highly varnished lithographic plan hanging up in the agent's counting-house in the city of London; that this room of state, in short, could be anything but a pleasant fiction and cheerful jest of the captain's, invented and put in practice for the better relish and enjoyment of the real state-room presently to be disclosed : these were truths which I really could not, for the moment, bring my mind at all to bear upon or comprehend. And I sat down upon a kind of horsehair slab, or perch, of which there were two within; and looked, without any expression of countenance whatever, at some friends who had come on board with us, and who were crushing their faces into all manner of shapes by endeavouring to squeeze them through the small doorway.

We had experienced a pretty smart shock before coming below, which, but that we were the most sanguine people living, might have prepared us for the worst. The imaginative artist to whom I have already made allusion, has depicted in the same great work, a chamber of almost interminable perspective, furnished, as Mr Robins would say, in a style of more than Eastern splendour, and filled (but not inconveniently so) with groups of ladies and gentlemen, in the very highest state of enjoyment and vivacity. Before descending into the bowels of the ship, we had passed from the deck into a long narrow apartment, not unlike a gigantic hearse with windows in the sides; having at the upper end a melancholy stove, at which three or four chilly stewards were warming their hands; while on either side, extending down its whole dreary length, was a long, long table, over each of which a rack, fixed to the low roof, and stuck full of drinking-glasses and cruet-stands, hinted dismally at rolling seas and heavy weather. I had not at that time seen the ideal presentment of this chamber which has since gratified me so much, but I observed that one of our friends who had made the arrangements for our voyage, turned pale on entering, retreated on the friend behind him, smote his forehead involuntarily, and said below his breath, 'Impossible! it cannot be!' or words to that effect. He recovered himself however by a great effort, and after a preparatory cough or two, cried, with a ghastly smile which is still before me, looking at the same time round the walls, 'Ha! the breakfast-room, steward – eh?' We all foresaw what the answer must be : we knew the agony he suffered. He had often spoken of *the saloon*; had taken in and lived upon the pictorial idea; had usually given us to understand, at home, that to form a just conception of it, it would be necessary to multiply the size and furniture of an ordinary drawing-room by seven, and then fall short of the reality. When the man in reply avowed the truth; the blunt, remorseless, naked truth; 'This is the saloon, Sir' – he actually reeled beneath the blow.

CHARLES DICKENS, American Notes, 1842

*

THE LOWER classes at Florence are in general ill-looking; nor have I seen one handsome woman since I came here. Their costume too is singularly unbecoming; but there is an airy cheerfulness and vivacity in their countenances, and a civility in their manners which is pleasing to a stranger. I was surprised to see the women, even the servant girls, decorated with necklaces of real pearl of considerable beauty and value. On expressing my surprise at this to a shopkeeper's wife, she informed me that these necklaces are handed down as a kind of heir-loom from mother to daughter; and a young woman is considered as dowered who possesses a handsome chain of pearl. If she has no hope of one in reversion, she buys out of her little earnings a pearl at a time, till she has completed the necklace.

The style of swearing at Florence is peculiarly elegant and

classical. I hear the vagabonds in the street adjuring Venus and
Bacchus; and my shoemaker swore 'by the aspect of Diana' that
he would not take less than ten pauls for what was worth about
three – yet was the knave forsworn.

ANNA JAMESON, *Diary of an Ennuyée,* 1826

*

MY ARRIVAL at Rotterdam presented me with a new scene of
pleasure. All the streets are paved with broad stones, and before
the meanest artificers' doors seats of various-coloured marbles,
and so neatly kept, that, I will assure you, I walked over almost
all the town yesterday, *incognita,* in my slippers, without receiving
one spot of dirt; and you may see the Dutch maids washing the
pavement of the street with more application than ours do our
bed-chambers. The town seems so full of people, with such busy
faces, all in motion, that I can hardly fancy that it is not some
celebrated fair; but I see it is every day the same. 'Tis certain no
town can be more advantageously situated for commerce. Here are
seven large canals, on which the merchants' ships come up to the
very doors of their houses. The shops and warehouses are of a
surprising neatness and magnificence, filled with an incredible
quantity of fine merchandise, and so much cheaper than what we
see in England, I have much ado to persuade myself I am still so
near it. Here is neither dirt nor beggary to be seen. One is not
shocked with those loathsome cripples, so common in London, nor
teazed with the importunities of idle fellows and wenches, that
choose to be nasty and lazy. The common servants and little shop-
women here are more nicely clean than most of our ladies; and
the great variety of neat dresses (every woman dressing her head
after her own fashion) is an additional pleasure in seeing the town.

LADY MARY WORTLEY MONTAGU, *Letters,* 1716

*

Thursday 13 September 1764 (Berlin)
I passed the morning with Burnett, who is now *chargé d'affaires*
here. I dined *chez* Castillon. At four he carried me to the Royal

How delightful the weather for the time of year! And how idyllic the scene beside our Alpine lake!

The photographer at Berchtesgaden contrived a most convincing pretence of the mines at Ober-salzburg. Do we not look adventurous?

Ernest reminded me that I must practise on my autoharp when we return.

How remarkable to be able to picnic in the very crater of Vesuvius!

We never go anywhere without our Kodak.

Do you not think, Mama, that Maud and I look rather BOLD? And the gentlemen rather PROMISING? But the sea was perfectly CALM.

Academy of Berlin. The building is large. Below are the King's stables, and above assemble his *literati,* which made a wag put this inscription on the Academy: *'Muis et mulis'*. [To the Muses and the mules.] I saw a poor collection of natural curiosities, except indeed the collection of dried plants of the Levant made by Tournefort. The Academy assembled before five. Formey read a letter from a physician at Truro in Cornwall concerning some astronomical phenomenon. He wrote sad Latin, and, when he wanted a word, mixed still worse Greek. I was ashamed of him. Monsieur Frencheville next read a dissertation on the art of making ambergris, with which I was not greatly edified. After he had done, not a word was said. The Academecians grinned and separated. A poor affair this.

I then went to Madame de Brandt's, where I imagined I was invited. But I had mistaken Tuesday for Thursday, and she punished me by a recital of the fine *partie* that she had, as it was her daughter's birthday. How she had a fine supper and a fine ball and all the company were dressed *à la turque;* and how a dress was ready for me. She asked me to stay this evening with her. Much she talked of gallantry and of the Duke of Portland, who was here some years ago. Young Comte Schaffgotsch supped with us, and after supper we played at 'seek the pin'. One is sent out of the room till the pin is hid, and when he enters he must seek it. In proportion as he approaches it, one beats harder and harder upon the table, till at last he finds it. Madame's daughter said, 'One gets terribly bored in Berlin'. I believe it.

On the way home I took up with a street girl. Black. But having no condom I disenchanted myself.

Friday 14 September
In the morning Castillon and I went and saw the collection of natural curiosities of Mr Gerhard. In metals, not amiss. I dined at Burnett's, where was Schmidt, the engraver. Burnett was hearty. At four Castillon and I went and saw the old Maggraf, the chemical professor, a very industrious and able man in his profession. But a strange old fellow. It thundered and lightened. He

cried, 'I love to see my God in flames', and he laughed always when he spoke. Such is man. He must have defects. He may have health and manners. But then he is ignorant. He may have knowledge. But then he is sick and awkward. Maggraf showed us glasses of his making, and a composition by which he can imitate all kinds of precious stones. He gave me a piece like sapphire. His minerals were very complete. I promised to send him some from Scotland.

Castillon went home with me. He said we ought to revere God; but all affectations exercised towards the supreme being were only in the fancy of fanaticks. He owned that the Gospels were all that he owned as truly Christian pieces. The Epistles he thought only good pieces which might be of use sometimes. He said the Christian religion had not added much to morality. What would he be at? He left me at eight. I amused myself with a street girl as in London. Idleness – no great harm.

Saturday 15 September

Some time ago I was taken in by Castillon for a dreary dinner at Treptow, of which Captain Durand of the artillery paid the expense. Castillon and I could not do less than give such another treat, so I could not shun once more being taken in. We went to Stralau and had a sad house. I tired terribly. At dinner I was sulky, and I railed against the French. Durand came and seated himself by me, saying, 'It is better that I, rather than my sister, should hear these little impertinences that are flying about'. 'Sir', said I, 'I hope that you have not been offended by what I have said.' 'Yes, Sir. You have spoken against the French. I, Sir, am a Frenchman; and no one can speak in such a way against an entire nation unless he is a scoundrel.' This last word gave me a blow on the heart. It was a clear affront which could not be put up. I bowed and said, 'I am sorry, Sir. I had no intention of being impertinent.' It happened luckily in the middle of dinner, so that I had time to think. I found fear working with me. I recalled old David, Laird of Auchinleck, my great-grandfather, and though he called to me to support the honour of my family,

I had also my honour as a Scotsman, my character as a man, at stake. I must do myself the justice to say that I was fully determined for the worst. Yet I wished that the affair could be made up, as I was really in the wrong. I felt myself in the situation which I have often fancied, and which is a very uneasy one. Yet upon my honour, so strong is my metaphysical passion that I was pleased with this opportunity of intimately observing the working of the human mind.

When dinner was over I took the Captain to a walk behind the house and said, 'I am very sorry, Sir, for what happened today. I was much in the wrong. I should wish, if it is possible, to avoid a quarrel. But you made use of an expression which a gentleman cannot endure, and I must have satisfaction.' 'Whatever you wish, Sir,' said he; 'I am ready for anything.' 'Sir', said I, 'I wish that you would own that you were in the wrong to speak to me as you did. I shall own first that I was impolite to speak as I did against the French.' By this time one of his brother officers and another gentleman came up to us. To excuse me, they said, 'The gentleman was only joking.' I replied, 'Excuse me. No, I shall not deny my feelings. I was in earnest, Sir. I own that I have an antipathy, or, if you wish, a prejudice against your nation. I own also that I ought not to mention it in a company I am not certain of. Sir, will you own that you were in the wrong?' He said, 'Sir, everything you wish. I am very sorry that I used such an expression; for you did not mean that, because I am French, I am not a gentleman.'

Castillon also came, and he owned his fault before three or four gentlemen, and Castillon said, 'Then everything is arranged. Mr Boswell, you could ask no more.' However, I was still uneasy. The affront had been given before all the company. It was necessary that all the company should see it repaired. Some went by land, the rest of us in the boat. I sat in great uneasiness. We supped all at Durand's very well. After supper I filled up a bumper of hock, and called to him, 'Sir, Captain Durand, I repeat here what we said in private. I am very sorry that I spoke today in an impolite manner. I hope that you will say as much.' He replied,

'I am very sorry, Sir, that I was so hot-headed and that I spoke to you in an impolite manner.' I cannot remember our very words. I said, 'Sir, I should only like to make you see that a man can speak as I have done and be imprudent or impolite, but not a scoundrel.' 'O, Monsieur', said he with concern. We drank to each other and all was fully and genteelly settled. When I got home I reflected with a Lucretian suavity on the *mare magnum* that I had escaped. In time coming, I shall be more on my guard, and be truly polite.

> JAMES BOSWELL, *On the Grand Tour:*
> *Germany and Switzerland,* 1764

*

OF GIORGIO, dragoman, cook, valet, interpreter, and guide, I have had as yet nothing to complain; he is at home in all kinds of tongues, speaking ten fluently, an accomplishment to many of the travelling oriental Greeks, for he is a Smyrniote by birth. In countenance my attendant is somewhat like one of those strange faces, lion or griffin, which we see on door-knockers or urn-handles, and a grim twist of his under-jaw gives an idea that it would not be safe to try his temper too much. In the morning he is diffuse and dilates on past journeys; after noon his remarks become short and sententious – not to say surly. Any appearance of indecision evidently moves him to anger speedily. It is necessary to watch the disposition of a servant on whom so much of one's personal comfort depends, and it is equally necessary to give as little trouble as possible, for a good dragoman always has enough to do without extra whims or worryings from his employer.

> EDWARD LEAR, *Journals of a Landscape Painter in*
> *Greece and Albania,* 1851

*

THIS MORNING we set off for the Falls of Terni (La cascata di Marmore) in two carriages and four: O such equipages! – such rat-like steeds! such picturesque accoutrements! and such poetical looking guides and postilions, ragged, cloaked and whiskered! –

but it was all consistent : the wild figures harmonized with the wild landscape. We passed a singular fortress on the top of a steep insulated rock, which had formerly been inhabited by a band of robbers and their families, who were with great difficulty, and after a regular siege, dislodged by a party of soldiers, and the place dismantled. In its present ruined state, it has a very picturesque effect; and though the presence of the banditti would no doubt have added greatly to the romance of the scene, on the present occasion we excused their absence.

We visited the falls both above and below, but unfortunately we neither saw them from the best point of view, nor at the best season. The body of water is sometimes ten times greater, as I was assured – but can scarce believe it possible. The words 'Hell of waters', used by Lord Byron, would not have occurred to me while looking at this cataract, which impresses the astonished mind with an overwhelming idea of power, might, magnificence, and impetuosity; but blends at the same time all that is most tremendous in sound and motion, with all that is most lovely in forms, in colours, and in scenery.

As I stood close to the precipice's edge, immediately under the great fall, I felt my respiration gone : I turned giddy, almost faint, and was obliged to lean against the rock for support. The mad plunge of the waters, the deafening roar, the presence of a power which no earthly force could resist or control, struck me with an awe, almost amounting to terror. A bright sunbow stood over the torrent, which, seen from below, has the appearance of a luminous white arch bending from rock to rock. The whole scene was – but how can I say what it was? I have exhausted my stock of fine words; and must be content with silent recollections, and the sense of admiration and wonder unexpressed.

ANNA JAMESON, *Diary of an Ennuyée,* 1826

*

Nice, Jan. 15, 1765
Dear Sir, – It is not without reason that Genoa is called *La Superba.* The city itself is very stately; and the nobles are very

proud. Some few of them may be proud of their wealth; but, in general, their fortunes are very small. My friend Mr R—— assured me that many Genoese noblemen had fortunes of half a million of livres per annum. But the truth is, the whole revenue of the state does not exceed this sum; and the livre of Genoa is but about ninepence sterling. There are about half-a-dozen of their nobles who have ten thousand a year; but the majority have not above a twentieth part of that sum. They live with great parsimony in their families and wear nothing but black in public; so that their expenses are but small. If a Genoese nobleman gives an entertainment once a quarter, he is said to live upon the fragments all the rest of the year. I was told that one of them lately treated his friends, and left the entertainment to the care of his son, who ordered a dish of fish that cost a zechine, which is about equal to ten shillings sterling. The old gentleman no sooner saw it appear on the table, than, unable to suppress his concern, he burst into tears, and exclaimed, *Ah Figliuolo indegno! Siamo in Rovina! Siamo in precipizio!* [Ah base child! We are in ruins! We are brought to downfall!]

TOBIAS SMOLLETT, Travels in Italy 1766

*

THE *French* are generally of middling stature, more robust and better made than the *Spaniards* and *Italians,* but inferior in this respect to the *English, Germans* and *Flemmings.* The women are handsomer in some provinces than others, as in part of *Guienne,* towards *Bordeaux,* part of *Dauphiné, Languedoc,* and *Provence.* They are a people of quick understanding and nice taste, of an active and enterprizing disposition, and generally very capable of whatever they undertake with respect either to arts, sciences or arms. They are ready at imitating foreign inventions, and quick themselves at inventing, especially with regard to modes, dresses, and manner of living. They are brave and valiant, particularly the better sort, extremely fond of their prince, polite and affable to strangers, so as to be looked upon as matters of complaisance and good breeding.

But these virtues are balanced by several vices; for they are generally reckoned fiery, impatient, inconstant, and of a restless disposition, which involves them either in continual law-suits, and civil broils at home, or obliges their princes to engage them in foreign parts in foreign wars. They are much addicted to gaming, which is the soul of all their assemblies, and the only means for a foreigner to ingratiate himself in their company. The young people are debauched and irreligious; but we must own that this is compensated by the solidity, piety, and good behaviour of the maturer sort. They are very talkative, especially those of the female Sex, who are nevertheless not only very pleasing in discourse, but also of a graceful and winning deportment. Their fiery temper hurries them often into quarrels and duels; but the latter are not so frequent since the late king's severe edicts against this barbarous and *Gothic* custom. They are charged likewise with insincerity in their complaisance, and with being little better than genteel hypocrites in their cringes and impertinent ceremonies.

THOMAS NUGENT, *The Grand Tour,* 1749

*

Jan. 4th 1790. After breakfast, walk in the gardens of the Tuileries, where there is the most extraordinary sight that either French or English eyes could ever behold at Paris. The King, walking with six grenadiers of the *milice bourgeoise,* with an officer or two of his household, and a page. The doors of the gardens are kept shut in respect to him, in order to exclude everybody but deputies, or those who have admission-tickets. When he entered the palace, the doors of the garden were thrown open for all without distinction, though the Queen was still walking with a lady of her court. She also was attended so closely by the *gardes bourgeoises,* that she could not speak, but in a low voice, without being heard by them. A mob followed her, talking very loud, and paying no other apparent respect than that of taking off their hats wherever she passed, which was indeed more than I expected. Her Majesty does not appear to be in health;

she seems to be much affected, and shows it in her face; but the King is as plump as ease can render him. By his orders, there is a little garden railed off for the Dauphin to amuse himself in, and a small room is built into it to retire to in case of rain; here he was at work with his little hoe and rake, but not without a guard of two grenadiers. He is a very pretty, good-natured-looking boy, of five or six years old, with an agreeable countenance; wherever he goes, all hats are taken off to him, which I was glad to observe. All the family being kept thus close prisoners (which they are in effect), affords, at first view, a shocking spectacle; and is really so, if the act were not really necessary to effect the revolution; this I conceive to be impossible; but if it were necessary, no one can blame the people for taking every measure possible to secure that liberty they had seized in the violence of revolution.

Arthur Young, Travels in France, 1792

*

The Austrians, who are paramount here [Naples], allow masks only twice a week, Sundays and Thursdays. The people seem determined to indemnify themselves for this restriction on their pleasures by every allowed excess during the two days of merriment, which their despotic conquerors have spared them ... Whatever the gaieties of the carnival may have been formerly, it is scarce possible to conceive a more fantastic, a more picturesque, a more laughable scene than the Strado di Toledo exhibited today; the whole city seemed to wear 'one universal grin'; and such an incessant fire of sugar-plums (or what seemed such) was carried on, and with such eagerness and mimic fury, that when our carriage came out of the conflict, we all looked as if a sack of flour had been shaken over us. The implements used in this ridiculous warfare, are, for common purposes, little balls of plaster of Paris and flour, made to resemble small comfits: friends and acquaintances pelted each other with real confetti, and those of the most delicious and expensive kinds. A double file of carriages moved in a contrary direction along the Corso; a space in the middle and on each side being left for horsemen and pedestrians, and the most exact order was maintained by the guards and police; so that if by chance a carriage lost its place in the line it was impossible to recover it, and it was immediately obliged to leave the street, and re-enter by one of the extremities. Besides the warfare carried on below, the balconies on each side were crowded with people in gay or grotesque dresses, who had *sacks* of bonbons before them, from which they showered vollies on those beneath, or aimed across the street at each other: some of them filled their handkerchiefs, and then dexterously loosening the corners, and taking certain aim, flung a volley at once. This was like a cannon loaded with grapeshot, and never failed to do the most terrific execution.

ANNA JAMESON, *Diary of an Ennuyée,* 1826

*

I AM at this present writing in a house situated on the banks of the Hebrus, which runs under my chamber window. My garden is full of tall cypress-trees, upon the branches of which several couples of true turtles are saying soft things to one another from morning till night. How naturally do boughs and vows come into my head at this minute! and must not you confess, to my praise, that 'tis more than ordinary discretion that can resist the wicked suggestions of poetry, in a place where truth, for once, furnishes all ideas of the pastoral? The summer is already far advanced in this part of the world; and, for some miles round Adrianople, the whole ground is laid out in gardens, and the banks of the river set with fruit trees, under which all the most considerable Turks divert themselves every evening; not with walking, that is not one of their pleasures, but a set party of them choose out a green spot, where the shade is very thick, and there they spread a carpet, on which they sit drinking their coffee, and generally attended by some slave with a fine voice, or that plays on some instrument. Every twenty paces you may see one of these little companies listening to the dashing of the river; and this taste is so universal, that the very gardeners are not without it. I have often seen them and their children sitting on the banks, and playing on a rural instrument, perfectly answering the description of the ancient *fistula,* being composed of unequal reeds, with a simple but agreeable softness in the sound.

Mr Addison might here make the experiment he speaks of in his travels; there not being one instrument of music among the Greek or Roman statues, that is not to be found in the hands of the people of this country. The young lads generally divert themselves with making garlands for their favourite lambs, which I have often seen painted and adorned with flowers, lying at their feet while they sung or played. It is not that they ever read romances, but these are the ancient amusements here, and as natural to them as cudgel-playing and foot-ball to our British swains; the softness and warmth of the climate forbidding all rough exercises, which were never so much as heard of amongst them, and naturally inspiring a laziness and aversion to labour, which the great plenty indulges. These gardeners are the only happy race of country people in Turkey. They furnish all the city with fruit and herbs, and seem to live very easily. They are most of them Greeks, and have little houses in the midst of their gardens, where their wives and daughters take a liberty not permitted in the town, I mean, to go unveiled. These wenches are very neat and handsome, and pass their time at their looms under the shade of the trees.

LADY MARY WORTLEY MONTAGU, *Letters,* 1717

*

WHILE TAKING a parting cup of coffee with the postmaster I unluckily set my foot on a handsome pipe-bowl (pipe-bowls are always snares to near-sighted people moving over Turkish floors, as they are scattered in places quite remote from the smokers, who live at the farther end of the prodigiously long pipe-sticks) – crash; but nobody moved; only on apologizing through Giorgio, the polite Mohammedan said: 'The breaking of such a pipe-bowl would indeed, under ordinary circumstances, be disagreeable; but in a friend every action has its charm!'

EDWARD LEAR, *Journals of a Landscape Painter in Greece and Albania,* 1851

I EXPRESSED some inclination to publish an account of my Travels upon the continent of Europe, for which I had a variety of materials collected. JOHNSON: 'I do not say, Sir, you may not publish your travels; but I give you my opinion, that you would lessen yourself by it. What can you tell of countries so well known as those upon the continent of Europe, which you have visited?' BOSWELL: 'But I can give an entertaining narrative, with many incidents, anecdotes, *jeux d'esprit*, and remarks, so as to make very pleasant reading.' JOHNSON: 'Why, Sir, most modern travellers in Europe, who have published their travels, have been laughed at: I would not have you added to the number. The world is now not contented to be merely entertained by a traveller's narrative; they want to learn something. Now some of my friends asked me, why I did not give some account of my travels in France. The reason is plain: intelligent readers had seen more of France than I had. *You* might have liked my travels in France, and THE CLUB might have liked them; but, upon the whole, there would have been more ridicule than good produced by them.' BOSWELL: 'I cannot agree with you, Sir. People would like to read what you say of anything. Suppose a face has been painted by fifty painters before; still we love to see it done by Sir Joshua.' JOHNSON: 'True, Sir, but Sir Joshua cannot paint a face when he has not time to look on it.' BOSWELL: 'Sir, a sketch of any sort by him is valuable. And, Sir, to talk to you in your own style (raising my voice and shaking my head), you *should* have given us your Travels in France. I am *sure* I am right, and *there's an end on't.*'

JAMES BOSWELL, *Tour to the Hebrides,* 1785

*

ROME, *March* 31, 1766.
SIR,

The Holy Week, with all its Functions, ended last night. These ceremonies, like the spectacles of the ancient *Romans,* serve to entertain the people, and keep them in good humour, who, otherwise, would be as mutinous in these days for want of bread, as they used to be in the times of the first Consuls. Wherever I travel, I find the multitude discontented with their governors, and I suppose it must be always the case, sometimes with, and sometimes without foundation; therefore, some plaything or another must be thrown out to them to prevent their petulancy. A good Catholick would be shocked to hear me treat these Functions, where they think the Salvation of Souls is concerned, as having a temporal and political use; but we Hereticks, who are denied Grace, esteem it the most favourable construction that can be given to all these raree-shows : A sour Mahometan, whose religion consists in prayers, fastings, and ablutions would treat the exhibitions of Saints, Relicks, Virgins, Crucifixes, &c. with more rigour, and call the whole Profaneness, Blasphemy, and Idolatry.

Last *Thursday* the Pope, according to annual custom, pronounced his Benediction from a balcony in St *Peter's,* which overlooks the churchyard, where a monstrous crowd of people was collected on the occasion. The manner of the form is more suitable to the holiness of his character, than I was aware of; for I had understood, he cursed all Turks, Hereticks, &c. on the face of the earth; whereas, that part of the function is performed by the two Deacons, (Cardinals) who read the Curse, one in *Italian,* the other in *Latin*; and the words are no sooner out of their mouths, than he pronounces the Benediction, and wipes off all the efficacy of the Curse : The Pope is, during the whole ceremony, supported on the shoulders of twelve men, in an armed chair, holding in his hand a large lighted wax taper; and, in the very instant that the last words of the Curse are uttered, the bell tolls, and he throws it down among the people : which circumstance clearly explains the sense of a proverb well known in *England,* of swearing or cursing, by bell, book, and candle. I had the good fortune to be placed close to his Holiness's elbow; and, whilst he read the blessing, and three or four prayers, or exhortations previous to it, I overlooked the office; and, I confess to you, was edified by the modesty and decorum of the form, as well as by his Holiness's manner of chanting them. The exhortations are of the declaratory kind; that if the assembly would repent sincerely of their sins, and sin no more, there was room for absolution; and the Benediction seemed to be as little arrogant as that pronounced by our Ministers at the end of the Liturgy, viz. *The Grace of our Lord Jesus Christ, &c.* In the moment that he is speaking the Benediction, the bells toll, the drums beat, and the cannon at the castle of St *Angelo* fire, which adds to the awefulness of the scene, and renders the performance truely solemn.

Yesterday (*Easter-Sunday*) the same Function was repeated, with this difference, that there was no Curse, but only the Benediction. The concourse of people was greater, all the Peasants from the adjacent countries being more at leisure on a *Sunday,* to come and partake of the blessing. As it is a religious ceremony, and the mob make all their religion consist in ceremony, and a due submission to the church and the priesthood, there are no riots here, as there would be with us; but they are peaceable and silent from the beginning to the end of the Function, as an elegant audience at *Drury Lane,* when *Garrick* is on the stage. The moment the cannon at St *Angelo* fire, the good people in the neighbourhood of *Rome,* who hear them, prostrate themselves, and are supposed to have the benefit of the benediction. There are both days two squadrons of horse, and a small battalion of foot, drawn out before the church, which are not a little ornament to the Festival; for, tho' his Holiness's troops might possibly have made no great figure in the fields of *Minden,* they are very well cloathed, and add much to the glory of the day, and the beauty of St *Peter's* church-yard.

I shall not describe any of the other Functions, such as feeding Pilgrims, washing their feet by people of quality; and again the same ceremony performed by his Holiness, with Priests and Cardinals.

Yesterday he celebrated Mass in St *Peter's* before he pronounced the Benediction, a very tedious and tiresome service both for the poor old man and his congregation; yet these things are worth seeing once, and were a man to chuse a month in the year to spend at *Rome,* I would recommend that month, in which the Holy Week is included.

I am, Sir, &c.

SAMUEL SHARP, *Letters from Italy,* 1767

*

PISA HAS a look of elegant tranquillity, which is not exactly *dullness,* and pleases me particularly : if the thought of its past independence, the memory of its once proud name in arts, arms, and literature, come across the mind, it is not accompanied by any painful regret caused by the sight of present misery and degradation, but by that philosophic melancholy with which we are used to contemplate the mutability of earthly greatness.

... The Leaning Tower should be contemplated from the portico of the church to heighten its effect : when the perpendicular column cuts it to the eye like a plumb line, the obliquity appears really terrific.

The Campo is an extraordinary place : it affects the mind like the cloisters of one of our Gothic cathedrals which resembles it in effect. Means have lately been taken to preserve the singular frescoes on the walls, which for five hundred years have been exposed to open air.

I remarked the tomb of that elegant fabulist Pignotti; the last personage of celebrity buried in the Campo Santo.

The university of Pisa is no longer what it was when France and Venice had nearly gone to war about one of its law professors, and its colleges ranked next to those of Padua : it has declined in fame, in riches, and in discipline. The Botanic Gardens were a few years ago the finest in Europe, and are still maintained with great cost and care : it contains a lofty magnolia, the stem of which is as bulky as a good sized tree : the gardener told us rather poetically, that when in blossom it perfumed the whole city of Pisa.

ANNA JAMESON, *Diary of an Ennuyée,* 1826

*

PARIS, 1841. Such a man of an engraver as I have found! I wish you could see him. He is abt. 28 has not a spark of genius : works 14 hours a day, never breakfasts except off cheese & bread in his atelier, dines in the same way, never goes out, makes about 3,000 francs a year, has a wife & child & is happy the whole day long – the whole house is like a cage of canaries, nothing but singing from morning till night. It goes to my heart to hear his little wife singing at her work – what noble characters does one light on in little nooks of this great world!

WILLIAM MAKEPEACE THACKERAY, *Letters,* 1841

*

CROSSING THE Esla at Mansilla, a loose broken road, dusty in summer and muddy in winter, leads to Mayorga, pop. 2,000, a mud-built village on the Cea, with a decent *posada.* Here Moore (Dec. 20, 1808) effected his junction with Baird, and here took place the first cavalry encounter, when Lord Paget, with 400 of the 15th, charged 600 splendid French dragoons, riding them down horse and man. In vain (as at Fuentes de Onoro) was brandy served out to the enemy; the better man prevailed, as must be the case, if the foe can only be grappled with at close quarters, either with sword, bayonet, or with the Nelsonic touch 'close action' and the boarding-pike. Then, in a bull-dog struggle for life or death, 'beef', blood, bone, and bottom must tell, and a purely *physical* superiority generates, from consciousness of its power, a *moral* confidence. Gen. Foy accordingly attributed the *accidental* success of the English horsemen, first to their invariably *vast superiority of number,* and next the larder. 'Le rhum vient à propos ranimer ses esprits dans le moment du danger.' Again, 'Nous avons vu plus d'une fois de faibles détachments charger nos battaillons à fond, mais en désordre. Le cavalier ivre de rhum lançait son cheval, et le cheval emportait le cavalier au delà du but.' Be that as it may, such was the moral superiority felt by our mounted beefeaters, that the Duke was obliged to issue a general order to prevent mere companies from charging whole French regiments. Such was, to use his words, 'The *trick* our officers of cavalry have acquired of galloping at everything e.g. Balaclava'.

On these very plains, ten short days afterwards, did Blake, with his whole army, run away, scared by one daring charge of Franceschi's dragoons, which two companies of British infantry would have riddled to shreds.

RICHARD FORD, Handbook for Travellers in Spain, 1855

*

I SHOULD abstain from mentioning the curious clock in Lyons Cathedral, if it were not for a small mistake I made, in connexion with that piece of mechanism. The keeper of the church was very anxious it should be shown; partly for the honour of the establishment and the town; and partly, perhaps, because of his deriving a percentage from the additional consideration. However that may be, it was set in motion, and thereupon a host of little doors flew open, and innumerable little figures staggered out of them, and jerked themselves back again, with that special unsteadiness of purpose, and hitching in the gait, which usually attaches to figures that are moved by clockwork. Meanwhile, the Sacristan stood explaining these wonders, and pointing them out, severally, with a wand. There was a centre puppet of the Virgin Mary; and close to her, a small pigeon-hole, out of which another and a very ill-looking puppet made one of the most sudden plunges I ever saw accomplished: instantly flopping back again at sight of her, and banging his little door violently after him. Taking this to be emblematic of the victory over Sin and Death, and not at all unwilling to show that I perfectly understood the subject, in anticipation of the showman, I rashly said, 'Aha! The Evil Spirit. To be sure. He is very soon disposed of.' 'Pardon, Monsieur,' said the Sacristan, with a polite motion of his hand towards the little door, as if introducing somebody – 'The Angel Gabriel!'

CHARLES DICKENS, Pictures From Italy, 1846

*

I SAW in this hospital [Santa Maria Nuove, Florence] a shocking object; a man with a tumour on his arm that was swelled as

128

big as his body: no chance of suppuration – amputation impossible: no rest, night nor day: a probability of living some months – and the certainty of a painful death! A thought of such an unfortunate being might render us easy under those trifles, which, for want of greater evils, we call sufferings. It has since occurred to me in riding by, that if an accident was then to happen, I should prefer the hospital to my own house : – that surrounded by miseries greater than my own, and perhaps less merited, I should receive more comfort than from the sight of pleasures I could not enjoy, and yet might envy. Not that I should choose to be carried thither, like the man I met yesterday, on a bier, covered with black; supported and attended by a parcel of dismal figures in long black growns and black masks, looking more like devils than men : if the poor fellow had weak nerves, he might fancy himself already both dead and damned. Count——, just arrived in Florence, meeting with an accident at Fiesole, the Misericordia were sent for to carry him home; but when he saw the apparatus, and the dismal appearance it made, he fancied they thought him dead, and intended to bury him. It was to no purpose he was assured to the contrary, and told how handy they are in their operations; he still persisted that not one of them should touch him; he put himself in a posture of defence; and they were obliged to return as they came.

PETER BECKFORD, *Familiar Letters From Italy,* 1805

*

I SUPPOSE you have read, in most of our accounts of Turkey that their houses are the most miserable pieces of building in the world. I can speak very learnedly on that subject, having been in so many of them; and I assure you 'tis no such thing. We are now lodged in a place belonging to the Grand Signior. I really think the manner of building here very agreeable, and proper for the country. 'Tis true they are not all solicitous to beautify the outsides of their houses, and they are generally built of wood, which I own is the cause of many inconveniences; but this is not to be charged on the taste of the people, but the oppression

E

of the government. Every house upon the death of its master is at the disposal of the Grand Signior's disposal; and, therefore, no man cares to make a great expense, which he is not sure his family will be the better for. All their design is to build a house commodious, that will last their lives; and they are very indifferent if it falls down the year after.

Every house, great and small, is divided into two distinct parts, which only join together by a narrow passage. The first house has a large court before it, and open galleries all round it, which is to me a thing very agreeable. This gallery leads to all the chambers, which are commonly large, and with two rows of windows, the first being of painted glass : they seldom build above two stories, each of which has such galleries. The stairs are broad, and not above thirty steps. This is the house belonging to the lord, and the one adjoining is called the *harém,* that is, the ladies' apartment (for the name of *seraglio* is peculiar to the Grand Signior's); it has also a gallery running round it towards the garden, to which all the windows are turned, and the same number of chambers as the other, but more gay and splendid, both in painting and furniture. The second row of windows is very low, with grates like those of convents; the rooms are all spread with Persian carpets and raised at one end of them (my chamber is raised at both ends) about two feet. This is the sofa, and is laid with a richer sort of carpet, and all round it a sort of couch, raised half a foot, covered with rich silk according to the fancy or magnificence of the owner. Mine is of scarlet cloth with a gold fringe; round this are placed, standing against the wall, two rows of cushions, the first very large, and the next little ones; and here the Turks display their greatest magnificence. They are generally brocade, or embroidery of gold wire upon satin; – nothing can look more gay and splendid. These seats are so convenient and easy, I shall never endure chairs as long as I live. The rooms are low, which I think no fault, the ceiling is always of wood, generally inlaid and painted or gilded. They use no hangings, the rooms being all wainscoted with cedar set off with silver nails or painted with flowers, which open in many places with folding doors, and serve for cabinets, I think, more conveniently than ours. Between the windows are little arches to set pots of perfume, or baskets of flowers. But what pleases me best is the fashion of having marble fountains in the lower part of the room, which throw up several spouts of water, giving at the same time an agreeable coolness, and a pleasant dashing sound, falling from one basin to another. Some of these fountains are very magnificent. Each house has a bagnio, which is generally two or three little rooms, leaded on the top, paved with marble, with basins, cocks of water, and all conveniences for either hot or cold baths.

LADY MARY WORTLEY MONTAGU, *Letters*, 1717

*

IN THIS, the first town I had seen in Northern Albania, the novelty of the costumes is striking; for, rich as is the clothing of all these people, the tribes of Ghegheria surpass all their neighbours in gorgeousness of raiment, by adding to their ordinary vestments a long surtout of purple, crimson, or scarlet, trimmed with fur, or bordered with gold thread, or braiding. Their jackets and waistcoats are usually black, and their whole outer man contrasts strongly with that of their white neighbours of Berát, or many-hued brethren of Epirus. Other proofs were not wanting of my being in a new land; for as we advanced slowly through the geese-frequented kennels (a running stream with *trottoirs* on each side and crossed by stepping stones is a characteristic of this place) my head was continually saluted by small stones and bits of dirt, the infidel air of my white hat courting the notice and condemnation of the orthodox Akridhani. 'And', quoth Giorgio, 'unless you take to a fez, Vossignoria will have no peace and possibly lose an eye in a day or two.'

EDWARD LEAR, *Journals of a Landscape Painter in Greece and Albania*, 1851

*

NEXT MORNING, when we set forth on the Willebroek Canal, the rain began heavy and chill. The water of the canal stood at

about the drinking temperature of tea; and under this cold asper-
sion, the surface was covered with steam. The exhileration of
departure, and the easy motion of the boats under each stroke of
the paddles, supported us through this misfortune while it lasted;
and when the clouds passed and the sun came out again, our
spirits went up above the range of stay-at-home humours. A
good breeze rustled and shivered in the rows of trees that bordered
the canal. The leaves flickered in and out of the light in tumul-
tuous masses. It seemed sailing weather to eye and ear; but down
between the banks, the wind reached us only in faint and desul-
tory puffs. There was hardly enough to steer by. Progress was
intermittent and unsatisfactory. A jocular person, of marine ante-
cedents, hailed us from the tow-path with a *'C'est vite, mais c'est
long.'*

The canal was busy enough. Every now and then we met or
overtook a long string of boats, with great green tillers; high
sterns with a window on either side of the rudder, and perhaps
a jug or a flower-pot in one of the windows; a dinghy following
behind; a woman busied about the day's dinner, and a handful
of children. These barges were all tied one behind the other with
tow ropes, to the number of twenty-five or thirty; and the line was
headed and kept in motion by a steamer of strange construction. It
had neither paddle-wheel or screw; but by some gear not rightly
comprehensible to the mechanical mind, it fetched up over its bow
a small bright chain which lay along the bottom of the canal, and
paying it out again over the stern, dragged itself forward, link by
link, with its whole retinue of loaded skows. Until one had
found out the key to the enigma, there was something solemn and
uncomfortable in the progress of one of these trains, as it moved
gently along the water with nothing to mark its advance but an
eddy alongside dying away into the wake.

R. L. STEVENSON, An Inland Voyage, 1908

*

HAVING RESOLVED to explore the island of Rasay, which could
be done only on foot, I last night obtained my fellow-traveller's

permission to leave him for a day, he being unable to take so hardy a walk. Old Mr Malcolm M'Cleod, who had obligingly promised to accompany me, was at my bedside between five and six. I sprang up immediately, and he and I, attended by two other gentlemen, traversed the country during the whole of this day. Though we had passed over not less than four-and-twenty miles of very rugged ground, and had a Highland dance on the top of Dun Can, the highest mountain in the island, we returned in the evening not at all fatigued, and piqued ourselves at not being outdone at the nightly ball by our less active friends, who had remained at home.

My survey of Rasay did not furnish much which can interest my readers; I shall therefore put into as short a compass as I can, the observations upon it, which I find registered in my journal. It is about fifteen English miles long, and four broad. On the south side is the laird's family seat, situated on a pleasing low spot. The old tower of three stories, mentioned by Martin, was taken down soon after 1746, and a modern house supplies its place. There are very good grass-fields and corn-lands about it, well-dressed. I observed, however, hardly any inclosures, except a good garden plentifully stocked with vegetables, and strawberries, raspberries, currants, etc.

On one of the rocks just where we landed, which are not high, there is rudely carved a square, with a crucifix in the middle. Here, it is said, the Lairds of Rasay, in old times, used to offer up their devotions. I could not approach the spot, without a grateful recollection of the event commemorated by this symbol.

A little from the shore, westward, is a kind of subterraneous house. There has been a natural fissure, or separation of the rock, running towards the sea, which has been roofed over with long stones, and above them turf has been laid. In that place the inhabitants used to keep their oars. There are a number of trees near the house, which grow well; some of them of a pretty good size. They are mostly plane and ash. A little to the west of the house is an old ruinous chapel, unroofed, which never has been very curious. We here saw some human bones of an uncommon size. There was a heel-bone, in particular, which Dr Macleod said was such, that if the foot was in proportion, it must have been twenty-seven inches long. Dr Johnson would not look at the bones. He started back from them with a striking appearance of horror. Mr M'Queen told us, it was formerly much the custom, in these isles, to have human bones lying above ground, especially in the windows of churches. On the south of the chapel is the family burying-place. Above the door, on the east end of it, is a small bust or image of the Virgin Mary, carved upon a stone which makes part of the wall. There is no church upon the island. It is annexed to one of the parishes of Sky; and the minister comes and preaches either in Rasay's house, or some other house, on certain Sundays. I could not but value the family seat more, for having even the ruins of a chapel close to it. There was something comfortable in the thought of being so near a piece of consecrated ground. Dr Johnson said, 'I look with reverence upon every place that has been set apart for religion;' and he kept off his hat while he was within the walls of the chapel.

The eight crosses, which Martin mentions as pyramids for deceased ladies, stood in a semicircular line, which contained within it the chapel. They marked out the boundaries of the sacred territory within which an asylum was to be had. One of them, which we observed upon our landing, made the first point of the semicircle. There are few of them now remaining. A good way further north, there is a row of buildings about four feet high : they run from the shore on the east along the top of a pretty high eminence, and so down to the shore on the west, in much the same direction with the crosses. Rasay took them to be the marks for the asylum; but Malcolm thought them to be false sentinels, a common deception, of which instances occur in Martin, to make invaders imagine an island better guarded. Dr Donald M'Queen, justly in my opinion, supposed the crosses which form the inner circle to be the church's land-marks.

The south end of the island is much covered with large stones or rocky strata. The laird has enclosed and planted part of it with firs, and he showed me a considerable space marked out for additional plantations.

Dun Can is a mountain three computed miles from the laird's house. The ascent to it is by consecutive risings, if that expression may be used when valleys intervene, so that there is but a short rise at once; but it is certainly very high above the sea. The palm of altitude is disputed for by the people of Rasay and those of Sky; the former contending for Dun Can, the latter for the mountains in Sky, over against it. We went up the east side of Dun Can pretty easily. It is mostly rocks all around, the points of which hem the summit of it. Sailors, to whom it was a good object as they pass along, call it Rasay's Cap. Before we reached this mountain, we passed by two lakes. Of the first, Malcolm told me a strange fabulous tradition. He said, there was a wild beast in it, a sea-horse, which came and devoured a man's daughter; upon which the man lighted a great fire, and had a sow roasted at it, the smell of which attracted the monster. In the fire was put a spit. The man lay concealed behind a low wall of loose stones, and he had an avenue formed for the monster, with two rows of large flat stones, which extended from the fire over the summit of the hill, till it reached the side of the loch. The monster came, and the man with the red-hot spit destroyed it. Malcolm showed me the little hiding-place, and the rows of stones. He did not laugh when he told this story. I recollect having seen in the 'Scots Magazine', several years ago, a poem upon a similar tale, perhaps the same, translated from the Erse, or Irish, called 'Albin and the Daughter of Mey'.

There is a large tract of land, possessed as a common, in Rasay. They have no regulations as to the number of cattle. Every man puts upon it as many as he chooses. From Dun Can northward, till you reach the other end of the island, there is much good natural pasture unencumbered by stones. We passed over a spot, which is appropriated for the exercising ground. In 1745, a hundred fighting men were reviewed here, as Malcolm told me, who was one of the officers that led them to the field. They returned home all but about fourteen. What a princely thing is it to be able to furnish such a band! Rasay has the true spirit of a chief. He is, without exaggeration, a father to his people.

There is plenty of limestone in the island, a great quarry of freestone, and some natural woods, but none of any age, as they cut the trees for common country uses. The lakes, of which there are many, are well stocked with trout. Malcolm catched one of four-and-twenty pounds weight in the loch next to Dun Can, which, by the way, is certainly a Danish name, as most names of places in these islands are.

The old castle, in which the family of Rasay formerly resided, is situated upon a rock very near the sea. The rock is not one mass of stone, but a concretion of pebbles and earth, so firm that it does not appear to have mouldered. In this remnant of antiquity I found nothing worthy of being noticed, except a certain accommodation rarely to be found at the modern houses of Scotland, and which Dr Johnson and I sought for in vain at the Laird of Rasay's new-built mansion, where nothing else was wanting. I took the liberty to tell the Laird it was a shame there should be such a deficiency in civilized times. He acknowledged the justice of the remark. But perhaps some generations may pass before the want is supplied. Dr Johnson observed to me, how quietly people will endure an evil, which they might at any time very easily remedy; and mentioned as an instance, that the present family of Rasay had possessed the island for more than four hundred years, and never made a commodious landing-place, though a few men with pickaxes might have cut an ascent of stairs out of any part of the rock in a week's time.

The north end of Rasay is as rocky as the south end. From it I saw the little isle of Fladda, belonging to Rasay, all fine green ground; and Rona which is of so rocky a soil that it appears to be a pavement. I was told however that it has a great deal of grass, in the interstices. The Laird has it all in his own hands. At this end of the island of Rasay is a cave in a striking situation. It is in a recess of a great cleft, a good way up from the sea. Before it the ocean roars, being dashed against monstrous broken rocks; grand and awful *propugnacula*. On the right hand of it is a longitudinal cave, very low at the entrance, but higher as you advance. The sea having scooped it out, it seems strange and un-accountable that the interior part, where the water must have operated with less force, should be loftier than that which is more immediately exposed to its violence. The roof of it is all covered with a kind of petrifications formed by drops, which perpetually distil from it. The first cave has been a place of much safety. I find a great difficulty in describing visible objects. I must own too that the old castle and cave, like many other things, of which one hears much, did not answer my expectations. People are every-where apt to magnify the curiosities of their country.

The island has an abundance of black cattle, sheep, and goats; a good many horses, which are used for ploughing, carrying out dung, and other works of husbandry. I believe the people never ride. There are indeed no roads through the island, unless a few detached beaten tracks deserve that name. Most of the houses are upon the shore; so that all the people have little boats, and catch fish. There is great plenty of potatoes here. There are black-cock in extraordinary abundance, moor-fowl, plover and wild pigeons, which seemed to me to be the same as we have in pigeon-houses, in their state of nature. Rasay has no pigeon-house. There are no hares nor rabbits in the island, nor was there ever known to be a fox, till last year, when one was landed on it by some malicious person, without whose aid he could not have got thither, as that animal is known to be a very bad swimmer. He has done much mischief. There is a great deal of fish caught in the sea round Rasay; it is a place where one may live in plenty, and even in luxury. There are no deer; but Rasay told us he would get some.

They reckon it rains nine months in the year in this island, ow-ing to its being directly opposite to the western coast of Sky, where the watery clouds are broken by high mountains. The hills here, and indeed all the healthy grounds in general, abound with the sweet-smelling plant which the Highlanders call *gaul*, and, I think, with dwarf juniper in many places. There is enough of turf, which is their fuel, and it is thought there is a mine of coal. Such are the observations which I made upon the island of

Rasay, upon comparing it with the description given by Martin, whose book we had with us.

JAMES BOSWELL, *Tour to the Hebrides,* 1785

*

IT WAS as late as half past nine AM when I left Tirana, and one consolation there was in quitting its horrible khan, that travel all over the world a worse could not be met with. Various delays prevented an early start; the postmaster was in the bath, and until he came out no horses could be procured; then a dispute with the Khanjí, who, like many of these provincial people, insisted on counting the Spanish dollar as twenty-three instead of twenty-four Turkish piastres. Next followed a row with Békír of Akridha, who vowed he would be paid and indemnified for the loss of an imaginary amber pipe, which he declared he had lost in a fabulous ditch, while holding my horse at Elbasán; and lastly, and not the least of the list, the crowd around the khan gave way at the sound of terrific shrieks and howlings, and forth rushed my spinning neighbour, the mad dervísh, in the most foaming state of indignation. First he seized the bridles of the horses; then, by a frantic and sudden impulse, he began to prance and circulate in the most amazing manner, leaping and bounding and shouting 'Allah!' with all his might, to the sound of a number of little bells, which this morning adorned his brass-hooked weapon. After this he made an harangue for ten minutes, of the most energetic character, myself evidently the subject; at the end of it he advanced towards me with furious gestures, and bringing his hook to within two or three inches of my face, remained stationary, in a Taglioni attitude. Knowing the danger of interfering with these privileged fanatics, I thought my only and best plan was to remain unmoved, which I did, fixing my eye steadily on the ancient buffoon, but neither stirring nor uttering a word; whereon, after he had screamed and foamed at me for some minutes, the demon of anger seemed to leave him at a moment's warning; for yelling forth discordant cries and brandishing his stick and bells, away he ran, as if he were really possessed. Wild

and savage were the looks of many of my friend's excited audience,
their long matted black hair and brown visage giving them an air
of ferocity which existed perhaps more in the outward than the
inner man; moreover, these Gheghes are all armed, whereas out
of Ghegheria no Albanian is allowed to carry so much as a knife.

EDWARD LEAR, *Journals of a Landscape Painter in*
Greece and Albania, 1851

*

FOR ME, I am not ashamed to own I took more pleasure in
looking on the beauteous Fatima, than the finest piece of sculpture
could have given me. Her fair maids were ranged below the sofa,
to the number of twenty, and put me in mind of the pictures of
ancient nymphs. I did not think all nature could have furnished
such a scene of beauty. She made them a sign to play and dance.
Four of them immediately began to play some soft airs on instruments, between a lute and a guitar, which they accompanied
with their voices, while the others danced by turns. This dance
was very different from what I have seen before. Nothing could
be more artful, or more proper to raise certain ideas. The tunes so
soft! – the motions so languishing! – accompanied by pauses and
dying eyes! half falling back, and then recovering themselves in
so artful a manner, that I am very positive the coldest and most
rigid prude upon earth could not have looked upon them without
thinking of something not to be spoken of. I suppose I must have
read that the Turkas have no music but what is shocking to the
ears; but this account is from those who never heard any but what
is played in the streets, and is just as reasonable as if a foreigner
should take his ideas of the English music from the bladder and
string, and marrow-bones and cleavers. I can assure you that the
music is extremely pathetic; 'tis true I am inclined to prefer the
Italian, but perhaps I am partial. I am acquainted with a Greek
lady who sings better than Mrs Robinson, and is very well skilled
in both, who gives the preference to the Turkish. 'Tis certain they
have very fine natural voices; these were very agreeable. When
the dance was over, four fair slaves came into the room with
silver censers in their hands, and perfumed the air with amber,

aloes-wood, and other scents. After this they served me coffee upon their knees in the finest japan china, with *soucoupes* of silver gilt. The lovely Fatima entertained me all this time in the most polite agreeable manner, calling me often *Guzél sultanum,* or the beautiful sultana, and desiring my friendship with the best grace in the world, lamenting that she could not entertain me in my own language.

LADY MARY WORTLEY MONTAGU, *Letter to the Countess of Mar,* 18 April 1717

*

AT FIVE I went to a bawdy-house. I was shown upstairs and had a bottle of claret and a *juffrouw.* But the girl was much fitter for being wrapped in the blankets of salivation than kissed between the sheets of love. I had no armour, so did not fight. It was truly ludicrous to talk in Dutch to a whore. This scene was to me a rarity as great as peas in February. Yet I was hurt to find myself in the sinks of great debauchery. This was a proper way to consider the thing. But so sickly was my brain that I had the low scruples of an Edinburgh divine.

I went to Blinshall's at eight. He talked of religious melancholy like a good sound fellow. He pleased me by saying it was bodily. I was so fretted as to be glad of any relief. I supped with Blinshall's landlord, Connal, am Irish peruke-maker who it seems was once a young fellow of fortune in London, and acquainted with Pope and many more men of genius. It was a queer evening. At six I had been so tired as to go...and drink among blackguards a bottle of wine. I shall never forget that lowness; for low it was indeed. At eleven we parted. I resolved to go to a *speelhuis* but had no guide. I therefore very madly sought for one myself and strolled up and down the Amsterdam streets, which by all accounts are very dangerous at nights. I began to be frightened and to think of Belgic knives. At last I came to a *speelhuis,* where I entered boldly. I danced with a fine lady in laced riding-clothes, a true blackguard minuet. I had my pipe in my mouth and performed like any common sailor. I had near quarrelled with one of the musicians. But I was told to take care, which I wisely did.

I spoke plenty of Dutch but could find no girl that elicited my
inclinations. I was disgusted with this low confusion, came home
and slept sound.

JAMES BOSWELL, *Boswell in Holland,* 1763–4

*

ALL HURRY and confusion – just on the point of setting off for
Naples. Made several visits and after a d—d squabble about the
post chaise of which we were disappointed 20 times, we at length
procured a good looking one, and set out at ½ past 4 for Villetri
on our way to Naples. It soon grew dark and we could see nothing
of the country, but at setting off from the *porta di S. Giovanni,*
there seemed but little to regret. The wind was violently high and
at the end of the 1st post it began to rain. This was only a single
house, called *il tor di mezza via* [Alla Torre]. The next post was
Marino, a town which I had seen when I visited the environs of
Albano. The 3rd Faiola and the 4th Vellatri. In the morning
(MONDAY) which was a very bad one, the first thing we were able
to see, was the famous or rather infamous Palus Pontina or marsh
of Pontini now called by the Italians Paludi Pontine, which
extends more than 30 miles on the left hand of the road, and
which has never yet been drained, not withstanding the repeated
attempts made both by the ancients and moderns. It is to this stag-
nant water and uncultivated land that the mall'aria on this side
the Campagna of Rome is attributed and one shudders with hor-
rour at the sight of this bog and the sickly and putrid hue of
the inhabitants. I am rather of the opinion of Padri Ximenes
and Contatori, in their history of Terracina, that the obstacles
must be insurmountable, as the ancients, who were so industrious and who performed such great works in aqueducts, roads
and fortifications have failed in this project, and am inclined to
think with this last author that the springs and quick-sands are
so innumerable that the draining of this country is not practic-
able. The road to Naples lies between this fen, and the Appenine
Mountains which are on the left. Here buffalos and black
pigs abound – both of the colour and ugliness of the d—l.

The towns and posts we stopt at to change horses on this marsh were Cisterna, Sermonetta, Casenuove, Piperno, and Terracina. The woods on the hills by Sermonetta are very pretty – on the right is seen the promontory of Monte Circello [Circeo] where Circe is said to have changed Scylla into a sea monster, and Ulysses' companions into sea-hogs. This country was inhabited by the ancient Volsci and Sezze, then *Setia,* was their capital. Terracina was the Anxur of the ancients and belonged to the Volsci. Here we came to the Mediterranean Sea, and travelled near it all the way to Naples, generally on the shore. It was very windy and the sea foamed and beat against the rocks which are here very high in a very grand and terrible manner – I never had seen it so enraged. Here we paid the gabella of 3 pauls to the Pope and soon after entered the Kingdom of Naples, where the finest road begins I ever had travelled; it was made 2 years ago for the new Queen when she came from Vienna. It is is smoother than our best turn-pike roads and in general, covered with excellent gravel. At the town dell'Epitasio, we were not asked to shew our pasports but our money : from hence to Fondi we travelled thro' a grove of myrtles of all sorts, very beautiful though not now in blossom. The weather cleared up and we found the air pure and delightful. At Itri, a populous town, we were obliged to stop to have a buckle mended in the harness, and had a mob of more than 100 miserable looking wretches round us, who eyed us as curiously as if we had been wild beasts. There were several ruins of ancient buildings, sepulchres etc. It grew darkish ere we reached Mola [-di-Gaeta], a Neapolitan sea port on the Mediterranean, where we lay. 'Tis a remarkable dear place to strangers; but we escaped for $\frac{2}{3}$ of what the landlord asked. We were obliged to go to the custom house on getting out of the chaise, and underwent a severe visiting of our baggage which was all a farce to draw money from us. We paid here in different fees to officers, porters etc, of the custom house 12 carlins. In the night there was a dreadful storm of thunder, wind and rain.

CHARLES BURNEY, *Men, Music and Manners,* 1773

*

THE LAST appearance of Cerito [an operatic soprano] in Milan was before an entirely English audience. They had bought every seat in the house as soon as the announcement was made. The occasion was marked by an enthusiasm which we may say is fortunately unknown in England. She was called upon the stage fifty-two times, and 1,494 bouquets and 836 garlands were thrown to her. Among the bouquets was one of such gigantic proportions that it required two porters to carry it to the theatre. As well, perhaps, that the tributes were thrown to her and not at her. To buy up all the hothouses and flower gardens of Lombardy is something Englishmen do only when they are abroad and their blood is heated by dangerous southern suns.

The Pictorial Times, 29 April 1843

*

Nice, Jan. 20, 1764

Dear Sir, – Last Sunday I crossed Montalban on horseback, with some Swiss officers, on a visit to our consul, Mr B—d, who lives at Ville Franche, about half a league from Nice. It is a small town, built upon the side of a rock at the bottom of the harbour, which is a fine basin, surrounded with hills on every side, except to the south, where it lies open to the sea. If there was a small island in the mouth of it, to break off the force of the waves when the wind is southerly, it would be one of the finest harbours in the world; for the ground is exceeding good for anchorage. There is sufficient depth of water and room enough for the whole navy of England. On the right hand as you enter the port, there is an elegant fanal or light-house, kept in good repair. But in all the charts of this coast which I have seen, this lanthorn is laid down to the westward of the harbour; an error equally absurd and dangerous, as it may mislead the navigator, and induce him to run his ship among the rocks to the eastward of the light-house, where it would undoubtedly perish. Opposite to the mouth of the harbour is the fort, which can be of no service but in defending the shipping and the town by sea; for, by land, it is commanded by Montalban, and all the hills in the neighbourhood. In the war of 1744, it was taken and retaken. At present it is in tolerable good repair. On the left of the fort is the basin for the gallies, with a kind of dock, in which they are built, and occasionally laid up to be refitted. This basin is formed by a pretty stone mole; and here his Sardinian Majesty's two gallies lie perfectly secure, moored with their sterns close to the jetty. I went on board one of these vessels and saw about two hundred miserable wretches chained to the banks, on which they sit and row when the galley is at sea. This is a sight which the British subject, sensible of the blessing he enjoys, cannot behold without horror and compassion. Not but that, if we consider the nature of the case with coolness and deliberation, we must acknowledge the justice and even sagacity of employing for the service of the public, those malefactors who have forfeited their title to the privileges of the community. Among the slaves at Ville Franche is a Piedmontese count, condemned to the gallies for life, in consequence of having been convicted of forgery. He is permitted to live on shore, and gets money by employing the other slaves to knit stockings for sale. He appears always in the Turkish habit, and is in a fair way of raising a better fortune than that which he has forfeited.

TOBIAS SMOLLETT, Travels in Italy, 1766

*

I WENT yesterday with the French embassadress to see the Grand Signior in his passage to the mosque. He was preceded by a numerous guard of janissaries, with vast white feathers on their heads, *spahis* and *bostangees* (these are foot and horse guard), and the royal gardeners, which are a very considerable body of men, dressed in different habits of fine lively colours, that, at a distance, they appeared like a parterre of tulips. After them the aga of the janissaries, in a robe of purple velvet, lined with silver tissue, his horse led by two slaves richly dressed. Next him the *kyzlár-aga* (your ladyship knows this is the chief guardian of the seraglio ladies) in a deep yellow cloth (which suited very well to his black face) lined with sables, and at last his Sublimity himself, in green lined with the fur of a black Muscovite fox, which is sup-

Cook's Nile Service

Cook's Nile Service

M. S. "HATASOO"

M. S. "HATASOO"

LIST OF PASSENGERS PER M. S. "HATASOO"
Leaving Cairo 15th February 1896

1 Miss H. C. Fane	20 Lady Mc Double
2 Mr. H. Brooks Broadhurst	21 Miss A. Oswald
3 Mrs. Broadhurst	22 Dr. F. R. Martine
4 Hon. Catherine Beresford	23 Mr. L. C. Wakefield
5 Maid	24 Mrs. Wakefield
6 Rev. C. J. Rowland Berkeley	25 Miss Wakefield
7 Mr. P. M. Berkeley	26 Miss J. Blunt
8 Mr. J. Mc Lachlan	27 Mr. Murray Ind
9 Mrs. Napier Sturt	28 Mrs. Murray Ind
10 Miss Astley Sparke	29 Maid
11 Maid	30 Lady Decies
12 Mr. Oakley Maund	31 Lady Ramsden
13 Manservant	32 Maid
14 Capt. Fairholme	33 Mrs. Stevenson
15 Miss Pereira	34 Miss Stevenson
16 Maid	35 Maid
17 Mrs. Holford	36 Mr. Fernando Freire
18 Mrs. Stanley	37 Mr. Patrizio Larrain
19 Maid	38 Mr. Aurelio Fernandez

The potential troublemakers are Nos. 36, 37 and 38. Damned foreigners with their foreign names and waxed moustaches. They'll wheedle themselves to the Captain's table, I'll be bound.

Cairo is extremely warm. Wish you were here. Our room is the fourth from the right on the top floor and has every elegant convenience.

The hotel staff are most respectful. We had scarcely arrived before the English EFFENDI and his party were asked to pose for the photographer.

I thought the camel unseemly and indelicate in its behaviour and said so. I insisted on a mule for myself, not being inclined to foreign ways.

Mr Cook's courier explained something of the curious religion of the ancient Egyptians while we were at the temple. We listened carefully but were not amused.

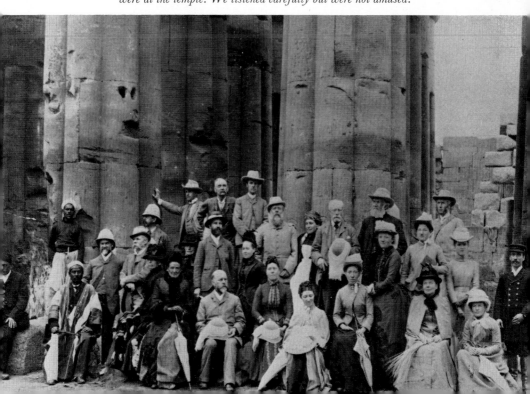

At the commencement of our tour of Tunis my guide Ahmed took me firmly by the hand and said he was my brother. One does not take these people too seriously.

posed worth a thousand pounds sterling, mounted on a fine horse, with furniture embroidered with jewels. Six more horses richly furnished were led after him; and two of his principal courtiers bore, one his gold, and the other his silver coffee-pot, on a staff; another carried a silver stool on his head for him to sit on.

LADY MARY WORTLEY MONTAGU, *Letters,* 1717

*

OSMÁN PASHÁ, the dignitary who at present governs the city of Skódra and its surrounding district, is a Bosnaic by birth, and is said to be in great favour with the Porte from having, while in his present command, made some successful warfare against the Montengríni, who are ever at feud with the Mohammedan government. His Highness is short and fat, with an intelligent and amiable expression of countenance; and spite of his Oriental attitude as he squatted in his corner, a pale frock-coat and European-made trousers gave him little of the air of the Turk. Beside him sat an individual, whose closely buttoned grey vest, clerical hat, gold chain and cross proclaimed the Roman Catholic bishop; this was Monsignore Topicka, the diocesan of Lissus, in which is included the district of Skódra. By means of the Vice-Consular dragoman, the conversation became animated. The pashá was remarkably affable, and asked me to dine with him on the 5th. And then came pipes and coffee – pipes, pipes, sweetmeats – pipes, sherbet, and pipes; throughout which ceremony discourse was extremely plentiful compared with the usual run of Turkish visits.

They call this place the Siberia or exile of Turkey in Europe; and indeed it must be little less than banishment for those who have lived in Stamboul. The Pashá made several remarks, showing that he was by no means an ill-informed man. He asked if 'Lord' Cook had left any children, and if so they also went round the world. Various anecdotes – some very facetious – at which His Highness laughed immoderately, were told by the Consul and bishop; and on the whole the visit, though rather long, was a merry one. There was much talk also regarding reports of battles between the Cattarési and Montenegrini on the far side of the lake.

After the departure of the Vescovo I was invited to walk on the ramparts; and, said the Pashá, 'You may note down all the state of the fortress, if you please; you may look at everything, for your Sovereign is a friend of ours.' It would have been in vain to have said that I had no commission to report upon fortresses or that I was totally incapable of doing so : any attempt to disabuse the august mind of so natural a conception would have had no other result than that of appearing to confirm it. After this I had hoped the visit was over, and was horrified to find that we returned to the divan, when fresh pipes and rose-water ensued, and pipes – pipes – like Banquo's posterity, till I was utterly weary; by the time we had taken leave and repassed the galleries full of retainers the sun had set, and it was dark ere we reached the plain, where we fell in with long lines of Scutarini leaving the bazaars and returning home, each with his empty sack.

> EDWARD LEAR, *Journals of a Landscape Painter in*
> *Greece and Albania,* 1851

*

I WENT to Notre Dame to hear high Mass. I had great difficulty to get there – coaches are not allowed, till all the processions with which the streets swarm, are over. The streets through which they are to pass in the way to the churches are all lined with tapestery, or, for want of that, with bed curtains and old peticoats. I find the *Gens comme il faut* all go out of town on these days to avoid the *embarras* of going to Mass, or the ennui of staying at home. Whenever the Host stops which is frequent for the priests to sing a psalm, all the people fall on their knees in the middle of the street, be it dirty or clean. I readily complied with this ceremony rather than give offence or become remarkable.

> CHARLES BURNEY, *Men, Music and Manners,* 1773

*

THIS IS the great fountain-head and focus of the Carnival. But all the streets in which the Carnival is held, being vigilantly kept by dragoons, it is necessary for carriages, in the first instance, to pass, in line, down another thoroughfare, and so come into the Corso at the end remote from the Piázza del Popolo; which is one of its terminations. Accordingly, we fell into the string of coaches, and, for some time, jogged on quietly enough; now crawling on at a very slow walk; now trotting half-a-dozen yards; now backing fifty; and now stopping altogether: as the pressure in front obliged us. If any impetuous carriage dashed out of the rank and clattered forward, with the wild idea of getting on faster, it was suddenly met, or overtaken, by a trooper on horseback, who, deaf as his own drawn sword to all remonstrances, immediately escorted it back to the very end of the row, and made it a dim speck in the remotest perspective. Occasionally, we interchanged a volley of confétti with the carriage next in front, or the carriage next behind; but as yet, this capturing of stray and errant coaches by the military, was the chief amusement.

Presently, we came into a narrow street, where, besides one line of carriages going, there was another line of carriages returning. Here the sugar-plums and the nosegays began to fly about, pretty smartly; and I was fortunate enough to observe one gentleman attired as a Greek warrior, catch a light-whiskered brigand on the nose (he was in the very act of tossing up a bouquet to a young lady in a first-floor window) with a precision that was much applauded by the bystanders. As this victorious Greek was exchanging a facetious remark with a stout gentleman in a doorway – one-half black and one-half white, as if he had been peeled up the middle – who had offered him his congratulations on this achievement, he received an orange from a house-top, full on his left ear, and was much surprised, not to say discomfited. Especially, as he was standing up at the time; and in consequence of the carriage moving on suddenly, at the same moment, staggered ignominiously, and buried himself among his flowers.

Some quarter of an hour of this sort of progress, brought us to the Corso; and anything so gay, so bright, and lively as the whole scene there, it would be difficult to imagine. From all the innumerable balconies: from the remotest and highest, no less than from the lowest and nearest: hangings of bright red, bright green, bright blue, white and gold, were fluttering in the brilliant sunlight. From windows, and from parapets, and tops of houses, streamers of the richest colours, and draperies of the gaudiest and most sparkling hues, were floating out upon the street. The buildings seemed to have been literally turned inside out, and to have all their gaiety towards the highway. Shop-fronts were taken down, and the windows filled with company, like boxes at a shining theatre; doors were carried off their hinges, and long tapestried groves, hung with garlands of flowers and evergreens, displayed within; builder's scaffoldings were gorgeous temples, radiant in silver, gold, and crimson; and in every nook and corner, from the pavement to the chimney-tops, where women's eyes could glisten, there they danced, and laughed, and sparkled, like the light in water. Every sort of bewitching madness of dress was there. Little preposterous scarlet jackets; quaint old stomachers more wicked than the smartest bodices; Polish pelisses, strained and tight as ripe gooseberries; tiny Greek caps, all awry, and clinging to the dark hair, Heaven knows how; every wild, quaint, bold, shy, pettish, madcap fancy had its illustration in a dress; and every fancy was as dead forgotten by its owner, in the tumult of merriment, as if the three old aqueducts that still remain entire had brought Lethe into Rome, upon their sturdy arches, that morning.

The carriages were now three abreast; in broader places four; often stationary for a long time together; always one close mass of variegated brightness; showing, the whole streetful, through the storm of flowers, like flowers of a larger growth themselves. In some, the horses were richly caparisoned in magnificent trappings; in others they were driven by coachmen with enormous double faces: one face leering at the horses: the other cocking its extraordinary eyes into the carriage: and both rattling again, under the hail of sugar-plums. Other drivers were attired as women, wearing long ringlets and no bonnets, and looking more ridiculous in any real difficulty with the horses (of which, in such a concourse, there were a great many) than tongue can tell, or pen describe. Instead of sitting *in* the carriages, upon the seats, the handsome Roman women, to see and to be seen the better, sit in the heads of the barouches, at this time of general licence, with their feet upon the cushions – and oh the flowing skirts and dainty waists, the blessed shapes and laughing faces, the free, good-humoured, gallant figures that they make! There were great vans, too, full of handsome girls – thirty, or more together, perhaps – and the broadsides that were poured into, and poured out of, these fairy fire-shops, splashed the air with flowers and bon-bons for ten minutes at a time. Carriages, delayed long in one place, would begin a deliberate engagement with other carriages, or with people at the lower windows; and the spectators at some upper balcony or window, joining in the fray, and attacking both parties, would empty down great bags of confétti, that descended like a cloud, and in an instant made them white as millers. Still, carriages on carriages, dresses on dresses, colours on colours, crowds upon crowds, without end. Men and boys clinging to the wheels of coaches, and holding on behind, and following in their wake, and diving in among the horses' feet to pick up scattered flowers to sell again; maskers on foot (the drollest generally) in fantastic exaggerations of court-dresses, surveying the throng through enormous eye-glasses, and always transported with an ecstasy of love, on the discovery of any particularly old lady at a window; long strings of Policinelli, laying about them with blown bladders at the ends of sticks; a waggonful of madmen, screaming and tearing to the life; a coachful of grave Mamelukes, with their horse-tail standard set up in the midst; a party of gipsy-women engaged in terrific conflict with a shipful of sailors; a man-monkey on a pole, surrounded by strange animals with pigs' faces, and lions' tails, carried under their arms, or worn gracefully over their shoulders; carriages on carriages, dresses on dresses, colours on colours, crowds upon crowds, without end.

CHARLES DICKENS, *Pictures From Italy,* 1846

*

Now I have mentioned the Armenians, perhaps it will be agreeable to tell you something of that nation, with which I am sure you are utterly unacquainted. I will not trouble you with the geographical account of the situation of their country, which you may see in the map, or a relation of their ancient greatness, which you may read in the Roman history. They are now subject to the Turks; and, being very industrious in trade, and increasing and multiplying, are dispersed in great numbers through all the Turkish dominions. They were, as they say, converted to the Christian by St Gregory, and are perhaps the devoutest Christians in the whole world. The chief precepts of their priests enjoin the strick keeping of their lents, which are at least seven months in every year, and are not to be dispensed with on the most emergent necessity; no occasion whatever can excuse them, if they touch any more than mere herbs or roots (without oil) and plain dry bread. That is their lenten diet. Mr Wortley has one of his intrepreters of this nation; and the poor fellow was brought so low by the severity of his fasts, that his life was despaired of. Yet neither his master's commands, or the doctor's entreaties (who declared nothing else could save his life), were powerful enough to prevail with him to take two or three spoonfuls of broth. Excepting this, which may rather be called custom than an article of faith, I see very little in their religion different from ours . . .

What is most extraordinary in their customs, is their matrimony; a ceremony I believe unparallel'd all over the world. They are always promised very young; but the espoused never see one another till three days after their marriage. The bride is carried to church with a cap on her head, in the fashion of a large trencher, and over it a red silken veil which covers her all over to her feet. The priest asks the bridegroom, whether he is contented to marry that woman, be she deaf, be she blind? These are the literal words: to which having answered *yes*, she is led home to his house, accompanied with all the friends and relations on both sides, singing and dancing, and is placed on a cushion in the corner of the sofa; but her veil never lifted up, not even by her husband, till she has been three days married. There is something so odd and monstrous in these ways, that I could not believe them till I had enquired of several Armenians myself, who all assured me of the truth of them, particularly one young fellow, who wept when he spoke of it, being promised by his mother to a girl that he must marry in this manner, though he protested to me he had rather die than submit to this slavery, having already figured his bride to himself with all the deformities in nature.

LADY MARY WORTLEY MONTAGU, *Letters,* 1718

*

A DIADEM worn by Lady Castlereagh, and representing her husband's Order of the Garter, is the subject of general conversation at Vienna. The English ladies eclipse all the rest of the fair sex by the splendour of their dress; but the Polish women, of whom there is a great number, bear away the palm of beauty. The union of different nations necessarily requires one common language, and the French still maintains its universality, being nearly the one in which the English can make themselves understood by the Russians, Poles, Germans and the French. The ladies regard it as the natural language of gallantry, and those who have wished to introduce the Italian in its stead form but a minority.

Report on the Congress of Vienna in the *Examiner,*
8 January 1815

*

THIS IS the worst winter that has been seen in Holland for many years. We have had scarcely any frost, which is surely the best winter weather in this land. Whenever it freezes hard, so that the canals are covered with good ice, the Dutchmen are happy; then everybody goes out to skate. But this winter we have had nothing at all but rain and wind and thick fogs; weather indeed so unhealthy that a foreigner cannot stand it. I myself had had a bad cold for ten days. I had a severe headache, but I am so regular that I have not been absent a day from my college. Mynheer Trotz also had a cold, yet he gave his lectures, and I thought that it would be highly scandalous if the student should indulge himself more than the professor, who is much older.

Mynheer Trotz is certainly a most unusual man. He is a Prussian. But he has been many years in the Seven Provinces, first at Franeker in Friesland, then at Utrecht, having been professor of law in both places. He is an excellent jurist, having a profound knowledge of Roman and Dutch law, and having also much knowledge of history and philosophy. He is very lively and mingles many entertaining stories with lessons. He has a great desire to learn English. He began it some years ago, but he neglected it. However, he has begun it again. Mr Rose is his teacher, and goes to him twice a week, and really it is amazing to see with what attention and spirit the old professor can read.

JAMES BOSWELL, *Boswell in Holland,* 1763–4

*

26 *June* 1767

Moderate fine pleasant weather, with regular sea and Land breezes. We now prepared for Landing at the Watering place, to take possession of this Beautiful Island in his Majesty's name. We first hove taut upon the spring and brought the ship's broadside to bear on the head of the Bay, then manned and armed the Barge, Cutter and Launch, and Quartered all the hands on board at the Great Guns, to be ready to fire upon the natives if they attempted to prevent our Boats from Landing.

When all this precaution was taken, Mr Furneaux the second Lieut. was ordered to take the command of the party, and to Land with the serjeant and twelve marines and Eighteen able seamen, besides three young Gentlemen to assist him, and Mr Molyneux, one of the mates, had the command of the three boats, with orders to bring them all three to anchor, with their Grapnels in a line along shore.

The Instant that the Lieut. landed he was to keep four men in Each boat ready to fire the musquetoons upon the natives, if they attacked our men; and if the party was obliged to retreat to the Boats, Mr Molyneux was to take care to keep the boats in about four foot of water, that the men might be able to Jump in. After all these orders were given the Boats set out, and in a few minutes Landed and formed on the Beach, and took possession of the

Island In His Majesty's name, and Honoured it with the name of our Most Gracious soverign King George the third.

Soon after they Landed about four or five hundred of the Natives assembled within musket shot of our men and began to advance slowly towards the River-side, every man carrying the bow of a Plantain Tree in his hand as an Emblem of Peace. When they got to the River-side they all stopped and made several friendly signs to our people, but none of them attempted to cross the River until the Lieut. made a sign for some of them to come over. Then three Elderly Men set out directly and crossed the River, with a small pig in one hand and an Emblem of Peace in the other. When they got over the River the Lieut. made signs for one of the three to come up to him, and he Advanced about twenty yards from his party to meet the Old Man, who came up with his Emblem of Peace and the Young Pig by way of a Peace Offering.

When the Old Man came within a few Yards of the Lieut. he made a full stop, and talked for some time, then laid down the pig and laid the plantain bough on the top of it. Then the Lieut. made a short talk to the Old Man and ordered one of the seamen to receive the peace-offering, and the Lieut. paid the Old Man with Nails and Toys, and let him know that we wanted Water, which he made signs for us to take as much as we wanted. Then the Lieut. Ordered our men to roll two small casks in to the River, and fill them, which was immediately done, at same time he ordered some men to fix a long pole in the Ground, and hoisted a pendant on it in token of our having taken Possession of that place.

GEORGE ROBERTSON, *The Discovery of Tahiti,* 1780

*

CHRISTMAS IN THE ANTARCTIC

Thursday 22 June 1911 : MIDWINTER. The sun reached its maximum depression at about 2.30 PM on the 22nd, Greenwich Mean Time : this is 2.30 AM on the 23rd according to the local time of the 180th meridian which we are keeping. Dinner tonight is therefore the meal which is nearest the sun's critical change of course, and has been observed with all the festivity customary at Xmas at home.

At tea we broached an enormous Buszard cake, with much gratitude to its provider, Cherry-Garrard. In preparation for the evening our 'Union Jacks' and sledge flags were hung about the large table, which itself was laid with glass and a plentiful supply of champagne bottles instead of the customary mugs and enamel limejuice jugs. At seven o'clock we sat down to an extravagant bill of fare as compared with our usual simple diet.

Beginning on seal soup, by common consent the best decoction that our cook produces, we went on to roast beef with Yorkshire pudding, fried potatoes and Brussels sprouts. Then followed a flaming plum-pudding, and excellent mince pies, and thereafter a dainty savoury of anchovy and cod's roe. A wondrous attractive meal even in so far as judged by our simple lights, but with its garnishments a positive feast, for withal the table was strewn with dishes of burnt almonds, crystallized fruits, chocolates and such toothsome kickshaws, whilst the unstinted supply of champagne which accompanied the courses was succeeded by a noble array of liquer bottles from which choice could be made in the drinking of toasts.

I screwed myself up to a little speech which drew attention to the nature of the celebration as a half-way mark not only in our winter but in the plans of the Expedition as originally published. (I fear there are some who don't realize how rapidly time passes and who have barely begun work which by this time ought to be in full swing.)

We had come through a summer season and half a winter, and had before us half a winter and a second summer. We ought to know how we stood in every respect; we did know how we stood in regard to stores and transport, and I especially thanked the officer in charge of stores and the custodians of the animals. I said that as regards the future, chance must play a part, but that experience showed me that it would have been impossible to have chosen people more fitted to support me in the enterprise to the South than those who were to start in that direction in the spring. I thanked them all for having put their shoulders to the wheel and given me this confidence.

We drank to the Success of the Expedition.

Then everyone was called on to speak, starting on my left and working round the table; the result was very characteristic of the various individuals – one seemed to know so well the style of utterance to which each would commit himself.

Needless to say, all were entirely modest and brief; unexpectedly, all had exceedingly kind things to say of me – in fact, I was obliged to request the omission of compliments at an early stage. Nevertheless it was gratifying to have a really genuine recognition of my attitude towards the Scientific workers of the Expedition, and I felt very warmly towards all these kind, good fellows for expressing it.

If goodwill and happy fellowship count towards success, very surely shall we deserve to succeed. It was matter for comment, much applauded, that there had not been a single disagreement between any two members of our party from the beginning. By the end of dinner a very cheerful spirit prevailed, and the room was cleared for Ponting and his lantern, whilst the gramophone gave forth its most lively airs.

When the table was upended, its legs removed, and chairs arranged in rows, we had quite a roomy lecture hall. Ponting had cleverly chosen this opportunity to display a series of slides made from his own local negatives. I have never so fully realized his work as on seeing these beautiful pictures; they so easily outclass anything of their kind previously taken in these regions. Our audience cheered vociferously.

After this show the table was restored for snapdragon, and a brew of milk punch was prepared in which we drank the health of Campbell's Party and of our good friends in the *Terra Nova*. Then the table was again removed and a set of lancers formed.

By this time the effect of stimulating liquid refreshment on men so long accustomed to a simple life became apparent. Our biologist had retired to bed, the silent Soldier bubbled with humour and insisted on dancing with Anton. Evans, P.O., was imparting confidences in heavy whispers. 'Pat' Clissold sat with a constant expansive smile and punctuated the babble of conversation with an occasional 'Whoop' of delight or disjointed witticism. Other bright-eyed individuals merely reached the capacity to enjoy that which under ordinary circumstances might have passed without evoking a smile.

In the midst of the revelry Bowers suddenly appeared, followed by some satellites bearing an enormous Christmas Tree whose branches bore flaming candles, gaudy crackers, and little presents for all. The presents, I learnt, had been prepared with kindly thought by Miss Souper (Mrs Wilson's sister) and the tree had been made by Bowers of pieces of stick and string with coloured paper to clothe its branches; the whole erection was remarkably creditable and the distribution of the presents caused much amusement.

Whilst revelry was the order of the day within our hut, the elements without seemed desirous of celebrating the occasion with equal emphasis and greater decorum. The eastern sky was massed with swaying auroral light, the most vivid and beautiful display that I had ever seen – fold on fold the arches and curtains of vibrating luminosity rose and spread across the sky, to slowly fade and yet again spring to glowing life.

The brighter light seemed to flow, now to mass itself in wreathing folds in one quarter, from which lustrous streamers shot upward, and anon to run in waves through the system of some dimmer figure as if to infuse new life within it.

It is impossible to witness such a beautiful phenomenon without a sense of awe, and yet this sentiment is not inspired by its brilliancy but rather by its delicacy in light and colour, its transparency, and above all by its tremulous evanescence of form. There is no glittering splendour to dazzle the eye, as has been too often described; rather the appeal is to the imagination by the suggestion of something wholly spiritual, something instinct with a fluttering ethereal life, serenely confident yet restlessly mobile.

One wonders why history does not tell us of 'aurora' worshippers, so easily could the phenomenon be considered the manifestation of 'god' or 'demon'. To the little silent group which stood at gaze before such enchantment it seemed profane to return to the mental and physical atmosphere of our house. Finally when I stepped within, I was glad to find that there had been a general movement bedwards, and in the next half-hour the last of the roysterers had succumbed to slumber.

Thus, except for a few bad heads in the morning, ended the High Festival of Midwinter.

There is little to be said for the artificial uplifting of animal spirits, yet few could take great exception to so rare an outburst in a long run of quiet days.

After all, we celebrated the birth of a season which for weal or woe must be numbered amongst the greatest in our lives.

ROBERT FALCON SCOTT, *Diary of the Expedition,* 1912

*

AT BELGRADE we lodged with a great and rich effendi, a man of wit and learning, and of a very agreeable humour. We were in his house about a month, and he did constantly eat with us, drinking wine without any scruple. As I rallied him a little on this subject, he answered me, smiling, that all creatures in the world were made for the pleasure of man; and that God would not have let the wine grow, were it a sin to taste of its juice: but that nevertheless the law which forbids the use of it to the vulgar, was very wise, because such sort of folks have not enough sense to take it with moderation.

LADY MARY WORTLEY MONTAGU, *Letters,* 1718

*

THE FREQUENT change of coachmen works no change or variety in the coachman's character. He is always dirty, sullen, and taciturn. If he be capable of smartness of any kind, moral or physical, he has a faculty of concealing it which is truly marvellous. He never speaks to you as you sit beside him on the box, and if you speak to him, he answers (if at all) in monosyllables. He points out nothing on the road, and seldom looks at anything : being, to all appearance, thoroughly weary of it and of existence generally. As to doing the honours of his coach, his business, as I have said, is with the horses. The coach follows because it is attached to them and goes on wheels: not because you are in it. Sometimes, towards the end of a long stage, he suddenly breaks out into a discordant fragment of an election song, but his face never sings along with him: it is only his voice, and not often that.

He always chews and always spits, and never encumbers himself with a pocket-handkerchief. The consequences to the box passenger, especially when the wind blows towards him, are not agreeable.

Whenever the coach stops, and you can hear the voices of the inside passengers; or whenever any bystander addresses them, or any one among them; or they address each other; you will hear one phrase repeated over and over and over again to the most extraordinary extent. It is an ordinary and unpromising phrase enough, being neither more nor less than 'Yes, Sir;' but it is adapted to every variety of circumstance, and fills up every pause in the conversation. Thus:

The time is one o'clock at noon. The scene, a place where we are to stay and dine, on this journey. The coach drives up to the door of an inn. The day is warm, and there are several idlers lingering about the tavern, and waiting for the public dinner. Among them, is a stout gentleman in a brown hat, swinging himself to and fro in a rocking-chair on the pavement.

As the coach stops, a gentleman in a straw hat looks out of the window:

STRAW HAT. (To the stout gentleman in the rocking-chair.) I reckon that's Judge Jefferson, an't it?

BROWN HAT. (Still swinging, speaking very slowly; and without any emotion whatever.) Yes, Sir.

STRAW HAT. Warm weather, Judge.

BROWN HAT. Yes, Sir.

STRAW HAT. There was a snap of cold, last week.

BROWN HAT. Yes, Sir.

STRAW HAT. Yes, Sir.

A pause. They look at each other, very seriously.

STRAW HAT. I calculate you'll have got through that case of the corporation, Judge, by this time, now?

BROWN HAT. Yes, Sir.

STRAW HAT. How did the verdict go, Sir?

BROWN HAT. For the defendant, Sir.

STRAW HAT. (Interrogatively.) Yes, Sir?

BROWN HAT. (Affirmatively.) Yes, Sir.

BOTH. (Musingly, as each gazes down the street.) Yes, Sir.

Another pause. They look at each other again, still more seriously than before.

BROWN HAT. This coach is rather behind its time today, I guess.

STRAW HAT. (Doubtingly.) Yes, Sir.

BROWN HAT. (Looking at his watch.) Yes, Sir; nigh upon two hours.

STRAW HAT. (Raising his eyebrows in very great surprise.) Yes, Sir!

BROWN HAT. (Decisively, as he puts up his watch.) Yes, Sir.

ALL THE OTHER INSIDE PASSENGERS. (Among themselves.) Yes, Sir.

COACHMAN. (In a very surly tone.) No it an't.

STRAW HAT. (To the coachman.) Well, I don't know, Sir. We were a pretty tall time coming that last fifteen mile. That's a fact.

The coachman making no reply, and plainly declining to enter into any controversy on a subject so far removed from his sympathies and feelings, another passenger says, 'Yes, Sir;' and the gentleman in the straw hat in acknowledgment of his courtesy, says 'Yes, Sir,' to him, in return. The straw hat then inquires of the brown hat, whether that coach in which he (the straw hat) then sits, is not a new one? To which the brown hat again makes answer, 'Yes, Sir.'

STRAW HAT. I thought so. Pretty loud smell of varnish, Sir?

BROWN HAT. Yes, Sir.

ALL THE OTHER INSIDE PASSENGERS. Yes, Sir.

BROWN HAT. (To the company in gerneral.) Yes, Sir.

CHARLES DICKENS, *American Notes,* 1842

*

THE CLOCK of the city of Bâle is about an hour before all the clocks in the country, and indeed before the sun himself, by which they are regulated; so that when a stranger sets out from Bâle at noon, after travelling a league, he finds it noon still. Various are the causes assigned for this particularity of the Bâle clock. Some say there was a conspiracy of the citizens to rise in arms at a certain hour, and that the magistrates, having had notice of it, advanced the clock an hour; so that some of the conspirators came to the rendezvous too late, and others too soon, and in short all were in confusion. Some again maintain that the enemy were at their gates, and were to be let in at a certain time by some wicked malcontents, but that a miracle was wrought in the favour of Bâle, and the clock advanced an hour. This tradition is highly natural. It flatters their vanity and pleases their superstition to suppose such an interposition of Providence. No less a man than the late famous mathematician Bernoulli set himself to account for this strange mensuration of time. He supposed that they had taken a dial which was not just to regulate the clock of the cathedral by. By this means the Cathedral clock has been put wrong, and the others have followed. But this account will not suffice; for if the dial for the Cathedral clock had been bad, it would have been corrected by the others. Wolleb said that most probably the clock had been advanced during the Council of Bâle, that the ecclesiastics might meet an hour sooner, perhaps with design to be an hour sooner with their mistresses. As the Council lasted ten years, the irregularity of the clock became a custom. I asked if they did not think to correct this absurd custom. A grave gentleman of authority in the city gravely replied that not a year ago the affair had been debated in Council, and some of the members had maintained that the clock should not be changed, as it might perhaps bring ruin upon their republic. Is it possible that such darkness can remain in an age so enlightened? Wolleb said that the servants and workmen would lie abed longer by the change; as to rise at five would appear terrible, although they really rise at present at that hour by the name of six.

I must give a specimen of Wolleb's wit. When in England he

said, 'You English don't love the foreigners; and yet had it not been for a foreigner you would be damned. You own there is no salvation but through Jesus Christ'. – 'Yes, sure.' – 'Well, Jesus Christ was a foreigner. Ha! ha!'

JAMES BOSWELL, *On the Grand Tour:*
Germany and Switzerland, 1764

*

EARLY IN the morning we surveyed the remains of antiquity at this place, accompanied by an illiterate fellow, as cicerone, who called himself a descendant of a cousin of Saint Columba, the founder of the religious establishment here. As I knew that many persons had already examined them, and as I saw Dr Johnson inspecting and measuring several of the ruins of which he has since given so full an account, my mind was quiescent; and I resolved to stroll among them at my ease, to take no trouble to investigate minutely, and only receive the general impression of solemn antiquity, and the particular ideas of such objects as should of themselves strike my attention.

We walked from the monastery of Nuns to the great church or cathedral, as they call it, along an old broken causeway. They told us, that this had been a street; and that there were good houses built on each side. Dr Johnson doubted if it was anything more than paved road for the nuns. The convent of Monks, the great church, Oran's chapel, and four other chapels are still to be discerned. But I must own that Icolmkill did not answer my expectations; for they were high, from what I had read of it, and still more from what I had heard and thought of it, from my earliest years. Dr Johnson said, it came up to his expectations, because he had taken his impression from an account of it subjoined to Sacheverel's History of the Isle of Man, where it is said, there is not much to be seen here. We were both disappointed, when we were shown what are called the monuments of the kings of Scotland, Ireland, and Denmark, and of a king of France. There are only some gravestones flat on the earth, and we could see no inscriptions. How far short was this of marble monuments,

F

like those in Westminster Abbey, which I had imagined here! The gravestones of Sir Allan M'Lean's family, and of that of M'Quarrie, had as good an appearance as the Royal gravestones; if they were royal, we doubted.

My easiness to give credit to what I heard in the course of our Tour was too great. Dr Johnson's peculiar accuracy of investigation detected much traditional fiction, and many gross mistakes. It is not to be wondered at, that he was provoked by people carelessly telling him, with the utmost readiness and confidence, what he found, on questioning them a little more, was erroneous. Of this there were innumerable instances.

I left him and Sir Allan at breakfast in our barn, and stole back again to the cathedral, to indulge in solitude and devout meditation. While contemplating the venerable ruins, I reflected with much satisfaction, that the solemn scenes of piety never lose their sanctity and influence, though the cares and follies of life may prevent us from visiting them, or may even make us fancy that their effects are only 'as yesterday, when it is past', and never again to be perceived. I hoped, that, ever after having been in this holy place, I should maintain an exemplary conduct. One has a strange propensity to fix upon some point of time from whence a better course of life may begin.

Being desirous to visit the opposite shore of the island, where Saint Columba is said to have landed, I procured a horse from one M'Ginnis, who ran along as my guide. The M'Ginnises are said to be a branch of the clan of M'Lean. Sir Allan had been told that this man had refused to send him some rum, at which the knight was in great indignation. 'You rascal!' said he, 'don't you know that I can hang you if I please?' Not adverting to the Chieftain's power over his clan, I imagined that Sir Allan had known of some capital crime that the fellow had committed, which he could discover, and so get him condemned; and said 'How so?' 'Why,' said Sir Allan, 'are they not all my people?' Sensible of my inadvertency, and most willing to contribute what I could towards the continuation of feudal authority, 'Very true,' said I. Sir Allan went on: 'Refuse to send rum to me, you rascal!

Don't you know that, if I order you to go and cut a man's throat, you are to do it?' 'Yes, an't please your honour! and my own too, and hang myself too.' The poor fellow denied that he had refused to send the rum. His making these professions was not merely a pretence in presence of his Chief; for after he and I were out of Sir Allan's hearing, he told me, 'Had he sent his dog for the rum, I would have given it: I would cut my bones for him.' It was very remarkable to find such an attachment to a Chief, though he had then no connection with the island, and had not been there for fourteen years. Sir Allan, by way of upbraiding the fellow, said, 'I believe you are a *Campbell.*'

The place which I went to see is about two miles from the village. They call it Portawherry, from the wherry in which Columba came; though, when they show the length of his vessel, as marked on the beach by two heaps of stones, they say, 'Here is the length of the *Currach,*' using the Erse word.

Icolmkill is a fertile island. The inhabitants export some cattle and grain; and I was told, they import nothing but iron and salt. They are industrious, and make their own woollen and linen cloth; and they brew a good deal of beer, which we did not find in any of the other islands.

We set sail again about mid-day, and in the evening landed on Mull, near the house of the Reverend Mr Neal M'Leod, who having been informed of our coming, by a message from Sir Allan, came out to meet us. We were this night very agreeably entertained at his house. Dr Johnson observed to me, that he was the clearest-headed man that he had met with in the Western Islands. He seemed to be well acquainted with Dr Johnson's writings, and courteously said, 'I have been often obliged to you, though I never had the pleasure of seeing you before.'

He told us, he had lived for some time in St Kilda, under the tuition of the minister or catechist there, and had there first read Horace and Virgil. The scenes which they describe must have been a strong contrast to the dreary waste around him.

JAMES BOSWELL, Tour to the Hebrides, 1785

*

To BLOIS, an old town, prettily situated on the Loire, with a good stone bridge of eleven arches. We viewed the castle, for the historical monument it affords that has rendered it so famous. They show the room where the council assembled, and the chimney in it before which the Duke of Guise was standing when the king's page came to demand his presence in the royal closet; the door he was entering when stabbed; the tapestry he was in the act of turning aside; the tower where his brother the cardinal suffered; with a hole in the floor into the dungeon of Louis XI, of which the guide tells many horrible stories, in the same tone, from having told them so often, in which the fellow in Westminster Abbey gives his monotonous history of the tombs ... The murders, or political executions perpetrated in the castle, though not uninteresting, were inflicted on, and by men that command neither our love nor our veneration. The character of the period, and of the men that figured in it, were alike disgusting. Bigotry and ambition, equally dark, insidious, and bloody, allow no feelings of regret. The parties could hardly be better employed than in cutting each other's throats.

ARTHUR YOUNG, *Travels in France,* 1792

*

To THINK that I, an ordinary Englishman in the ordinary course of travel abroad, should have encountered the great Beethoven! The more the miracle because he is so withdrawn. Though not an old man he is lost to society in consequence of his extreme deafness, which has rendered him almost unsocial. So I was astonished when my friend Mr Dibdin bore me off to a beer hall where he might be seen. And indeed there he was! Though only the waiter would venture near him. The neglect of his person which he exhibits gives him a somewhat wild appearance. His features are strong and prominent; his eye is full of rude energy; his hair, which neither comb nor scissors seem to have visited for years, overshadows his broad brow in a quantity and confusion to which only the snakes round a Gorgon's head offer a parallel. His general behaviour does not ill accord with the uncompromising exterior. Except when he is among his chosen friends kindliness and affability are not his characteristics. The total loss of hearing had deprived him of all the pleasure which society can give, and perhaps soured his temper. He used to frequent a particular cellar, where he spent the evening in a corner, beyond the reach of all the chattering and disputation of a public room, drinking wine and beer, eating cheese and red herrings, and studying the news-papers. One evening a person took a seat near him whose counte-nance did not please him. He looked hard at the stranger, and spat on the floor as if he had seen a toad; then glanced at the newspaper, then again at the intruder, and spat again, his hair bristling gradually into more shaggy ferocity, till he closed the alternation of spitting and staring, by fairly exclaiming 'What a scoundrelly phiz!' and rushing out of the room. Fortunately no such embarrassing incident occurred during my visit with Mr Dibdin; for if Beethoven was at all aware of our presence, he was no doubt aware of our nationality also, and would not like to offend representatives of such an admiring nation.

SIR JOHN RUSSELL, *A Tour in Germany,* 1828

*

BOLOGNA BEING very full of tourists, detained there by an inundation which rendered the road to Florence impassable, I was quartered up at the top of an hotel, in an out-of-the-way room which I never could find : containing a bed, big enough for a boarding-school, which I couldn't fall asleep in. The chief among the waiters who visited this lonely retreat, where there was no other company but the swallows in the broad eaves over the window, was a man of one idea in connexion with the English; and the subject of this harmless monomania, was Lord Byron. I made the discovery by accidentally remarking to him, at breakfast, that the matting with which the floor was covered, was very comfortable at that season, when he immediately replied that Milor Beeron had been much attached to that kind of matting. Observing, at the same moment, that I took no milk, he exclaimed with enthusiasm, that Milor Beeron had never touched it. At first, I took it for granted, in my innocence, that he had been one of the Beeron servants; but no, he said, no, he was in the habit of speaking about my Lord, to English gentlemen; that was all. He knew all about him, he said. In proof of it, he connected him with every possible topic, from the Monte Pulciano wine at dinner (which was grown on an estate he had owned), to the big bed itself, which was the very model of his. When I left the inn, he coupled with his final bow in the yard, a parting assurance that the road by which I was going, had been Milor Beeron's favourite ride; and before the horses' feet had well begun to clatter on the pavement, he ran briskly upstairs again, I dare say to tell some other English-man in some other solitary room that the guest who had just de-parted was Lord Beeron's living image.

CHARLES DICKENS, *Pictures From Italy,* 1846

*

THE SECOND day after we set sail we passed Callipolis, a fair city, situate in the bay of Chersonesus, and much respected by the Turks, being the first town they took in Europe. At five the next morning we anchored in the Hellespont, between the castles of Sestos and Abydos, now called the Dardanelli. These are now two little ancient castles, but of no strength, being commanded by a rising ground behind them, which I confess I should never have taken notice of, if I had not heard it observed by our captain and officers, my imagination being wholly employed by the tragic story that you are well acquainted with :

> *The swimming lover, and the nightly bride,*
> *How Hero loved, and how Leander died.*

Verse again! – I am certainly infected by the poetical air I have passed through. That of Abydos is undoubtedly very amorous, since that soft passion betrayed the castle into the hands of the Turks, in the reign of Orchanes, who besieged it. The governor's daughter, imagining to have seen her future husband in a dream (though I don't find she had either slept upon bride-cake, or kept St Agnes' fast), fancied she saw afterwards the dear figure in the form of one of her besiegers; and being willing to obey her destiny, tossed note to him over the wall, with the offer of her person, and the delivery of the castle. He shewed it to his general, who consented to try the sincerity of her intentions, and withdrew his army, ordering the young man to return with a select body of men at midnight. She admitted him at the appointed hour; he destroyed the garrison, took her father prisoner, and made her his wife. This town is in Asia, first founded by the Milesians. Sestos is in Europe, and was once the principal city of Chersonesus. Since I have seen this strait, I find nothing improbable in the adventure of Leander, or very wonderful in the bridge of boats of Xerxes. 'Tis so narrow, 'tis not surprising a young lover should attempt to swim it, or an ambitious king try to pass his army over it. But then 'tis so subject to storms 'tis no wonder the lover perished, and the bridge was broken.

LADY MARY WORTLEY MONTAGU, *Letters*, 1718

*

THE HOUSES of Khimára are all of dark stone, and bear signs of having seen better days; on every side are heaps of ruin, and a great extent of rubbish, with walls of different dates, proclaims this remarkable Acropolis to have been once a considerable place. The people of Khimára are all of Greek origin, and speak Romaic, though those of the towns I have passed on my way, although Christian, are all Albanian with the exception of a few families such as the Kasnétzi. The Khimáriotes of this place declare that the town contains vestiges of sixty-two churches. There are some remains of fifteen or sixteen on the lower part of the rock, but all in a state of total ruin, and the appearance of the Ecónomo of Khimára is in complete accordance with that of his native ecclesiastical edifices.

As I walked slowly up the zigzag path to the entrance to the town, I had leisure to examine my numerous new acquaintance, whom I thought by far the most wild and most typical of Albanian character that I had yet seen; the men wear their hair extremely long, and walk with the complete strut of Albanian dignity – the loftiest and most sovereign expression of pride in every gesture. As for the females, I saw none, except a few of the heavy stick-laden, who were toiling up the hill, clad in dark blue dresses with red aprons (worn behind), and red-worked hose. Guided by Anastásio, who seemed, here as elsewhere, a general acquaintance and was greeted with excessive hilarity, we proceeded to a house where, in a dark room of great size, a mat and cushions were spread for me and there was no lack of company. A very aged man, more than a century old, occupied a bed in one corner; a screaming baby in a cradle on the opposite side illustrated another extreme point of the seven ages of the family; two or three women, retiring into the obscurest shade, seemed to be knitting, while circles of long-haired Khimáriotes thronged the floor.

Many of these, both outside and in the house, extended their hands for mine to shake, I supposed from being aware of Frank modes of salutation; but among them three or four gave me so peculiar a twist or crack of my fingers that I was struck by its singularity; though it was not until my hand had been held firmly for a repetition of this manoeuvre, accompanied by a look of interrogation from the holder, that the thought flashed on my mind, that what I observed was a concerted signal. I shortly became fully aware that I was among people who, from some cause or other, had fled from justice in other lands.

Of these was one who, with his face entirely muffled excepting one eye, kept aloof in the darker part of the chamber, until having thoroughly scrutinized me he came forward, and dropping his capote discovered to my horror and amazement features which, though disguised by an enormous growth of hair, I could not fail to recognize as typical. 'The world is my city now,' he said; 'I am become a savage like those with whom I dwell. What is life to me?' And covering his face again, he wept with a heart-breaking bitterness only life-exiles can know.

EDWARD LEAR, *Journals of a Landscape Painter in Greece and Albania,* 1851

*

IT IS certain that I have the greatest desire to learn French, but I fear that I am not learning it very quickly. Perhaps my keen desire makes me think myself worse in acquiring the language than I am. I certainly take a great deal of pains to improve. I write two pages of a theme every morning. I read for two hours in the works of Voltaire every evening. When I do not understand words perfectly, I look them up in the dictionary, and I write them down with their meanings. Every Wednesday I have the pleasure of passing the evening in a literary society where it is not permitted to speak a word of anything but French. Yet I cannot observe that I am making rapid progress. In writing, I am slow and clumsy, and in speaking I have great difficulty in expressing myself and often make terrible blunders. Instead of saying, 'Would you like to play at shuttlecock?' (*volant*), I said 'Would you like to play at robber?' (*voleur*); and instead of 'Mademoiselle, I am entirely at your service' (*tout ce qu'il vous plaira*), I said, 'Mademoiselle, I am something (*quelque chose*) that will please you.' Such blunders make a man very ridiculous.

JAMES BOSWELL, *Boswell in Holland*, 1763–4

*

IN THE pleasant Cemetery at Bologna, I found myself walking next Sunday morning, among the stately marble tombs and colonnades, in company with a crowd of Peasants, and escorted by a little Cicerone of that town, who was excessively anxious for the honour of the place, and most solicitous to divert my attention from the bad monuments: whereas he was never tired of extolling the good ones. Seeing this little man (a good-humoured little man he was, who seemed to have nothing in his face but shining teeth and eyes) looking wistfully at a certain plot of grass, I asked him who was buried there. 'The poor people, Signore,' he said, with a shrug and a smile, and stopping to look back at me – for he always went on a little before, and took off his hat to introduce every new monument. 'Only the poor, Signore! It's very cheerful. It's very lively. How green it is, how cool! It's like a meadow! There are five,' – holding up all the fingers of his right hand to express the number, which an Italian peasant will always do, if it be within the compass of his ten fingers, – 'there are five of my little children buried there, Signore; just there; a little to the right. Well! Thanks to God! It's very cheerful. How green it is, how cool it is! It's quite a meadow!'

He looked me very hard in the face, and seeing I was sorry for him, took a pinch of snuff (every Cicerone takes snuff), and made a little bow; as neat as ever man made. Immediately afterwards, he took his hat off altogether, and begged to introduce me to the next monument; and his eyes and his teeth shone brighter than before.

CHARLES DICKENS, *Pictures From Italy,* 1846

*

A NIGHTCAP is a most excellent invention, for nothing is more wholesome than to have the head well covered from the dampness of the night air, especially when the pores are open and the whole body relaxed by sleep. It is highly necessary in order to preserve the teeth, and the teeth are highly necessary to man. Without those useful members he cannot speak gracefully, for he whistles like an old woman of eighty. And besides (a thing even more to be deplored) he cannot eat meat. Monsieur Castillon, although a very learned man, is a sad example of this. His teeth are so bad that for several years he has eaten nothing but hash. Unknown to him are the joys of greedily devouring a great piece of beef or mutton. Poor man!

JAMES BOSWELL, *Boswell in Holland,* 1763–4

*

I PUT up at the Hotel of the Golden Lion, and was in my own room arranging plans with the brave Courier, when there came a modest little tap at the door, which opened on an outer gallery surrounding a court-yard; and an intensely shabby little man looked in, to inquire if the gentleman would have a Cicerone to show the town. His face was so very wistful and anxious, in the half-opened doorway, and there was so much poverty expressed in his faded suit and little pinched hat, and in the threadbare worsted glove with which he held it– not expressed the less, because these were evidently his genteel clothes, hastily slipped on – that I would as soon have trodden on him as dismissed him. I engaged him on the instant, and he stepped in directly.

While I finished the discussion in which I was engaged, he stood, beaming by himself in a corner, making a feint of brushing my hat with his arm. If his fee had been as many napoleons as it was francs, there could not have shot over the twilight of his shabbiness such a gleam of sun, as lighted up the whole man, now that he was hired.

'Well!' said I, when I was ready, 'shall we go out now?'

'If the gentleman pleases. It is a beautiful day. A little fresh, but charming; altogether charming. The gentleman will allow me to open the door. This is the Inn Yard. The court-yard of the Golden Lion! The gentleman will please to mind his footing on the stairs.'

We were now in the street.

'This is the street of the Golden Lion. This, the outside of the Golden Lion. The interesting window up there, on the first *piano*, where the pane of glass is broken, is the window of the gentleman's chamber!'

Having viewed all these remarkable objects, I inquired if there were much to see in Mantua.

'Well! Truly, no. Not much! So, so,' he said, shrugging his shoulders apologetically.

'Many churches?'

'No. Nearly all suppressed by the French.'

'Monasteries or convents?'

'No. The French again! Nearly all suppressed by Napoleon.'

'Much business?'

'Very little business.'

'Many strangers?'

'Ah Heaven!'

I thought he would have fainted.

'Then, when we have seen the two large churches yonder, what shall we do next?' said I.

He looked up the street, and down the street, and rubbed his chin timidly; and then said, glancing in my face as if a light had broken on his mind, yet with a humble appeal to my forbearance that was perfectly irresistible :

'We can take a little turn about the town, Signore!'

CHARLES DICKENS, *Pictures From Italy,* 1846

*

DON'T FANCY, however, that I am infected by the air of these popish countries; though I have so far wandered from the discipline of the Church of England, to have been last Sunday at the Vienna Opera, which was performed in the garden of the Favorita; and I was so much pleased with it, I have not yet repented my seeing it. Nothing of that kind ever was more magnificent; and I can easily believe what I am told, that the decorations and habits cost the emperor thirty thousand pounds sterling. The stage was built over a very large canal, and, at the beginning of the second act, divided into two parts, discovering the water, on which there immediately came, from different parts, two fleets of little gilded vessels, that gave the representation of a naval fight. It is not easy to imagine the beauty of the scene, which I took particular notice of. But all the rest were perfectly fine in their kind. The story of the opera is the enchantments of Alcina, which gives opportunities for a great variety of machines, and changes of the scene, which are performed with a surprising swiftness. The theatre is so large, that it is hard to carry the eye to the end of it; and the habits in the utmost magnificence, to the number of one hundred and eight. No house could hold such large decorations; but the ladies all sitting in the open air, exposes them to great inconveniences, for there is but one canopy for the imperial family; and the first night it was represented, a shower of rain happening, the opera was broken off, and the company crowded away in such confusion, I was almost squeezed to death.

LADY MARY WORTLEY MONTAGU, *Letter to Pope,*
14 September 1716

*

ON SUNDAY, the Pope assisted in the performance of High Mass at St Peter's. The effect of the Cathedral on my mind, on that second visit, was exactly what it was at first, and what it remains after many visits. It is not religously impressive or affecting. It is an immense edifice, with no one point for the mind to rest upon; and it tires itself with wandering round and round. The very purpose of the place, is not expressed in anything you see there, unless you examine its details – and all examination of details is incompatible with the place itself. It might be a Pantheon, or a Senate House, or a great architectural trophy, having no other object than an architectural triumph. There is a black statue of St Peter, to be sure, under a red canopy; which is larger than life, and which is constantly having its great toe kissed by good Catholics. You cannot help seeing that : it is so very prominent and popular. But it does not heighten the effect of the temple, as a work of art; and it is not expressive – to me at least – of its high purpose.

A large space behind the altar, was fitted up with boxes, shaped like those at the Italian Opera in England, but in their decoration much more gaudy. In the centre of the kind of theatre thus railed off, was a canopied dais with the Pope's chair upon it. The pavement was covered with a carpet of the brightest green; and what with this green, and the intolerable reds and crimsons, and gold borders of the hangings, the whole concern looked like a stupendous Bonbon. On either side of the altar, was a large box for lady strangers. These were filled with ladies in black dresses and black veils. The gentlemen of the Pope's guard, in red coats, leather breeches, and jack-boots, guarded all this reserved space, with drawn swords that were very flashy in every sense; and from the altar all down the nave, a broad lane was kept clear by the Pope's Swiss guard, who wear a quaint striped surcoat, and striped tight legs, and carry halberds like those which are usually shouldered by those theatrical supernumeraries, who never *can* get off the stage fast enough, and who may be generally observed to linger in the enemy's camp after the open country, held by opposite forces, has been split up the middle by a convulsion of Nature.

I got upon the border of the green carpet, in company with a great many other gentlemen, attired in black (no other passport is necessary), and stood there at my ease, during the performance of Mass. The singers were in a crib of wirework (like a large meat-safe or bird-cage) in one corner; and sang most atrociously. All about the green carpet, there was a slowly moving crowd of people: talking to each other: staring at the Pope through eye-glasses; defrauding one another, in moments of partial curiosity, out of precarious seats on the bases of pillars: and grinning hideously at the ladies. Dotted here and there, were little knots of friars (Francescáni, or Cappuccíni, in their coarse brown dresses and peaked hoods) making a strange contrast to the gaudy ecclesiastics of higher degree, and having their humility gratified to the utmost, by being shouldered about, and elbowed right and left, on all sides. Some of these had muddy sandals and umbrellas, and stained garments: having trudged in from the country. The faces of the greater part were as coarse and heavy as their dress; their dogged stupid, monotonous stare at all the glory and splendour, having something in it, half miserable, and half ridiculous.

Upon the green carpet itself, and gathered round the altar, was a perfect army of cardinals and priests, in red, gold, purple, violet, white, and fine linen. Stragglers from these, went to and fro among the crowd, conversing two and two, or giving and receiving introductions, and exchanging salutations; other functionaries in black gowns, and other functionaries in court-dresses, were similarly engaged. In the midst of all these, and stealthy Jesuits creeping in and out, and the extreme restlessness of the Youth of England, who were perpetually wandering about, some few steady persons in black cassocks, who had knelt down with their faces to the wall, and were poring over their missals, became, unintentionally, a sort of humane man-traps, and with their own devout legs, tripped up other people's by the dozen.

There was a great pile of candles lying down on the floor near me, which a very old man in a rusty black gown with an open-work tippet, like a summer ornament for a fireplace in tissue-paper, made himself very busy in dispensing to all the ecclesiastics: one-apiece. They loitered about with these for some time, under their arms like walking-sticks, or in their hands like truncheons. At a certain period of the ceremony, however, each carried his candle up to the Pope, laid it across his two knees to be blessed, took it back again, and filed off. This was done in a very attenuated procession, as you may suppose, and occupied a long time. Not because it takes long to bless a candle through and through, but because there were so many candles to be blessed. At last they were all blessed; and then they were all lighted; and then the Pope was taken up, chair and all, and carried round the church.

I must say, that I never saw anything, out of November, so like the popular English commemoration of the fifth of that month. A bundle of matches and a lantern, would have made it perfect. Nor did the Pope, himself, at all mar the resemblance, though he has a pleasant and venerable face; for, as this part of the ceremony makes him giddy and sick, he shuts his eyes when it is performed : and having his eyes shut and a great mitre on his head, and his head itself wagging to and fro as they shook him in carrying, he looked as if his mask were going to tumble off. The two immense fans which are always borne, one on either side of him, accompanied him, of course, on this occasion. As they carried him along, he blessed the people with the mystic sign; and as he passed them, they kneeled down. When he had made the round of the church, he was brought back again, and if I am not mistaken, this performance was repeated, in the whole, three times. There was, certainly, nothing solemn or effective in it; and certainly very much that was droll and tawdry. But this remark applies to the whole ceremony, except the raising of the Host, when every man in the guard dropped on one knee instantly, and dashed his naked sword on the ground; which had a fine effect.

The next time I saw the cathedral, was some two or three weeks afterwards, when I climbed up into the ball; and then, the hangings being taken down, and the carpet taken up, but all the framework left, the remnants of these decorations looked like an exploded cracker.

CHARLES DICKENS, Pictures From Italy, 1846

*

'HOLLAND CERTAINLY has a very harsh climate, dangerous to strangers who have been brought up in a temperate region. There are terrible fogs and excessive cold, but especially a continuous dampness, except in the summer months.' Thus a discontented man might describe the United Provinces, and, I confess, with considerable justice. But when one has made the experiment of actually living there, one finds that there is no great difference between Holland and other countries; that is to say, if a stranger lives well, eats well, drinks well and dresses well – and also takes a good deal of exercise, which in Holland is absolutely necessary to give a brisk circulation to the blood and consequently an agreeable liveliness of mind. If one lives after that fashion and has a suitable occupation, one can be very well satisfied. I speak positively, for I speak from experience.

Nevertheless, I dare not be so bold as to deny that in Holland it begins to get cold early in the year. I have had experience of that too. If I should deny it, my hands and feet would cry out against their master and give him the lie. The fact is that I had made a resolution not to have a fire in my rooms before the month of November, and for several evenings I have studied three or four hours on end shivering like an Italian greyhound, and sometimes I have sat up to one o'clock in the morning enduring the most disagreeable sensations. But finally I had the honour of dining with the Count of Nassau, the Grand Bailiff of Utrecht, where I found a good fire so comfortable that I began that same evening to indulge myself with the like satisfaction; and tell me if I have not done well!

JAMES BOSWELL, *Boswell in Holland*, 1763–4

*

THE WHOLE party on board were made merry by these unexpected supplies; but none more so than a loquacious little Frenchman, who got drunk in five minutes, and a sturdy Cappuccino Friar, who had taken everybody's fancy mightily, and was one of the best friars in the world, I verily believe.

He had a free, open countenance; and a rich brown, flowing

Papa, greatly daring, bestrode a camel 'like a colossus' as the bard says. William and I preferred to stand. I cannot think but that the creature is extremely uncomfortable.

Note, if you please, the varied vehicles of South Africa, Somaliland, Japan and Iceland. How strange, when you come to consider it, they would all appear in Tufnell Park. But 'other lands, other customs', as they say.

Paris is bedecked and gay for the Exposition, and the hotel attendants are most solicitous. The omnibuses being so crowded they have provided Bath chairs. So amusing!

beard; and was a remarkably handsome man, of about fifty. He had come up to us, early in the morning, and inquired whether we were sure to be at Nice by eleven; saying that he particularly wanted to know, because if we reached it by that time he would have to perform Mass, and must deal with the consecrated wafer, fasting; whereas, if there were no chance of his being in time, he would immediately breakfast. He made this communication, under the idea that the brave Courier was the captain; and indeed he looked much more like it than anybody else on board. Being assured that we should arrive in good time, he fasted, and talked, fasting, to everybody, with the most charming good humour; answering jokes at the expense of friars, with other jokes at the expense of laymen, and saying that, friar as he was, he would engage to take up the two strongest men on board, one after the other, with his teeth, and carry them along the deck. Nobody gave him the opportunity, but I dare say he could have done it; for he was a gallant, noble figure of a man, even in the Cappuccino dress, which is the ugliest and most ungainly that can well be.

All this had given great delight to the loquacious Frenchman, who gradually patronised the Friar very much, and seemed to commiserate him as one who might have been born a Frenchman himself, but for an unfortunate destiny. Although his patronage was such as a mouse might bestow upon a lion, he had a vast opinion of its condescension; and in the warmth of that sentiment, occasionally rose on tiptoe, to slap the Friar on the back.

When the baskets arrived: it being then too late for Mass: the Friar went to work bravely: eating prodigiously of the cold meat and bread, drinking deep draughts of the wine, smoking cigars, taking snuff, sustaining an uninterrupted conversation with all hands, and occasionally running to the boat's side and hailing somebody on shore with the intelligence that we *must* be got out of this quarantine somehow or other, as he had to take part in a great religious procession in the afternoon. After this, he would come back, laughing lustily from pure good humour: while the Frenchman wrinkled his small face into ten thousand creases, and said how droll it was, and what a brave boy was that Friar! At length the heat of the sun without, and the wine within, made the Frenchman sleepy. So, in the noontide of his patronage of his gigantic protégé, he lay down among the wool, and began to snore.

CHARLES DICKENS, *Pictures From Italy,* 1846

4. The Guides

A word that will soothe all spirits throughout France is *rapprochement*. After any altercation or difference of opinion it may be mentioned with the entire object of international amity. But do not make the mistake of referring to anyone's *Yeux rapproches,* which is the equivalent in English of calling someone 'pig-eyes', an appelation no more appreciated there than here; and it may result in *invoquer l'aide de la justice* – a course most earnestly to be eschewed.

> Hugo's *Advice to Those Touring upon the Continent,* 1900

The Germans speak boisterously and with much laughter. Ladies should bow gravely as if in complete comprehension. This would be greatly appreciated, even if the many compound words are difficult.

> Introduction to Hilpert's *English-German Dictionary,* 1884

Ch'ü pa, pu yáo shán-pin-chiu, nà-lai yi p'ing-tzu p'i-chiu. Go away. I do not wish champagne, bring a bottle of beer, it is the English way.

> Professor H. A. Giles, *Chinese without a Teacher,* 1908

The best of them were far more than guides : they were historians,
statisticians, linguists, analysts of character, helpmeets, philosophers
and friends. 'Everyman, I will go with thee and be thy guide;
In thy most need to be by thy side.' So they were. Their stout
volumes, sometimes 'with soft linen covers for convenient packing
in the valise', were stuffed with help for the needy. What is it
but helpful to be told laconically by Richard Ford that in Spain
you should look for your letter in the *poste restante* not only
under the initials of your christian and surnames but also under
E for Esquire, since that nomenclative decoration was unknown
to the Spaniards? One wonders how many travellers were
mystified by the non-arrival of letters that remained for years filed
under E.

Ford was one of many authors commissioned by the publisher
John Murray, who had himself inaugurated, in 1836, with his
Handbook for Holland, Belgium and North Germany, the
series of guide-books bearing his name. Like the *Good Food
Guide* of today it was compiled from information collected by
friends and fellow travellers. It was followed by handbooks
covering the whole of western Europe and Egypt. Baedeker soon
came along with his guide to the Rhine, and in English trans-
literations soon rivalled Murray in popularity. So did Muirhead
with his Blue Guides (a title recently borrowed and tacked on
to a guide through London's porn-belt); and of course Thomas
Cook, whose *Travellers' Handbooks* were an essential part of
the Victorian tourist scene.

As tourists' historians they rarely failed. They assumed in their
flocks a good standard of education, a curiosity about works of
art, and a reverent attitude towards the past. It would be difficult
to find a better short account of the history of Pompeii than that
quoted from Murray, or a more comprehensive description of
St Peter's than comes from the same source. Compare the
subjective comments by Dickens but remember that he
was reporting his own reactions, not guiding; also that as an art
critic his views are worthless, since he had neither the training
nor the sensitivity to make them valuable.

It was the demand created by the proliferating train tourist that resulted in the splendid compendiums of Baedeker *et al.*; but guide books as such had of course existed since time immemorial. Virtually any set of directions as to how to get from one place to another can be considered a guide book. One of the earliest English printed books was *Informacon for pylgrymes unto the holy londe*; and all the great travellers and explorers in and out of Hakluyt's *Voyages* left accounts helpful to those who trailed after them. The fashionable Grand Tour of the eighteenth century gave Mr Thomas Nugent the opportunity to produce the first lavish *vade mecum* in his four famous volumes; and in the same century Joseph Addison, Samuel Sharp and Tobias Smollett recorded much about their travels in France and Italy. Some of the plums from their fruitful trees of knowledge are displayed here and elsewhere in this anthology. But for every plum displayed there were a dozen others of equally luscious bloom.

*

According to an old historical distribution, which, however, is falling more and more into desuetude, Moscow, which has developed in concentric circles round its centre the Kremlin, is divided into five main parts, separated from each other by walls or boulevards. 1. The *Kremlin,* the oldest part of the city. – 2. *Kitái-Gorod* (i.e. 'fortified city', Tartar Kitái), the crowded and irregularly-built centre of business, with the Exchange, the Trading Rows, and so forth. The Kremlin and Kitái-Gorod are now combined to form the *Gorodskáya Tchast* (i.e. the 'City Quarter'). This inner city, generally known simply as *Gorod* ('City'), is surrounded by a whitewashed wall (built in 1534), about $1\frac{1}{2}$ M. in length and relieved by numerous towers (chiefly of a bright green colour), turrets, and decorations. – 3. In a semicircle round the inner city stretches the *Byeli Gorod,* or *'White City'*, the most elegant quarter of Moscow, with wide streets radiating from the Kremlin, numerous palaces and public buildings, and the most attractive shops. The 'White City', now embraces the Tverskáya Tchast and the Myasnitzkaya Tchast and is enclosed by a wide girdle of handsome *Boulevards*, 4½ M. in length. –4. The 'White City' is adjoined by the *Zemlyanói Gorod,* or 'Earth City', so named after the earthen ramparts thrown up by Tzar Mikhail Feódorovitch, the site of which is now occupied by the boulevard-like *Garden Street (Sadóvaya)*, 11 M. long. –5. The outer-most zone is formed by the *Suburbs,* which occupy three-fourths of the total area of Moscow and are surrounded by the Maker-Kollézhski ramparts, erected in 1742 but now fallen to decay. Of the 14 former Zastávas or barriers, the names alone remain. The suburbs contain many manufactories (particularly on the banks of the Yáuza), several barracks, and the railway stations. They are mainly occupied by the poorer classes.

If ever a city expressed the character and peculiarities of its inhabitants, that city is Moscow, the 'heart of Russia', in which the Russian 'wide nature' is abundantly obvious. The characteristic life and tendencies of the people are seen in much greater purity here than in St Petersburg and are much less influenced by W. Europe, though even Moscow is rapidly becoming modernized of late years.

The TRAFFIC in the ill-paved streets is extraordinarily animated. What is here known as the 'German' dress is predominant; but side by side with it we see the bearded muzhik in his bast slippers, patched caftan, and gray armyák or sheepskin; the Russian pope in his long brown robe, with his black hat and long hair and beard; the merchant in his old-Russian fur cap, and his wife adorned with strings of genuine pearls; Circassians, Tartars, and Bokhariots, all in their national dress; Greeks in red fezes; Persians with high conical caps of black sheepskin; and other types too numerous to mention. The various costumes of the lower classes are best seen at the POPULAR FESTIVALS and in the MARKETS. Of the latter the most interesting is the *Okhótni Ryad* ('Hunter's Line'), or market for vegetables, eggs, poultry, and game, held in the square of that name, near the Imperial Theatres. The Sunday market in the Súkharev Square is also notable. The most important market for fruit and flowers is held in the *Bolótnaya Square;* the chief flower-market is held in the *Tzvyetnói*

Boulevard; the horse-market takes place in the *Kónnaya Square* while birds and dogs are bought and sold on Sun. in the Trúbnaya Square.

The Kremlin

In the centre of the city, on a hill rising 130 ft. above the Moskvá and dominating the whole of Moscow, rises the *Kremlin,* in which all the reminiscences of Moscow's past are united. For the Russian the Kremlin is a holy spot. It is in the Kremlin that the power of the Tzars first receives the sanction of the church when the bells of Iván Velíki announce to all Russia that the Tzar has ascended the throne of his ancestors. 'There is nothing above Moscow', says the proverb, 'except the Kremlin, and nothing above the Kremlin except Heaven.'

From the Krásnaya Plóshtchad or Red Square we enter the Kremlin by the Spásskiya Gate or Gate of the Redeemer, a tower-gateway 205 ft. in height, surmounded by the Russian eagle. The lower part of the tower was built by Pietro Antonio of Milan in 1491; the belfry was added by the English architect Galloway in 1626; the present clock dates from 1737. Outside the gate, on the right and left, are two small chapels; above the entrance is the *Picture of the Saviour* placed here by Tzar Alexis Mikháilo-vitch, in 1647, and regarded as the Palladium of the Kremlin. The decree of Alexis that no man should pass through this gateway with his hat on is still strictly enforced. . . .

The View from the top is especially beautiful by evening light. From this point Joseph II. viewed Moscow in 1780, Napoleon and his Marshals in 1812. We not only overlook the whole of the city and its suburbs, but also its environs for a distance of about 20 M., while we see the long windings of the Moskvá, which inter-sects the landscape like a shining, silver ribbon. At our feet lies the Kremlin, surrounded by the wall separating it from the city. Within these walls are the cathedrals, with their gilded domes; to the S.W. are the huge Imperial Palace, the Church of the Redeemer, and (more distant) the Convent of the Maidens and the Sparrow Hills; to the N. are the gleaming white Court of

Justice, the Historical Museum, the Great Theatre, and the Súk-harev Tower; to the E. are the Trading Rows, the Cathedral of St Basil, the Monument of Alexander II., and the Foundling Hospital. On all sides the Kremlin is surrounded by an ocean of houses, with numberless gaily-coloured church-domes, gradually losing themselves in the hilly and wooded environs, until all is merged in the blue horizon.

KARL BAEDEKER, *Russia,* 1914

*

AS REGARDS post-offices and letters, the general correspondence of Spain is tolerably well regulated; a single letter, *una carta sencilla,* must not exceed *six adarmes,* or half an ounce; the charge for postage increases with the weight. The English system has been recently introduced; a uniform charge for postage – by weight – now prevails over Spain, irrespective of distance. The stamps are called *sellos.* English newspapers, when not prohibited, are free to Spain; pamphlets and papers fastened like ours, with an open band or *faja* for directing, are charged at the rate of four reals the pound. As private letters are opened with very little scruple in Spain, correspondents should be cautious, especially on political subjects. Letters *from* England must be prepaid. A traveller may have his addressed to him at the post-office, but it is better to have them directed to some friend or banker, to whom subsequent instructions may be given how and where to forward them. In the large towns the names of all persons for whom any letters may have arrived which are not specially directed to a particular address, are copied and exposed on boards called *las tablas* at the post-offices, in lists arranged alphabetically. The inquirer is thus enabled to see at once if there be any one for him by referring to the list containing the first letter of his name, and then asking for the letter by its number, for one is attached to each according to the order it stands in the list. He should also look back into the old lists, for after a certain time names are taken from the more recent arrivals and placed among those which have remained some weeks on the unclaimed board. He should look over the alphabetical classifications of both his Christian and surname, as ludicrous mistakes occur from the difficulty Spaniards have in reading English handwriting and English names. Their post-masters – no decypherers of hieroglyphics – are sorely perplexed by our truly Britannic terminal title *Esq.*: and many a traveller gets scheduled away under the letter E. Prudent tourists should urge home correspondents, especially their fair ones, to direct simply, and to write the surname in large and legible characters. The best mode, while travelling in Spain, is to beg them to adopt the Spanish form – 'Señor Don Plantagenet Smytheville, Caballero Ingles.' This *'tablas'* system occasions loss of time, temper, and *letters,* for any one may ask for those of any other person and get it, so few precautions are taken. As a rule, Plantagenet Smythe-ville, Esq., should look if there be a letter for him under P. for Plantagenet, and under S. for Smytheville, and under E. for Esquire. It is always best to go to the post-office and make these inquiries in person, and, when applying for letters, to write the name down legibly, and give it to the *empleado,* rather than ask for it *vivâ voce.* The traveller should always put his own letters into the post-office himself, especially those which require prepay-ment, *'que deben franquearse'.* Foreign servants, and still less those hired during a few days' stay in a place, do not always resist the temptation of first destroying letters, and then charging the postage as paid, and pocketing the amount. Travellers, when settled in a town, may, by paying a small fixed sum to the post-office clerks, have a separate division, *'el apartado',* and an earlier delivery of their letters. Letters are generally sent for; if, however, they be specially directed, they are left by a postman, *'el cartero'.*

RICHARD FORD, *Handbook for Travellers in Spain,* 1855

*

FRIBOURG, BERN, SOLEURRE, ZURICH,
ST CAUL, LINDAW, &c.

From *Geneva* I travelled to *Lausanne,* and thence to *Fribourg,* which is but a mean Town for the Capital of so large a Canton: Its Situation is so irregular, that they are forced to climb up to several Parts of it by Stair-Cases of a prodigious Ascent. This Inconvenience however gives them a very great Commodity in case a Fire breaks out in any Part of the Town, for by reason of several Reservoirs on the Tops of these Mountains, by the opening of a Sluce they convey a River into what Part of the Town they please. They have Four Churches, Four Convents of Women, and as many for Men. The little Chappel, called the *Salutation,* is very neat, and built with a pretty Fancy. The College of Jesuits is, they say, the finest in *Switzerland.* There is a great deal of Room in it, and several beautiful Views from the different Parts of it. They have a Collection of Pictures representing most of the Fathers of their Order, who have been Eminent for their Piety or Learning. Among the rest many *English* men whom we name Rebels, and they Martyrs. *Henry Garnet's* inscription says, That when the Hereticks could not prevail with him either by Force or Promises, to change his Religion, they Hanged and Quartered him. At the *Capucins* I saw the Escargatoire, which I took the more notice of because I do not remember to have met with any thing of the same in other Countries. It is a square Place boarded in, and filled with a vast quantity of large Snails, that are esteemed excellent Food when they are well dressed. The Floor is strowed about half a Foot deep with several kinds of Plants, among which the Snails nestle all the Winter Season. When *Lent* arrives they open their Magazines, and take out of them the best meagre Food in the World, for there is no Dish of Fish that they reckon comparable to a Ragoût of Snails.

About Two Leagues from *Fribourg* we went to see a Hermitage, that is reckon'd the greatest Curiosity of these Parts. It lyes in the prettiest Solitude imaginable, among Woods and Rocks, which at first Sight dispose a Man to be serious. There has lived in it a Hermite these Five and Twenty Years, who with his own Hands has worked in the Rock a pretty Chappel, a Sacristie, a Chamber, Kitchin, Cellar, and other Conveniences. His Chimney is carry'd up through the whole Rock, so that you see the Sky through it, notwithstanding the Rooms lye very deep. He has cut the Side of the Rock into a Flat for a Garden, and by laying on it the waste Earth that he has found in several of the neighbouring Parts, has made such a Spot of Ground of it as furnishes out a kind of Luxury for a Hermite. As he saw Drops of Water distilling from several Parts of the Rock, by following the Veins of them, he has made himself Two or Three Fountains in the Bowels of the Mountain, that serve his Table, and water his little Garden.

We had very bad Ways from hence to *Bern,* a great Part of them through Woods of Fir-trees. The great Quantity of Timber they have in this Country makes them mend their High-ways with Wood instead of Stone. I could not but take notice of the Make of several of their Barns I here saw. After having laid a Frame of Wood for the Foundation, they place at the Four Corners of it Four huge blocks, cut in such a Shape as neither Mice nor any other sort of Vermin can creep up the Sides of them, at the same time that they raise the Corn above the Moisture that might come into it from the Ground. The whole weight of the Barn is supported by these Four Blocks.

What pleased me most at *Bern* was their publick Walks by the Great Church. They are raised extremely high, and that their Weight might not break down the Walls and Pilasters which sur-round them, they are built upon Arches and Vaults. Tho' they are, I believe, as high as most Steeples in *England* from the Streets and Gardens that lye at the Foot of them, yet about Forty Years ago a Person in his Drink fell down from the very Top to the Bottom, without doing himself any other Hurt than the Breaking of an Arm. He dy'd about Four Years ago. There is the noblest Summer-Prospect in the World from this Walk, for you have a full View of a huge Range of Mountains that lye in the Country of the *Grisons,* and are bury'd in Snow. They are about Twenty Five Leagues distance from the Town, though by Reason of their Height and their Colour they seem much nearer. The Cathedral Church stands on one side of these Walks, and is perhaps the most Magnificent of any Protestant Church in *Europe* out of *England.* It is a very bold Work, and a Master-piece in *Gothic* Architecture.

I saw the Arsenal of *Bern,* where they say there are Arms for Twenty Thousand Men. There is indeed no great Pleasure in visiting these Magazines of War after one has seen Two or Three of them, yet it is very well worth a Traveller's while to look into all that lye in his Way; for besides the Idea it gives him of the Forces of a State, it serves to fix in his Mind the most considerable Parts of its History. Thus in that of *Geneva* one meets with the Ladders, Petard, and other Utensils which were made use of in their Famous Escalade, besides the Weapons they took of the *Savoyards, Florentines,* and *French* in the several Battels mentioned in their History. In this of *Bern,* you have the Figure and Armour of the Count who founded the Town, of the Famous *Tell,* who is represented as shooting at the Apple on his Son's Head. The Story is too well known to be repeated in this Place. I here likewise saw the Figure and Armour of him that headed the Peasants in the War upon *Bern,* with the several Weapons which were found in the Hands of his Followers. They show too abundance of Arms that they took from the *Burgundians* in the Three great Battels which established them in their Liberty, and destroy'd the Great Duke of *Bergundy* himself, with the bravest of his Subjects. I saw nothing remarkable in the Chambers where the Council meet, nor in the Fortifications of the Town. These last were made on Occasion of the Peasants Insurrection, to defend the Place for the future against the like sudden Assaults.

JOSEPH ADDISON, *Remarks on Italy,* 1718

*

TOMSK IS a government town, standing on the right bank of the Tom at its junction with the river Usháika (56° 29′ N. lat. 54° 37½′ E. long). The locality occupied by the town is formed partly by the low branches of the Kuznétsk Alatáu (343 feet), and partly by lowland lying at the foot of these branches. The river Tom skirts the town, forming an almost regular semicircle from the south-west and western side. The population of the town was given at 52,430 by the census of 1897 (27,140 males, 25,290 females). In this respect Tomsk holds the first place among the towns of Siberia.

The town was founded at the beginning of the XVII century.

By command of the Tsar Boris Godunóv, the Cossack Major Pisarev and the noble's son Tyrkov, established the Tomsk stockaded post, which received its name from the river Tom and stood in a locality resorted to by the wandering Tartar tribe of Yeushtintsy ruled by the Prince Tayán. The entrenched post soon became of great importance for the subjection of the native tribes. In 1629, the Tomsk post was transformed into a town: in 1708, after the organisation of a Siberian government with the chief town of Tobólsk, it ranked as a district town; in 1719, Tomsk was included in the Yeniséisk province, in 1726, in the Tobólsk government; in 1782, after the establishment of the Tobólsk vicegerency, it ranked again as a district town; in 1797, it was transformed into a district town of the Tobólsk government, and in 1804, after the organisation of a special Tomsk government, it became its capital.

The climate of Tomsk is rather severe. The mean annual temperature is 0.7. The ice on the river Tom near the town breaks on the 30 April, and sets again on the 2 November; thus the river remains free of ice of 186 days in the year. Southern winds prevail. At the present date, Tomsk is a well built town containing many fine edifices of stone, fitted with electric light and telephones; some of the streets are paved. The total number of buildings in the town exceeds 13,000, there are over 3,200 estates. Tomsk possesses 2 orthodox monasteries and 23 churches, including 8 parish churches.

Charitable institutions: a charity board, hospital, poorhouse, a lunatic asylum (founded 1805) maintained at the cost of the board and from sums obtained by taxation. The hospital of the board, being situated close to the clinic of the University, serves the same purpose. The Mary children's home under the patronage of the Empress Mary, founded in 1844 at the cost of Commercial Councillor Popóv. This establishment owns a capital of R. 140,000, given by the goldminer Astashóv and Mrs Zybúlsky; the Mary orphanage, founded by the honorary citizen Púshnikov and his wife, in commemoration of the miraculous escape of the Imperial family from the railway accident which happened on the

17 October, 1888. The orphanage is provided with a capital of
R. 60,000; foundlings and orphans are admitted to it. The Vladí-
mir Home, founded in 1869 in commemoration of the Grand
Duke Vladimir Alexándrovich's visit to Tomsk, is under the control
of the Empress Mary Department. The building of the home
was constructed at the cost of the merchants Petróv and Mikháilov.
The institution possesses a capital of R. 80,000. There are further
a poorhouse for the lower class citizens; the Pokróv poorhouse;
the poorhouse of the Jewish Society; a night-shelter near the
landing-place of Cheremoshnikí; a home for emigrants' children,
founded in 1898 on the initiative of Mrs Lomachévsky, wife of
the Tomsk governor, by voluntary donations.

The town of Tomsk presented long ago an important commercial centre of Siberia, on account of its favourable position and as
the eastern terminus of the navigable route of the Ob basin.
Having been avoided by the railway, it was apprehended that the
further progress of the town would be stopped and that it would
become exclusively a centre of administration; these surmises however have proved untrue, and the town continues to grow and
extend its commercial operations. Having lost part of the goods in
transit by the railway, Tomsk in return has widened its local operations, the railway enlarging more and more the local demand.
The navigation commencing at the town of Tomsk receives as well
a further development thanks to the progress of the productive
capacity of the country caused by the railway. The establishment
of an exchange for ascertaining the general commercial conditions
of Siberian trade will greatly influence the growth of the town
and exert its effect upon trade and industry.

Guide to the Great Siberian Railway, 1900

*

THE CHIEF street in Zaragoza is *el Coso;* the houses are still
pitted and riddled with shot-marks, the honourable scars of the
memorable sieges. Here are many good specimens of Zaragozan
architecture: observe No. 168, and *la Casa de los Gigantes.*
Among other houses are *la del Comercio, Calle Santa Maria*

mayor, with fine *azulejos,* ceilings, and spiral pillars, windows, and delicate open work, in the *patio;* also those of *Castel Florit* and the Duque del Hijar, and No. 26, *Calle Zaporta,* with fine mouldings. *The* house, however, which no amateur or architect should fail to visit, is that of the *Infanta,* No. 77, Calle de San Pedro, which was built, in 1550, by the wealthy merchant Gabriel Zaporta, in the richest Arragonese cinque-cento style. Enter the beautifully-decorated *patio,* and observe the fluted pillars and torsos, the projecting medallions with most Italian-like heads. The magnificent staircase has a rich roof with groups of musicians, but all is hastening to decay.

Among the churches, visit *San Pablo,* A.D. 1259, with its brick octangular tower, fine façade, and columns : the high altar, a grand specimen of the plateresque, is the work of the illustrious Damian Forment. In the *Capilla de San Miguel* is the tomb of Diego de Monreal, bishop of Huesca, ob. 1607. The cupola is painted by Geronimo Secano. Inquire for the silver *Gancho.* Visit also the church of *Santiago*; a chapel marks the site where the Apostle lodged when on his tour to Zaragoza. This church glories in the possession of his pilgrim's staff, and also boasts of a *Campana Goda,* or bell, cast by the Goths. The *Musco Nacional,* in the old convent of *Santa Fé,* contains some 300 indifferent pictures.

Visit the *Torre Neuva, plaza San Felipe.* The view from it, especially of different points of the siege, is extensive. This octangular clock-tower for the city, built in 1504, leans some 9 feet out of the perpendicular, like those of Pisa and Bologna, which is unpleasing, as conveying a feeling of insecurity opposed to the essence of architectural principle. It seems to totter to its fall – Ruituraque semper, stat mirum! Here this want of the perpendicular is not the silly triumph of an architect, but has arisen from the sinking of a faulty foundation; and there has been some talk of taking it down; it is richly ornamented with brickwork, which at a distance looks Moorish, but it is much coarser both in design and execution. The noble university, with its precious library, was destroyed by the invaders, but a new one has been partly constructed with a fine quadrangle. The grand Hospital, *el general,* is dedicated to the Virgin, and is one of the largest in Spain. The former one was burnt by the enemy with its patients in it alive. In vain a white flag was hoisted, imploring mercy for the wretched inmates, for that very flag was made the especial mark for their bombs; but the enemy spared nothing, and when the town was entered, the sick, and even lunatics, were massacred in their beds. The *Casa de Misericordia* – there was no mercy then – is a sort of large hospital and poor-house, in which some 600 to 700 young and old are taken in and employed at most trades; the funds, however, are inadequate. Near it is the *Plaza de Toros,* and the grand fights are in honour of the Virgin, when the profits go to aid the hospitals. The N.W. gate, *el Portillo,* is the spot where *Agustina,* the maid of Zaragoza, snatched the match from a dying artilleryman's hand, and fired at the invaders; hence she was called *la Artillera.* This Amazon, although a mere itinerant seller of cool drinks, vied in heroism with the noble Condesa de Burita, who amid the crash of war tended the sick and wounded, resembling in looks and deeds a ministering angel.

Outside the *Portillo* is the *Aljaferia,* the old irregular citadel, built, for the city's *Alcazar,* by the Moor Abu *Giafar* Ahmed, king of Zaragoza, and hence called *Giafariya*; this palatial fortress was assigned to the Inquisition by Ferdinand the Catholic, partly to invest the hated tribunal with the prestige of royalty, and partly as the strong walls offered a security to the judges after the murder of Arbes. Here also Antonio Perez was confined in 1591, and liberated by the populace. Suchet having first damaged the palace with his bombs, used it as a barrack; afterwards it became a military hospital, and was degraded into a prison during the civil wars, hence its present deplorable condition. It is a true type of dilapidated Spain, fallen from its pride of place; some *talk* of restoration has taken place, but *'no funds'* – the old story – has allowed decay to be let alone; nothing has been done, barring some white-washing, and a burial of his baby by a Captain-General. Observe the once splendid staircase, adorned with the badges of Ferdinand and Isabella. One room is called *el Salon de Santa Isabel,* because the sainted queen of Hungary was born in it in 1271 : above hangs, luckily out of reach, and in contrast with present decay, the glorious blue and gold *artesonado* roof with stalactical ornaments; notice an elegant gallery, and a rich cornice with festoons of grape leaves; a Gothic inscription bears the memorable date 1492, which was that of the conquest of Granada, and of the discovery of the new world : and the first gold brought from it was employed by Ferdinand in gilding this ceiling.

The other gates of Zaragoza best worth notice, are that of *Toledo,* used as a prison, as a Newgate, and that of *La Ceneja,* so called from the ashes of martyrs found there in 1492, when it was rebuilt by Ferdinand. The public walks, with long lines of poplars, extend on this side of the city, close under the walls, and up to *La Casablanca,* a house placed on the canal, where there is a decent *Fonda,* much frequented by the Zaragozans, who dance and junket here on the festivals of *San Juan,* June 24, and *San Pedro,* June 29. *El Canal de Aragon* was one of the first to be *begun* in Europe, as it probably will be the last to be finished. This grand conception was projected in 1528 by Charles V., in order to connect the Mediterranean with the Atlantic : vast in promise, slow in execution, and impotent in conclusion, only 8 leagues were cut by 1546; then the affair was dropped and languished until 1770, when one Ramon Pignatelli advanced it a few more leagues. It now connects Zaragoza with Tudela, and a boat plies backwards and forwards with passengers. This canal suggested that of the *Canal du Midi* to, Louis XIV., which was begun in 1681, and finished with Roman magnificence : thus is Spain ever outstript by those to whom she sets an example. A foreign company, they say, is to finish it, and make the Ebro navigable. Veremos.

RICHARD FORD, *Handbook for Travellers in Spain,* 1855

*

POMPEII WAS situated on an elevated ground of trachytic lava, which appears to have formed a peninsula, surrounded on two

sides by the sea, which almost washed the walls of the city on the
W. and S., and bounded on the E., by the Sarno, which was
formerly navigable for a short distance above its mouth. The
position of the city must have given it some importance as a
commercial port, and also as an agreeable watering-place. Although Seneca calls it 'a celebrated city', we know little of its
history. Its origin is generally ascribed to the Oscans. It was
subsequently occupied by the Etruscans and the Samnites. In the
Social War it was besieged by Sylla after he had destroyed Stabiæ,
and was only saved by the diversion made by Gluentius, who
compelled the Roman general to give him battle in the neighbourhood of Nola. After this, the proceedings of Publius Sulpicius,
the tribune, compelled Sylla to return to Rome to quell the sedition
excited by the intrigues of Marius. Pompeii afterwards made
her peace with Rome, was admitted to the rank of a municipium,
and, like Herculaneum, was allowed to retain the privilege of being
governed by her own laws. Sylla, however, appears to have dismantled the fortifications, and to have established a military colony
in the suburbs, to keep the citizens in check, – a proceeding which
gave rise to frequent disturbances, followed by appeals to the
Roman senate, in which Cicero took a conspicuous share. Under
Augustus the city received another colony, consisting chiefly of dis-
banded veterans, who were located with the colony of Sylla in the
suburb outside the walls, which became known as *Augusta Felix*.
Under Nero, A.D. 55, Pompeii became a Roman colony. Long,
however, before this event, it was one of the favourite resorts of the
aristocracy of Rome. Cossinius, the Roman general, made it his
headquarters in the Servile War, and was nearly surprised and
captured by Spartacus while he was bathing on the beach. Cicero
had a villa in the Augustan suburb, in which he composed his
'Offices' and received Augustus, Balbus, Hirtius, and Pansa as his
guests. Claudius took refuge within its walls from the tyranny of
Tiberius, and his son Drusus lost his life here by suffocation from
swallowing a pear. During the same reign Phædrus resided here as
a refugee from the persecutions of Sejanus; and Seneca himself tells
us that all his early youth was passed at Pompeii. Tacitus states

that in A.D. 59 a quarrel, occasioned by some provincial sarcasms, took place in the amphitheatre between the people of Nuceria and those of Pompeii, which ended in a sanguinary fight (*atrox cædes*) in which the former were beaten with great loss. They went to law, and finally appealed to Nero, who gave judgment against the Pompeians. He sentenced Regulus and the other ringleaders to be banished, and ordered all public spectacles and theatrical amusements to be suspended in the city for the space of ten years. There is still extant in the Street of Mercury a rude drawing, a political caricature, commemorating the event, with the inscription, *Campani, victoria una cum Nucerinis periistis.*

Destruction. – While under this interdict, the city was visited by the earthquake of Feb. 5, 63. Tacitus says that it threw down the greater part of the city. Seneca adds that it damaged many places in its neighbourhood, swallowed up 600 sheep, and deprived many people of their reason. So great was the terror which it inspired that the Pompeians abandoned the city for a time. They returned, however, in the course of a few months, and began to repair the damage. Another earthquake in the following year appears to have done still greater mischief, for we find many of the floors out of their level, the columns bear evidence of having been violently dislocated, and the walls of the public buildings still show marks of having been split or overthrown. The citizens were rebuilding the shattered edifices when the eruption of Aug. 24, 79, occurred, the details of which are given in our account of Vesuvius. Pompeii was overwhelmed by showers of red-hot scoriæ, pumice, and ashes, no lava having ever reached it. The roofs of the houses, being mostly of wood, were burnt by the heated matter, or broken down by its weight. The number of skeletons hitherto discovered is extremely small, a fact which proves that the inhabitants succeeded in escaping : and as the lowest strata which now cover the ruins are found to have been disturbed in many places, it is supposed that many of the citizens revisited the site and removed such property as could be easily reached. In some instances the houses have been found disturbed in a much rougher manner than their owners would have been likely to adopt; in one remarkable case, in the house of Castor and Pollux, we shall find that considerable ingenuity was exercised to reach two chests containing money. For these explorations, facilities were afforded by the partial re-occupation of the site, for it appears that many of the lower classes built villages upon the ruins after Vesuvius had relapsed into inactivity, and that these villages were destroyed by the eruption of 472, after which the site was abandoned for ever. Subsequent eruptions deposited successive layers of volcanic matter, and we may now see at least seven distinct strata of scoriæ, tufa, and lapilli, varying in thickness according to the violence of the eruption which produced them, and covered by about 2 ft. of rich vegetable mould. The name, however, appears never to have been lost, for the term *Campus Pompeius* occurs frequently in the chronicles and ecclesiastical documents of the middle ages. With such a record perpetuated in the living language of the country, and with the upper wall of the Great Theatre still visible above the surface (for there is abundant proof that it was never entirely buried), it seems almost incredible that Pompeii should have remained undiscovered and forgotten until the middle of the last century. Still more extraordinary is the fact that the architect Domenico Fontana, when employed by the Count di Sarno in 1592 to form an aqueduct for conveying the water of the Sarno to Torre dell' Annunziata, could have carried his subterranean channel under the city, traversing the Forum and three Temples, and sinking his airshafts over more than a mile of its surface, without having his curiosity excited by the foundations of ancient buildings which must have impeded the progress of his work. Another century elapsed before Macrini, observing numerous traces of houses and walls in the more exposed portions of the surface, conjectured that they might possibly mark the side of the long-lost city of Pompeii.

Murray's Handbook to Southern Italy, 1855

*

SPAIN IS not a land of fleshly comforts, or of social sensual civilization. *Oh! dura tellus Iberiæ!* – God there sends the meat, and the evil one cooks: there are more altars than kitchens – *des milliers de prêtres et pas un cuisinier.*

Life in the country, there, is a Bedouin Oriental existence. The inland unfrequented towns are dull and poverty-stricken. *Bore* is the Genius Loci. Boasted Madrid itself is but a dear, second-rate, inhospitable city; the maritime seaports, as in the East, from being frequented by the foreigner, are more cosmopolitan, more cheerful and amusing. Generally speaking, in Spain, as in the East, public amusements are rare. The calm contemplation of a cigar, Mass and telling of beads, and a *dolce far niente, siestose* indolence, appear to suffice; while to some nations it is a pain to be out of pleasure, to the Spaniard it is a pleasure to be out of painful exertion: leave me, leave me, to repose and tobacco. When however awake, the *Alameda,* or church show, and the bullfight, are the chief relaxations. These will be best enjoyed in the Southern provinces, the land also of the song and dance, of bright suns and eyes, wholesale love making, and of not the largest female feet in the world.

Before pointing out other objects to be observed in Spain, and there only, it may be as well to mention what is *not* to be seen, as there is no worse loss of time than finding this out oneself, after weary chace and wasted hours. Those who expect to find well-garnished arsenals, libraries, restaurants, charitable or literary institutions, canals, railroads, tunnels, suspension-bridges, polytechnic galleries, pale-ale breweries, and similar appliances and appurtenances of a high state of political, social, and commercial civilization, had better stay at home. In Spain there are few turnpike-trust meetings, quarter-sessions, courts of *justice,* according to the real meaning of that word, no tread-mills or boards of guardians, no chairmen, directors, masters-extraordinary of the court of chancery, no assistant poor-law commissioners. There are no anti-tobacco-teetotal-temperance-meetings, no auxiliary missionary propagating societies, no dear drab doves of peace societies, or African slave emancipationists, nothing in the blanket and lying-in asylum line, little, in short, worth a quaker's or a revising barrister of three years' standing's notice. Spain may perhaps interest a political economist, as affording an example of the decline of the wealth of nations, and offering a fine example of errors to be avoided, and a grand field for theories and experimental plans of reform and amelioration. Here is a land where Nature has lavished her prodigality of soil and climate, and which man has for the last four centuries been endeavouring to counteract. *El cielo y suelo es bueno, el entresolo malo.* Here the tenant for life and the occupier of the peninsular *entresol,* abuses with incurious apathy the goods with which the gods have provided him, and 'preserves the country' as a *terra incognita* to naturalists and every branch of ists and ologists. All these interesting branches of inquiry, healthful and agreeable, as being out-of-door pursuits, and bringing the amateur in close contact with nature, offer to embryo authors, who are ambitious to *book something new,* a more worthy subject than the *decies repetita* descriptions of bull-fights and the natural history of mantillas, ollas, and ventas. Those who aspire to the romantic, in short, to any of the sublime and beautiful lines (feelings unknown to the natives, and brought in by foreigners themselves), will find subjects enough in wandering with lead-pencil and note-book through this singular country, which hovers between Europe and Africa, between civilization and barbarism; this land of the green valley and ashy mountain, of the boundless plain and the broken sierra; those Elysian gardens of the vine, the olive, the orange, and the aloe, those trackless, silent, uncultivated wastes, the heritage of the bustard and bittern; – striking indeed and sudden is the change, in flying from the polished monotony of England, to the racy freshness of that still original country where antiquity treads on the heels of to-day, where Paganism disputes the very altar with Christianity, where indulgence and luxury contend with privation and poverty, where a want of much that is generous, honest, or merciful is blended with the most devoted heroic virtues, where the cold-blooded cruelty is linked with the fiery passions of Africa, where ignorance and erudition stand in violent and striking contrast.

RICHARD FORD, *Handbook for Travellers in Spain,* 1855

5. *Criticisms and Complaints*

It is important to remember that in Finland the lavatory for men is called *Miehille,* and for women *Naiselle.* For a gentleman to say *Viekää minut Naiselle* ('Guide me to the women') is to court disaster; and in any case the beds are very lumpy.

Baedeker's *Guide to Russia,* 1914

In Persian the accent generally falls on the ultimate syllable even when the words are compound. The English lady or gentleman is advised to keep to the simplest words, to enunciate clearly, and make a small genuflexion when speaking the word *heft* (the number 7) for this is a word with sacred connotations and much mystery. The genuflexion may be suitably contemptuous and may even be accompanied by a snarl; but it should be made.

Rosen's *Modern Persian Colloquial Grammar,* 1898

The most important word in the Polish language, as in all languages, is *Angelski.* The language surpasses all other Slav tongues in richness, flexibility and conciseness. But *Angelski* (I am English) means everything. If anything else is needed say *Prose zaprowadzic mnie do hotelu.* (Please take me to the hotel). There they will understand.

Baedeker's *Poland,* 1911

There were always those who didn't like it abroad. They probably didn't like it at home either, but damned foreigners were sitting ducks for darts of criticism : they were a different breed – not quite gentlemen, however grand their titles or magnificent their houses. The fifth Earl of Cadogan scooped all criticism of foreign travel into one nutshell : 'Never go abroad. It's a dreadful place.' Noël Coward looked from the other direction : 'There's nothing funnier than an Englishman travelling abroad.' But, such sweeping statements apart, there were many more detailed analyses made by the petulant, the outraged, and those who, like Samuel Sharp, were continually comparing conditions with those in England. I find petulance too shrill a voice for my taste, but examples of the others are here.

Dickens, in two of the most horrifying of his *American Notes,* makes scarcely any direct comment but by straight quotation reveals two facets of the social scene that the interested Englishman could have observed in America in the middle of the nineteenth century. Thomas Cook is outraged for reasons that can draw no more than a smile from today's readers; but it is interesting to compare Dickens's somewhat similar attitude when turning the pages of the *graffiti* albums at Table Rock. The unfortunate businessman-courier John Bowring writes in restrained terms considering the circumstances of his arrest at Calais; and it is gratifying to know that as a result of the publicity afforded by the *Sunday Times*'s scoop in publishing his appeal to the Home Secretary his release was immediate and was accompanied by a sugary letter of apology from Louis XVIII's *éminence grise* Joseph Villèle.

I do not know anything about Archie Grant beyond the fact that his letter (it was sent to a friend called Jim who lived at 146 Church Road, Upper Norwood, S.E. 19) came into my hands in a pile of junk I bought at a jumble sale; but one sees him as a man hell-bent on fleshpots and disappointed of them in a country where they were tucked under the ashes of contrition. I doubt if the same difficulty would be encountered by any tourist nowadays.

I included the complaint of Herr Farina, originator of 4711

Eau de Cologne, because it was addressed specifically to the Englishman abroad, who was his best customer and whom he justifiably didn't want to be misled by imitators who coincidentally bore his un-Germanic name and by no means coincidentally traded on it.

In the travel literature of 1700–1914 there are many critical comments about food. The Englishman was obsessional about it. Offered *Matjes Herring Hausfrauen art* he'd scream blue murder about 'foreign muck'; the sight of a finger bowl sent him with curling lip into transports of contempt; fried mushrooms referred to as *champignons frites* were to him as falsely described as a spade masquerading under the name of a bloody shovel. Much of this criticism was caused by his scorn for languages other than his own – which, he conveniently forgot, had been built up from half the tongues of other nations. His blinkered vision failed to see why *thé* should be decorated with an accent or simple roast beef turned into *boeuf de roti*. But in any case the culinary art was not, as today's idiom has it, his scene. Hence his endless boring comments on the food served up to him abroad – which, except they have the strength of their own indignation, like Sharp's, I have deliberately omitted. I found too many moans and niggles about food too indigestible. Better, I think, to have chosen more trenchant stuff. Which I hope I have.

* * *

ROME, *Oct.* 1765.

SIR,

We arrived at this place, after a journey of seven days, with accommodations uncomfortable enough. Give what scope you please to your fancy, you will never imagine half the disagreeableness that *Italian* beds, *Italian* cooks, *Italian* post-horses, *Italian* postilions, and *Italian* nastiness, offer to an *Englishman*, in an autumnal journey; much more to an *English* woman.

At *Turin, Milan, Venice, Rome*, and, perhaps, two or three other towns, you meet with good accommodation; but no words can express the wretchedness of the other inns. No other bed than one of straw, with a matrass of straw, and next to that a dirty sheet, sprinkled with water, and, consequently, damp; for a covering you have another sheet, as coarse as the first, and as coarse as one of our kitchen jack-towels, with a dirty coverlet. The bedsted consists of four wooden forms, or benches : an *English* Peer and Peeress must lye in this manner, unless they carry an upholsterer's shop with them, which is very troublesome. There are, by the bye, no such things as curtains, and hardly, from *Venice* to *Rome,* that cleanly and most useful invention, a privy; so that what should be collected and buried in oblivion, is for ever under your nose and eyes. Take along with you, that in all these inns the walls are bare, and the floor has never once been washed since it was first laid. One of the most indelicate customs here, is, that men, and not women, make the ladies beds, and would do every office of a maid servant, if suffered. To sum up, in a word, the total of *Italian* nastiness, your chamber, which you would wish to be the sweetest, is by far the most offensive room in the house, for reasons I shall not explain. I must tell you, that they never scour their pewter, and unless you were to see it, you will not conceive how dirty and nauseous it grows in thirty or forty years. Their knives are of the same colour as their pewter, and their table-cloths and napkins such as you see on joint-stools in *Bartholomew-Fair,* where the mob eat their sausages. In these inns they make you pay largely, so much a head, and send up ten times as much as you can eat. For example, this is almost constantly the fare. – A soop like wash, with pieces of liver swimming in it; a plate full of brains, fried in the shape of fritters; a dish of livers and gizzards; a couple of fowls (always killed after your arrival) boiled to rags, without any the least kind of sauce, or herbage; another fowl, just killed, stewed as they call it; then two more fowls, or a turkey roasted to rags. I must not omit to mention, that all over *Italy,* I mean on their roads, the chickens and fowls are so stringy, you may divide the breast into as many filaments as you can a halfpennyworth of thread. Now and then we get a little piece of mutton, or veal, and generally speaking, it is the most eatable morsel that falls in our way. I should mention, that pigeons boiled and roasted, often supply the place of some of the above-mentioned dishes. The bread all the way is exceedingly bad, and the butter so rancid, it cannot be touch'd, or even borne within the reach of our smell. We procured the other day, a pint of cream, and made a little extempore butter, which proved almost as good as any we eat in *England,* so that the fault seems to lye in the manufacture, and not in the milk; yet such is the force of education and custom that the people here do not wish to have it better than it is. In *Savoy,* amongst the *Alps,* we were often astonished at the excellence of their diet; so great is the disparity betwixt *French* and *Italian* cooks, on the *Savoy* and the *Loretto* roads.

But what is a greater evil to travellers than any of the above recited, though not peculiar to the *Loretto* road, is the infinite number of gnats, bugs, fleas, and lice, which infest us by night and by day.

You will grant, after this description of the horrors of an *Italian* journey, that one ought to take no small pleasure in treading on classic ground; yet, believe me, I have not caricatured; every article of it is literally true. If the subject of this Letter be disgustful, comfort yourself, that I shall seldom or never touch upon it more, during my absence.

> *I am, Sir, &c.*
> Samuel Sharp, *Letters from Italy,* 1767

*

We start at eight o'clock in the morning, in a great mail-coach, whose huge cheeks are so very ruddy and plethoric, that it appears to be troubled with a tendency of blood to the head. Dropsical it certainly is, for it will hold a dozen passengers inside. But, wonderful to add, it is very clean and bright, being nearly new; and rattles through the streets of Cincinnati gaily.

Our way lies through a beautiful country, richly cultivated, and luxuriant in its promise of an abundant harvest. Sometimes we pass a field where the strong bristling stalks of Indian corn look like a crop of walking-sticks, and sometimes an enclosure where the green wheat is springing up among a labyrinth of stumps; the primitive worm-fence is universal, and an ugly thing it is; but the farms are neatly kept, and, save for these differences, one might be travelling just now in Kent.

We often stop to water at a roadside inn, which is always dull and silent. The coachman dismounts and fills his bucket, and holds it to the horses' heads. There is scarcely ever any one to help him; there are seldom any loungers standing round; and never any stable-company with jokes to crack. Sometimes, when we have changed our team, there is a difficulty in starting again, arising out of the prevalent mode of breaking a young horse : which is to catch him, harness him against his will, and put him in a stage-coach without further notice : but we get on somehow or other, after a great many kicks and a violent struggle; and jog on as before again.

Charles Dickens, American Notes, 1842

*

It would be impossible for me to decide which was the worst operatic show I ever saw – the choice would be too embarrassing. But it occurred certainly either in Paris or Milan. I know that after a performance of *Siegfried* at the Paris Opera House I took an oath never again to enter the Paris Opera House. It was all bad, but especially the scenery and the 'production' were horrible. . . . The performance must count amongst the foulest and most ghastly artistic outrages in the history of music. . . . The truth is, that foreign operatic mismanagers are obsessed by the music, and they leave everything else to people who are either dead and have forgotten to get themselves buried, or who don't know the elements of their job.

Arnold Bennett, Things That Have Interested Me, 1911

*

IN THE former [Venice] I lost my handkerchief and in the latter [Pisa] my patience. I suffered too much to be easily pleased, and the music seemed more common than that I had before heard of this author. One of my gondolieri, upon my telling him I had had my pocket picked – said this was a fair for thieves and told me a great many stories concerning their dexterity upon such occasions. The weather grows hotter and hotter. However, if it was not for the bugs, mosquitoes, gnats and fleas I could bear it well enough, but I am devoured. The canals are crowded with *musical* people at night – banks of music – French horns – duet singers in every gondola.

CHARLES BURNEY, *Men, Music and Manners*, 1773

*

NAPLES, *Dec.* 1765

SIR,

It is the custom in Italy to light the stage only, which renders their spectacles frightfully dark and melancholy. They pretend it is an advantage to the performers and the stage; and so far it is true, that if there must be only such a small quantity of light in the house, it is much better to place it on the stage, than on any other part; but on *gala* nights, when it is illuminated in every part, the *Italians* seem as much pleased with it as a stranger, so that I imagine it is to save the expence of so many wax tapers, that the custom is continued. These tapers are almost as big as small torches, and are disposed very unartfully against the sides of the boxes, as high as the fourth range; so that the glare, the heat, and the smell of them, are very offensive to those who sit in the boxes, on which account, it is not unusual, on the *gala* nights, when the King is not there, to see the people in the boxes extinguish several of them. When his Majesty is present, they do not take that liberty; but if, instead of these tapers, there were a sufficiency of lustres hanging over the pit, the purpose would be answered without the least annoyance.

Dark as the boxes are, they would be still darker, if those who sit in them did not, at their own expence, put up a couple of candles, without which it would be impossible to read the opera; yet there are some so frugal, as not to light up their box, though the instances are rare. It is not the fashion here, nor to the best of my remembrance, in any part of *Italy,* to take a small wax light to the house, and, therefore, hardly any man has eyes good enough to make use of a book in the pit.

The Ladies in the boxes and pit of the Opera House in *London,* make a much more brilliant appearance than they would in the dark boxes at *Naples,* where, on common nights, it is not possible to distinguish a feature in the opposite boxes: Indeed the *London* theatres are much better contrived to render the spectators an ornament to the house; for even the galleries in my opinion, exhibit a prospect which enlivens, if it do not beautify, the scene; but were they ever so awkward, they are necessary in *England,* where so many hundreds of the middle rank of people, resort every evening to the Play-house. The theatres at *Paris,* from their enormous length, are rather worse shapen than those of *Italy*; but their amphitheatre behind the pit, somewhat resembling our front boxes, is a great relief to them, otherwise, being so narrow, they would appear extremly melancholy. It is wonderful, that so gay, so elegant a nation should be satisfied such a length of time with two Tennis-courts converted into Play-houses; but I am apt to suspect from some conversations I have had with *Frenchmen* on this subject that the force of a long habit, has led them into an opinion, that theatres should be constructed in that form, and possibly were they to build two theatres for their *French* and *Italian* plays, they would adopt the same plan. Were an audience to consist of the fine people only, *Palladio's* theatre at *Vicenza* would unquestionably be the proper model, where the plan is half an oval cut length ways, surrounded with boxes ranged in a colonade, and where all the seats rise above one another so artfully; as to make the spectators themselves a most pleasing part of the spectacle.

The men in the pit do not, upon the whole, make a good figure; for though there are many officers, who are well drest, yet they and the Gentlemen are much the smaller portion of the company there. There is a vulgar set of men who frequent the pit, and another set still more vulgar, who pay nothing for their entrance, such as the upper servants of the Ladies who have boxes, the upper servants of ambassadors, and sometimes, for a small fee to the door-keepers, those servants introduce their friends. It is not to be omitted, amongst the objections to the immense largeness of the house and stage, that, in windy weather, you would imagine yourself in the streets, the wind blows so hard both in the pit and boxes; and this seldom happens without causing colds and fevers.

The performers are not paid so liberally at *Naples* as at *London,* but considering the different expence of living in the two places, the proportion is not very short amongst the capital singers, as may be gathered from the salary of *La Gabrieli,* who received for sing-ing the last year, eighteen hundred sequins, (nine hundred pounds sterling) and has contracted for the same sum, the ensuing year. *Aprile,* the first man, has three thousand five hundred ducats. *Genaro,* the first dancer amongst the men, has two thousand ducats, and *La Morelli,* the first woman dancer, one thousand five hundred ducats. A ducat is worth about three shillings and ten pence.

The impressario, or manager, is bound to very bad terms, so that his profits are inconsiderable, and sometimes he is a loser. The theatre being a part of the palace, the King reserves for him-self, his Officers of State, and Train, fifteen boxes; nor does the King (or rather the Regency) pay the manager one farthing, whereas the late King used to present him annually four thousand ducats. The junto deputed by his Majesty to supervise the Opera, reserve to themselves the right of nominating singers and dancers, which obliges the manager sometimes to pay them an exorbitant price. Another disadvantage he lies under, is, the frequent delay of payment for the boxes, and a manager must not take the liberty to compel persons of quality to pay their just debts.

You will wonder how I became possessed of these particu-lars; accident threw them in my way, and you may depend on their authenticity.

The two burletta Opera Houses are not in much request, except when they happen to procure some favourite composition, the grand Opera being the only object of the *Neapolitans,* which, indeed, has such pre-eminent encouragement, that the others are forbidden, by authority, to bring any dancers on their stage, without a special licence, lest they should divert the attention of the public from the King's Theatre. I must not omit a foolish singularity, in relation to the women dancers at *Naples,* that, in consequence of an order from court, in the late King's time, they all wear black drawers. I presume it was from some conceit on the subject of modesty, but it appears very odd and ridiculous. I shall not enter into any detail of the two houses; but their dresses, their scenery, and their actors, are much more despicable than one could possibly imagine.

I am, Sir, &c.

SAMUEL SHARP, *Letters from Italy,* 1767

*

ONE NIGHT I went to the opera at Genoa, which was indifferent enough, but I understand it is a good deal better sometimes. The favourite composer here, and all over Italy, is Rossini, a truly national genius, full of the finest national spirits, yet capable of the noblest gravity. My northern faculties were scandalized at seeing men in the pit with *fans*! Effeminacy is not always incompatible with courage, but it is a very dangerous help toward it; and I wondered what Doria would have said, had he seen a captain of one of his galleys indulging his cheeks in this manner. Yet perhaps they did so in his own times. What would be effeminate in a man in the north, unaccustomed to it, may be a harmless trifle to a man in the south.

LEIGH HUNT, *Autobiography,* 1850

*

ON TABLE ROCK, there is a cottage belonging to a Guide, where little relics of the place are sold, and where visitors register their names in a book kept for the purpose. On the wall of the room in which a great many of these columes are preserved, the follow-

At Colombo we had the honour of being shown the actual carriage in which the Prince of Wales travelled.

The Darjeeling railway solves the problem of ascent up an incline very ingeniously. But of course the engineers were British.

How crowded are the trains in Canada! How smokey the compartments! And how indelicate the habits of nursing mothers!

On the Orient Express I encountered a gentleman who said he lived in Baker Street. His conversation was as strong as his tobacco.

The Russians are of a very religious turn. The church carriage on the Great Siberian Railway is of an elaborate nature and I am inclined to think our Pastor would disapprove; certainly of the elaboration if not of the principle.

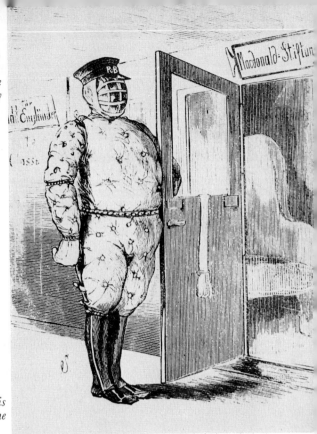

Against the blows of the englische Touristen our persons of the railway must protected be.

The englische Touristen is with his dog most alarming. It is alone that he wishes most assuredly to be.

ing request is posted : 'Visitors will please not copy nor extract the remarks and poetical effusions from the registers and albums kept here.'

But for this intimation, I should have let them lie upon the tables on which they were strewn with careful negligence, like books in a drawing-room : being quite satisfied with the stupendous silliness of certain stanzas with an anti-climax at the end of each, which were framed and hung up on the wall. Curious, however, after reading this announcement, to see what kind of morsels were so carefully preserved, I turned a few leaves, and found them scrawled all over with the vilest and the filthiest ribaldry that ever human hogs delighted in.

It is humiliating enough to know that there are among men, brutes so obscene and worthless, that they can delight in laying their miserable profanations upon the very steps of Nature's greatest altar. But that these should be hoarded up for the delight of their fellow-swine, and kept in a public place where any eyes may see them, is a disgrace to the English language in which they are written (though I hope few of these entries have been made by Englishmen), and a reproach to the English side, on which they are preserved.

CHARLES DICKENS, *American Notes*, 1842

*

Sir : – Although my French is still far from good, I cannot refrain from expressing the infinite gratitude I owe his Highness the Elector Palatine for the courtesies with which I have been honoured at his court.

I hope, Sir, that you will have the goodness to excuse my French. My expression will perhaps be very imperfect. But my feelings are very clear. Be assured, Sir, that they come from the heart.

It is a standing jest against the English that they are somewhat uncivilized because strangers who come among them do not find the most agreeable of receptions. I fear that this jest is only too true, but I like to think that with time our rude islanders will become more civilized. Let them come to Mannheim. Let them be presented to the Court there. They will see there perfect politeness of manners; they will experience the charm of that politeness, and when they return home, they will try to imitate so fine an example. It is at Mannheim that one sees a gracious prince. It is there that one is convinced that a great prince, by being affable, loses no portion of the respect due to him. It is true that at Brunswick his Grace the Duke speaks to strangers, and that he has an absurd idea that when a man keeps his mouth shut, strangers may suspect that it is more prudent for him to do so than to open it – and perhaps also his Highness thinks he does well to show a little good sense and wit, as if those qualities were not entirely useless in a prince. Besides, the family of Brunswick is only a minor family, almost unknown in Europe. It is true that it has produced heroes of the greatest distinction and that it has made the most illustrious of alliances. But that is nothing to the Elector Palatine. Show me another prince in Europe who has a face as black as his. No, Sir, you will not find one. It is that that constitutes his Highness's unique glory; and a stranger is sufficiently rewarded in coming to Mannheim if he obtains permission to look half an hour a day at the celebrated black face of the Elector Palatine. I shall never forgive a remark of one of my countrymen, a man who had been at other courts and imagined that he would find similar manners at the great Court of Mannheim. When some one asked him, 'Are you not satisfied? Did you not see his Highness's black face?' he replied brusquely, 'Black face? Black face? The devil take it! Can't I buy a negro who has a face two degrees darker than his?'

It is also true that at Brunswick strangers eat at the Duke's table. His Highness does not think that strangers come there to be fed, for if a man were looking for way to save money, he would hardly think of spending twenty louis on the road so as to be able to save five at Brunswick; but his Highness thinks that young noblemen on their travels would rather acquire polish in high company than pass their time at an inn. His Highness takes pleasure in helping young noblemen from abroad, and he finds that he has not diminished his grandeur in the least by having at his table people of good family who will everywhere express their delight at his goodness. But, as I have already had the honour to tell you, Brunswick is only a very, very small court. I hold in sovereign contempt the high officials, the ladies-in-waiting, and the gentlemen of the court who make it their business to speak immediately to strangers and to make their stay agreeable. But I admire the style of your antechamber, which resembles a café – I should say a very grand café. That's where one sees worthy people. You do not utter a word to a stranger, and no doubt he thinks you all oracles.

I commission you, Sir, to throw your self at the feet of the Elector Palatine and assure him of my gratitude in the terms which I have just stated to you. Do so, Sir, and you will infinitely oblige your most humble servant, J. Boswell.

> JAMES BOSWELL, *Letter to Baron von Wachtendonck,*
> *Grand Chambellan of the Court of Mannheim,*
> 8 November, 1764

*

Calais, Oct. 8, 1822
His Excellency Sir Charles Stuart, Bart.
Sir, – I have to entreat your Excellency's immediate interference on my behalf, in a case in which the rights of hospitality, and the protection of my passport endorsed by you, have been grossly and illegally violated.

I visited Paris for my commercial concerns, and left it by the diligence on Thursday last. On my arrival here, I obtained the endorsement of my passport and license for embarkation. When I reached the pier, I was arrested by agents of police, and conducted with my baggage to the Mairie, where I was told that an order from my government had arrived for the examination of all my papers. I requested the attendance of the British Consul, which was granted; my trunk was opened, my papers were all read and examined, and 15 sealed letters, with two sealed packets, one of them from the Portuguese Ambassador at Paris, to the Portuguese Minister at London, bearing the arms of Portugal, and delivered into my own hands by M. d'Oliveria himself, were forcibly taken from me.

I beg leave to premise that, of the contents of all or any of these letters or packets, I am wholly ignorant – a fact which I offered to depose upon oath. Notwithstanding this, my passport was taken from me, and after a detention of two days, I have been delivered over to the gendarmerie, to be conducted to Boulogne, and delivered up to the Procureur du Roi, without any legal proceeding against me, without the knowledge of any one circumstance to justify an act so arbitrary and so atrocious.

I have now to put myself under your powerful protection, and to solicit your instant interference to rescue my person from imprisonment, and to uphold the important character of that nation you represent, whose citizens no longer have any protection from the laws. I have also to entreat that you will consult with the Minister of his Faithful Majesty, as the means of vindicating those diplomatic privileges which have been so wantonly violated in his person, by seizing his official correspondence.

I have protested against acts which make your signature of no avail for the protection of British subjects; and though I know of no ground for apprehension that any part of the correspondence which was entrusted to me bears a political character, I have protested against the horrible principle, that the bearer of a sealed letter, whose contents are unknown to him, can be made responsible for those contents. I submit all this to your Excellency's consideration. My commercial affairs are dreadfully suffering from this violent detention : it is impossible to calculate the consequences. I venture, therefore, to hope, that your Excellency will take instant and effective measures for my release; and, referring to the report of the British Consul, I have the honour to be, your Excellency's

Most humble and obedient servant,

JOHN BOWRING

Letter to the Home Secretary, published in the *Sunday Times*, 20 October 1822

*

I WOULD not enter Norway again for all the firs in Scandinavia. The blight of Temperance has settled on the place. Half the towns have prohibition laws. The only art work of any consequence is Rodin's 'Man with the Key' and if there's anything but insipidity in any of the national music I have yet to detect it. Cold, clean living and scenery have killed the place – if it ever lived. Like Switzerland it is ruined by tidiness and order. Give me the flies and sweatiness of a Moroccan market rather than this land where the sun shines unnaturally at midnight and not even the pleasures of corruption enliven the morality of the people. The fault all stems from one of their damned kings, Olav the Holy, who was killed in battle about a thousand years ago and whose body refused to mortify after he was buried. They took this as a reproach for their wickedness and have been conscience-stricken ever since. Spare me from holiness when I travel abroad. Lust, drink and corruption are so much more interesting! But no one would want to lust with these Puritan dummies whose only word is a scream when you get a hand as far as the tapes of their drawers. I'd a sight rather have Wednesday afternoon in pouring rain in Macclesfield. At least you could have a quick success in the lobby of the Mechanics' Institute.

ARCHIE GRANT of Stroud, Gloucestershire, in a letter
to a friend, 1912

*

ONE CIRCUMSTANCE I must remark on .. is the taciturnity of the French. I came to the kingdom expecting to have my ears constantly fatigued with the infinite volubility and spirits of the people, of which so many persons have written, sitting, I suppose, by their English firesides. At Montpellier, though fifteen persons and some of them ladies were present, I found it impossible to make them break their inflexible silence with more than a monosyllable, and the whole company sat more like an assembly of tongue-tied Quakers, than the mixed company of a people famous for loquacity. Here also, at Nîmes, with a different party at every meal it is the same; not a Frenchman will open his lips. Today at dinner, hopeless of that nation, and fearing to lose the use of an organ they had so little inclination to employ, I fixed myself by a Spaniard, and having been so lately in his country, I found him ready to converse, and tolerably communicative; but we had more conversation than thirty other persons maintained among themselves.

ARTHUR YOUNG, Travels in France, 1792

*

NEXT TIME I submit (having the power to avoid it) to be crammed into a carriage, and carried from place to place, whether I would or not, and be set down at the stated *points de vue,* while a detestable laquais points out what I am to admire, I shall deserve to endure again what I endured today. As there was no possibility of relief I resigned myself to my fate, and was even amused by the absurdity of my own situation. We went to see the junction of the Arve and the Rhone: or rather to see the Arve pollute the rich, blue, transparent Rhone, with its turbid waters. The day was heavy, and the clouds rolled in prodigious masses along the dark sides of the mountains, frequently hiding them from our view, and substituting for their graceful outlines and ever-varying contrast of tint and shade, an impenetrable veil of dark grey vapour.

ANNA JAMESON, Diary of an Ennuyée, 1826

*

WHY ANYONE should desire to visit either Luc or Cheylard is more than my much-inventing spirit can suppose. For my part, I travel not to go anywhere, but to go. I travel for travel's sake. The great affair is to move; to feel the needs and hitches of our life more nearly; to come down off this feather-bed of civilization, and find the globe granite underfoot and strewn with cutting flints. Alas, as we get up in life, and are more preoccupied with our affairs, even a holiday is a thing that must be worked for. To hold a pack upon a pack-saddle against a gale out of the frozen north is no high industry, but it is one that serves to occupy and compose the mind. And when the present is so exacting, who can annoy himself about the future?

I came out at length above the Allier. A more unsightly prospect at this season of the year it would be hard to fancy. Shelving hills rose round it on all sides, here dabbled with wood and fields, there rising to peaks alternately naked and hairy with pines. The colour throughout was black or ashen, and came to a point in the ruins of the castle of Luc, which pricked up impudently from below my feet, carrying on a pinnacle a tall white statue of Our Lady, which, I heard with interest, weighed fifty quintals, and was to be dedicated on the 6th October. Through this sorry landscape trickled the Allier and a tributary of nearly equal size, which came down to join it through a broad nude valley in Vivarais. The weather had somewhat lightened, and the clouds massed in squadron; but the fierce wind still hunted them through heaven, and cast great ungainly splashes of shadow and sunlight over the scene.

Luc itself was a straggling double file of houses wedged between hill and river. It had no beauty, nor was there any notable feature, save the old castle overhead with its fifty quintals of brand-new Madonna. But the inn was clean and large. The kitchen, with its two box-beds hung with clean check curtains, with its wide stone chimney, its chimney-shelf four yards long and garnished with lanterns and religious statuettes, its array of chests and pair of ticking clocks, was the very model of what a kitchen ought to be; a melodrama kitchen, suitable for bandits and noblemen in disguise. Nor was the scene disgraced by the landlady, a handsome, silent, dark old woman, clothed and hooded in black like a nun. Even the public bedroom had a character of its own, with the long deal tables and benches, where fifty might have dined, set out as for a harvest-home, and the three box-beds against the wall. In one of these, lying on straw and covered with a pair of table-napkins, did I do penance all night long in goose-flesh, and sigh, from time to time as I awakened, for my sheepskin sack and the lee of some great wood.

R. L. STEVENSON, *Travels with a Donkey*, 1912

*

WHAT IS this dismal-fronted pile of bastard Egyptian, like an enchanter's palace in a melodrama! – a famous prison, called The Tombs. Shall we go in?

So. A long narrow lofty building, stove-heated as usual, with four galleries, one above the other, going round it, and communicating by stairs. Between the two sides of each gallery, and in its centre, a bridge, for the greater convenience of crossing. On each of these bridges sits a man: dozing or reading, or talking to an idle companion. On each tier, are two opposite rows of small iron doors. They look like furnace-doors, but are cold and black, as though the fires within had all gone out. Some two or three are open, and women, with drooping heads bent down, are talking to the inmates. The whole is lighted by a skylight, but it is fast closed; and from the roof there dangle, limp and drooping, two useless windsails.

A man with keys appears, to show us round. A good-looking fellow, and, in his way, civil and obliging.

'Are those black doors the cells?'

'Yes.'

'Are they all full?'

'Well, they're pretty nigh full, and that's a fact, and no two ways about it.'

'Those at the bottom are unwholesome, surely?'

'Why, we *do* only put coloured people in 'em. That's the truth.'

When do the prisoners take exercise?'

'Well, they do without it pretty much.'

'Do they never walk in the yard?'

'Considerable seldom.'

'Sometimes, I suppose?'

'Well, it's rare they do. They keep pretty bright without it.'

'But suppose a man were here for a twelvemonth. I know this is only a prison for criminals who are charged with grave offences, while they are awaiting their trial, or under remand, but the law here, affords criminals many means of delay. What with motions for new trials, and in arrest of judgment, and what not, a prisoner might be here for twelve months, I take it, might he not?'

'Well, I guess he might.'

'Do you mean to say that in all that time he would never come out at that little iron door, for exercise?'

'He might walk some, perhaps – not much.'

'Will you open one of the doors?'

'All, if you like.'

The fastenings jar and rattle, and one of the doors turns slowly on its hinges. Let us look in. A small bare cell, into which the light enters through a high chink in the wall. There is a rude means of washing, a table, and a bedstead. Upon the latter, sits a man of sixty; reading. He looks up for a moment; gives an impatient dogged shake; and fixes his eyes upon his book again. As we withdraw our heads, the door closes on him, and is fastened as before. This man has murdered his wife, and will probably be hanged.

'How long has he been here?'

'A month.'

'When will he be tried?'

'Next term.'

'When is that?'

'Next month.'

'In England, if a man be under sentence of death, even he has air and exercise at certain periods of the day.'

'Possible?'

With what stupendous and untranslatable coolness he says this, and how loungingly he leads on to the women's side: making, as he goes, a kind of iron castanet of the key and the stair-rail!

Each cell door on this side has a square aperture in it. Some of the women peep anxiously through it at the sound of footsteps; others shrink away in shame. – For what offence can that lonely child, of ten or twelve years old, be shut up here? Oh! that boy? He is the son of the prisoner we saw just now; is a witness against his father; and is detained here for safe keeping, until the trial; that's all.

But it is a dreadful place for a child to pass the long days and nights in. This is rather hard treatment for a young witness, is it not? – What says our conductor?

'Well, it an't a very rowdy life, and *that's* a fact!'

Again he clinks his metal castanet, and leads us leisurely away. I have a question to ask him as we go.

'Pray, why do they call this place The Tombs?'

'Well, it's the cant name.'

'I know it is. Why?'

'Some suicides happened here, when it was first built. I expect it come about from that.'

'I saw just now, that that man's clothes were scattered about the floor of his cell. Don't you oblige the prisoners to be orderly, and put such things away?'

'Where should they put 'em?'

'Not on the ground surely. What do you say to hanging them up?'

He stops and looks round to emphasise his answer:

'Why, I say that's just it. When they had hooks they *would* hang themselves, so they're taken out of every cell, and there's only the marks left where they used to be!'

The prison-yard in which he pauses now, has been the scene of terrible performances. Into this narrow, grave-like place, men are brought out to die. The wretched creature stands beneath the gibbet on the ground; the rope about his neck; and when the sign is given, a weight at its other end comes running down, and swings him up into the air – a corpse.

The law requires that there be present at this dismal spectacle, the judge, the jury, and citizens to the amount of twenty-five. From the community it is hidden. To the dissolute and bad, the thing remains a frightful mystery. Between the criminal and them, the prison-wall is interposed as a thick gloomy veil. It is the curtain to his bed of death, his winding-sheet, and grave. From him it shuts out life, and all the motives to unrepenting hardihood in that last hour, which its mere sight and presence is often all-sufficient to sustain. There are no bold eyes to make him bold;

no ruffians to uphold a ruffian's name before. All beyond the pitiless stone wall, is unknown space.

CHARLES DICKENS, *American Notes,* 1842

*

THE FOLLOWING are a few specimens of the advertisements in
the public papers. It is only four years since the oldest among them
appeared; and others of the same nature continue to be published
every day, in shoals.

'Ran way, Negress Caroline. Had on a collar with one prong
turned down.'

'Ran away, a black woman, Betsy. Had an iron bar on her
right leg.'

'Ran away, the negro Manuel. Much marked with irons.'

'Ran away, the negress Fanny. Had on an iron band about her
neck.' 'Ran away, a negro boy about twelve years old. Had round
his neck a chain dog-collar with 'De Lampert' engraved on it.'

'Ran away, the negro Hown. Has a ring of iron on his left foot.
Also, Grise, *his wife,* having a ring and chain on the left leg.'

'Ran away, a negro boy named James. Said boy was ironed
when he left me.'

'Committed to jail, a man who calls his name John. He has a
clog of iron on his right foot which will weigh four or five pounds.'

'Detained at the police jail, the negro wench, Myra. Has
several marks of LASHING, and has irons on her feet.'

'Ran away, a negro woman and two children. A few days before she went off, I burnt her with a hot iron, on the left side of
her face. I tried to make the letter M.'

'Ran away, a negro man named Henry; his left eye out, some
scars from a dirk on and under his left arm, and much scarred
with the whip.'

'One hundred dollars reward, for a negro fellow, Pompey. 40
years old. He is branded on the left jaw.'

'Committed to jail, a negro man. Has no toes on the left foot.'

'Ran away, a negro woman named Rachel. Has lost all her
toes except the large one.'

'Ran away, Sam. He was shot a short time since through the hand, and has several shots in his left arm and side.'

'Ran away, my negro man Dennis. Said negro has been shot in the left arm between the shoulder and elbow, which has paralysed the left hand.'

'Ran away, my negro man named Simon. He has been shot badly, in his back and right arm.'

'Ran away, a negro named Arthur. Has a considerable scar across his breast and each arm, made by a knife; loves to talk much of the goodness of God.'

'Twenty-five dollars reward for my man Isaac. He has a scar on his forehead, caused by a blow; and one on his back, made by a shot from a pistol.'

'Ran away, negro girl called Mary. Has a small scar over her eye, a good many teeth missing, the letter A is branded on her cheek and forehead.'

'Ran away, negro Ben. Has a scar on his right hand : his thumb and forefinger being injured by being shot last fall. A part of the bone came out. He has also one or two large scars on his back and hips.'

'Detained at the jail, a mulatto, named Tom. Has a scar on the right cheek, and appears to have been burned with powder on the face.'

'Ran away, a negro man named Ned. Three of his fingers are drawn into the palm of his hand by a cut. Has a scar on the back of his neck, nearly half round, done by a knife.'

'Was committed to jail, a negro man. Says his name is Josiah. His back very much scarred by the whip; and branded on the thigh and hips in three or four places, thus (J M). The rim of his right ear has been bit or cut off.'

'Fifty dollars reward, for my fellow Edward. He has a scar on the corner of his mouth, two cuts on and under his arm, and the letter E on his arm.'

'Ran away, negro boy Ellie. Has a scar on one of his arms from the bite of a dog.'

'Ran away, from the plantation of James Surgette, the following negroes: Randal, has one ear cropped; Bob, has lost one eye; Kentucky Tom, has one jaw broken.'

'Ran away, Anthony. One of his ears cut off, and his left hand cut away with an axe.'

'Fifty dollars reward for the negro Jim Blake. Has a piece cut out of each ear, and the middle finger of the left hand cut off to the second joint.'

'Ran away, a negro woman named Maria. Has a scar on one side of her cheek, by a cut. Some scars on her back.'

'Ran away, the Mulatto wench Mary. Has a cut on the left arm, a scar on the left shoulder, and two upper teeth missing.'

I should say, perhaps, in explanation of this latter piece of description, that among the other blessings which public opinion secures to the negroes, is the common practice of violently punching out their teeth. To make them wear iron collars by day and night, and to worry them with dogs, are practices almost too ordinary to deserve mention.

'Ran away, my man Fountain. Has holes in his ears, a scar on the right side of his forehead, has been shot in the hind parts of his legs, and is marked on the back with the whip.'

'Two hundred and fifty dollars reward for my negro man Jim. He is much marked with shot in his right thigh. The shot entered on the outside, halfway between the hip and knee joints.'

'Brought to jail, John. Left ear cropt.'

'Taken up, a negro man. Is very much scarred about the face and body, and has the left ear bit off.'

'Ran away, a black girl, named Mary. Has a scar on her cheek, and the end of one of her toes cut off.'

'Ran away, my Mulatto woman, Judy. She has had her right arm broke.'

'Ran away, my negro man, Levi. His left hand has been burnt, and I think the end of his forefinger is off.'

'Ran away, a negro man, NAMED WASHINGTON. Has lost a part of his middle finger, and the end of his little finger.'

'Twenty-five dollars reward for my man John. The tip of his nose is bit off.'

'Twenty-five dollars reward for the negro slave, Sally. Walks *as though* crippled in the back.'

'Ran away, Joe Dennis. Has a small notch in one of his ears.'

'Ran away, negro boy, Jack. Has a small crop out of his left ear.'

'Ran away, a negro man, named Ivory. Has a small piece cut out of the top of each ear.'

While on the subject of ears, I may observe that distinguished abolitionist in New York once received a negro's ear, which had been cut off close to the head, in a general post letter. It was forwarded by the free and independent gentleman who had caused it to be amputated, with a polite request that he would place the specimen in his 'collection'.

CHARLES DICKENS, *American Notes*, 1842

*

AT BENARES I saw a priest, or other official, ladling out to weary sin-sick pilgrims small doles of water of a 'holy' but filthy well, which sent up an effluvium like a common sewer, and the poor wretches drank, as fast as it could be handed to them, the dirty libation in the hope of obtaining forgiveness of sins: and around the filthy purlieus of that centre of idolatry hovered from windows and balconies shameless dancing girls, inviting the passers in the narrow streets to their dens.

In Bombay I saw in an evening ramble of observation, small shops with various coloured and various labelled bottles arrayed within reach of a priest of Bacchus, who sat cross legged on a barrel or other elevation, waiting to dispense the liquid of seduction, and from his shrine, either behind or from a side passage was a way to rooms above, from the windows and balconies of which lewd women were calling, singing and gesticulating to promenaders in the public street; and at the doors of some of the more fashionable resorts carriages were detained while their occupants were gone to worship at these double shrines of idolatry and vice.

THOMAS COOK, Letter to *The Times*, February 1873

*

SIR,

It must be in consequence of the precariousness of punishment, that this city furnishes many more delinquents, in proportion to its dimensions, than our wicked *London.* I think there are in the prisons here, about four or five thousand, (suppose two or three thousand) besides about two thousand in the galleys, lying in the harbour. Those in the galleys are chained two and two, and may be thought to suffer from lying on the decks; but their condition is far preferable to that of many of the poor, who lie in the streets; besides, that they have a certain allowance of bread from the King, and even some cloathing; but above all, and what renders the life of a poor *Neapolitan* happy, they are, in a manner, exempt from labour; for very few are employed in cruizing, or other business: What work they do aboard the vessels, is chiefly for their own benefit, and, I may say, luxury. If a taylor, a shoe-maker, or any other handicraftsman earns a few pence, he puts a part of it at least into his pocket, and purchases some rarity, the government, as I have intimated before, furnishing him with bread. The galleys lye very near my lodgings, and I have often diverted myself with speculating on the lives and manners of these slaves. The *Neapolitans* are not a gay mercurial people, but those aboard the galleys are by no means graver than those out of the galleys; and a man who has visited them so frequently as I have done, will never afterwards, when he means to picture extreme misery, represent it as the proverb does, in the shape of a galley-slave. I have seen a musician aboard, entertaining them with vocal and instrumental musick, whom I supposed one of their gang, but upon enquiry, found he was a poor man, they paid for his performances when they were disposed to be merry; and I do not doubt but this poor man styled those we call wretches, his good masters. If then so sober, so phlegmatic a nation as *Italy,* find such delights aboard a galley, what do you think of the lively skipping *Frenchmen* in the galleys at *Marseilles*? I should suppose, take one with another, they are a jollier, happier, set of people than our city *plumbs*. There are many services, however, to which these idle fellows might be very properly destined, such as mending the horrid roads of this kingdom, which could not fail to redound to the honour and profits of the nation, and at a very small immediate expence; but, as I told you before, the police here is not on a good footing.

I have, in some of my letters, mentioned how often murderers escape unpunished, and have assigned it as the obvious reason, why murders are so much more frequent in *Naples* than *London*. Would you believe it possible, that a magistrate of this city, a few days since, declared to a Gentleman who interrogated him on this subject, that the preceding week the populace had been very orderly, for that only four murders had been committed! I have this account from very good authority, a *Neapolitan,* of great birth, and a high station, who attests it to be a fact. Perhaps, however prone the populace are to so atrocious a deed as murder, the relation may be exaggerated; yet certainly, they do not here hold it in such horror as we do in the colder climates. A young Gentleman informs me, that, on the road to this place from *Rome,* he saw, at a distance, a scuffle amongst some postilions, in which, as it proved afterwards, one of them was stabbed dead. Upon an enquiry into the occasion of the tumult, his messenger was cooly answered, that it was a *colpo di coltello* (a stab with a knife.) If the guilty escape, or the innocent are convicted, you, an *Englishman,* will not admire at it, when I tell you that the plaintiff and defendant do not appear face to face before the judges, nor are the evidences confronted; but the method of trying criminal causes here, is, by the intervention of two *Scrivanos* (Attorneys) one on the side of the prosecutor, and the other of the delinquent, the first of which, states the accusation, and the other the defence; after that, the judges, by a plurality of voices, determine according to the nature of the evidence; a very loose vague manner of deciding causes of this nature, and which must leave a door open to a thousand subterfuges, chicaneries, and villanies; in fact, by this means justice is often eluded, either absolutely, or for a length of time; and the delays of criminal causes become as tedious as the delays of civil causes.

It a little hurts me, that so many of my accounts from this kingdom should seem severe. I desire, therefore, you will remark, that my censures regard chiefly the morals of the lower people, and the gallantry of the great. I wish I could always write panegyric; for, speaking as an *Englishman,* every partiality allowable should be admitted in their favour. I assure you, the politeness of the *Italians* towards our nation, is very extraordinary: Towards the *French* they are not so cordial; that people, by their frequent and wanton invasions of *Italy,* for some few centuries past, have given birth to a national animosity, which will not soon be appeased.

There are not, as I have said, many of the Nobility who keep any kind of open table; but those who do, never fail to invite such *English* whose quality, connections, or recommendatory letters, render them proper company for people of the first rank. The Prince of *Franca Villa* closed the carnival last week with a splendid dinner, (perhaps more splendid than any you see in *London,*) provided for eighteen guests, ten of which were the *English* Gentlemen on their travels. I do not find, by my observations, that foreigners think so abjectly of us as we do ourselves. It is much for our honour that they do not read our news-papers, so filled with groans, complaints and despair, on the subject of our present state; for abroad we are esteemed a happy, rich, triumphant nation. Madam ——, a *German* Lady of the first distinction, has lately procured the good opinion of the *English,* by a *repartee,* which, however, came better from her mouth than it does from my pen, as it owes some part of its beauty to the emphasis with which she uttered it. It seems she had fallen into a slight altercation with a *Frenchman* on national subjects, and being a little provoked by his manner, which she thought vain and overbearing, she told him with some indignation, *Sir, you Frenchmen, I know, despise every nation under the sun, except the* English, *and them you hate; but you would despise* them *if you could.*

I am, Sir, &c.

SAMUEL SHARP, *Letters from Italy,* 1767

*

AFTER PASSING through two little towns; in one of which, Acquapendente, there was also a 'Carnival' in progress: consisting of one man dressed and masked as a woman, and one woman dressed and masked as a man, walking ankle-deep through the muddy streets, in a very melancholy manner.

CHARLES DICKENS, Pictures From Italy, 1846

*

YESTERDAY AFTER a sad night of sickness from stomach disordered, you sprung up before seven, and taking a dram, went out to St Catherine Porte, where you made interest with honest German Carabineer and got into his box and saw Madame pass. She looked angelic, and that glimpse was ravishing. You then treated sentinel with Geneva [gin]. You stood on ramparts and saw her disappear. You was quite torn with love. Then you entered to fencing. You was very bad all day. Yet you was silent. At Madame Nassau's you was cheerful, yet on guard, but affected a little gloom. Mem., ill-humour is a crime; combat. Mademoiselle said you had much *bonheur,* and thought you content. Keep that character. Love has now fairly left you, and behold in how dreary a state you was in. At night you was listless and distressed and obliged to go crawling to bed. This day study hard; get firm tone; go on. Mademoiselle will be your friend.

JAMES BOSWELL, Boswell in Holland, 1763–4

*

COLOGNE O. RHINE

JOHN MARIA FARINA
(OPPOSITE THE JULICH'S PALACE),
Purveyor to H.M. Queen Victoria;
To H. M. F. W. III., King of Prussia;
The Emperor of Russia;
The King of Hanover, Etc., Etc.,
of the
ONLY GENUINE EAU DE COLOGNE

THE FREQUENCY of mistakes, which are sometimes accidental, but for the most part the result of deception practised by interested individuals, induces me to request the attention of English travellers to the following statement :

Since the first establishment of my house in 1709, there has never been any partner in the business who did not bear the name of FARINA, nor has the manufacture of a second and cheaper quality of EAU DE COLOGNE ever been attempted. Since 1828, however, several inhabitants of Cologne have entered into engagements with Italians of the name of Farina, and, by employing that name, have succeeded to a very great extent in foisting an inferior and spurious article upon the Public.

But they have in this rivalry in trade not been satisfied with the mere usurpation of my name; the concluding phrase, *'opposite the Julich's Palace,'* which had so long existed my special property, was not allowed to remain in its integrity. To deceive and lead astray again those of the public who are not fully conversant with the locality and circumstances, the competition seized hold of the word *'opposite'*, and more than once settled in my immediate neighbourhood, that they might avail themselves to the full extent of the phrase *'opposite the Julich's Palace.'* When tried before the courts, the use only of the word *'opposite'* was forbidden, which, however, has been supplied by the word *'at'* or *'near'*, with the addition of the number of their houses. It is true, another less flagrant, but not less deceitful invention, was, that several of my imitators established the sites of their manufactories in other public places of the town, to enable them to make use of the phrase *'opposite —— Place, or Market'*, on their address cards or labels, speculating, with respect to the proper name *'Julich'*, on the carelessness or forgetfulness of the consumer. I therefore beg to inform all strangers visiting Cologne that my establishment, which has existed since 1709, is exactly opposite the Julich's Palace, forming the corner of the two streets, Unter Goldschmidt and Oben Marspforten, No. 23; and that it may be the more easily recognised, I have put up the arms of England, Russia, &c. &c., in the front of my house. By calling the attention of the public to this notice, I hope to check that system of imposition which has been so long practised towards foreigners by coachmen, valets-de-place, and others, who receive bribes from the vendors of the many spurious compounds sold under my name.

A new proof of the excellence of MY manufacture has been put beyond all doubt by the fact of the Jury of the Great Exhibition in London having awarded ME the Prize Medal. – See the Official Statement in No. 20,934, page 6, of the '*Times*' of this month.

COLOGNE, *October,* 1851.   J.M. FARINA,
Opposite the Julich's Palace.
MURRAY'S *Handbook to Southern Italy,* 1855

*

I LEFT Paris in the diligence after Mass – it being Sunday. Unluckily once a week the vehicle of that name which goes to Lyons has ten passengers (a late Regulation – it used to have but eight) and this it was my lot to go in. Such a pack of legs etc., squeezed together, made it very fatiguing and disagreeable, and made all our legs swell terribly. Our company consisted of my friend the Captain and two cadets under his care, a *Chevalier de St Louis,* a gentleman of *Provence,* a young officer, an old wine merchant, a merchant of Amsterdam native of Milan, the Duke of Parma's surgeon and your Humble. We dined at *Fountaine-bleau* about 42 miles from Paris. By this time we were all acquainted and though there were no females, the conversation never slept if either the Chevalier or provençale gentleman were awake; for such eternal talkers and prosers the whole fair sex has never yet been able to boast. 1st night at Pont sur Yonne at a miserable village and Inn – but, compared with the English, the Inns throughout France are all miserable – and as to dirtiness one need only say once for all that the French are intolerable. The eating and drinking all the way was good enough for me though my countrymen would find fault with it, had it been better. Monday morning we set out at 4 and between 5 and 6 were at Sens, a large but ill built City, where we only stopped to change horses – dined at Joigny, passed through Auxerre another large old City, and at night lay at Vermonton – where I remembered with regret the company and evening I spent 4 years before. Dined on Tuesday at Rouvray by the waterside – where we saw the first pretty girl we had met with since we left Paris and the whole company was so struck with the novelty of the sight, that they all at the same instant applauded her by clapping hands violently. To say the truth as one goes towards the south the complexions are not only worse and worse but even the features. We got pretty soon into *Arnay le Duc* a small old fortified town – terribly mauled and tired. However after supper the company rallied their spirits and sung and danced till near 11 o'clock tho' we had been called up that morning at $\frac{1}{2}$ an hour past 2 and were to set off at the same time next day.

CHARLES BURNEY, *Men, Music and Manners*, 1773

*

THE INN to which we had been recommended at Quartes was full, or else the landlady did not like our looks. I ought to say, that with our long, damp india-rubber bags, we presented rather a doubtful type of civilization. 'These gentlemen are pedlars? – *Ces messieurs sont des marchands?*' asked the landlady. And then, without waiting for an answer, which I suppose she thought superfluous in so plain a case, recommended us to a butcher who lived hard by the tower, and took in travellers to lodge.

Thither we went. But the butcher was flitting, and all his beds were taken down. Or else he didn't like our look. As a parting shot we had 'These gentlemen are pedlars?'

It began to grow dark in earnest. We could no longer distinguish the faces of the people who passed us by with an articulate good-evening. And the householders of Pont seemed very economical with their oil; for we saw not a single window lighted in all that long village. I believe it is the longest village in the world; but I daresay in our predicament every pace counted three times over. We were much cast down when we came to the last auberge; and looking in at the dark door, asked timidly if we could sleep there for the night. A female voice assented in no very friendly tones. We clapped the bags down and found our way to chairs.

The place was in total darkness, save a red glow in the chinks and ventilators of the stove. But now the landlady lit a lamp to see her new guests; I suppose the darkness was what saved us another expulsion; for I cannot say she looked gratified at our appearance. We were in a large bare apartment, adorned with two allegorical prints of Music and Painting, and a copy of the law against public drunkenness. On one side, there was a bit of a bar, with some half-a-dozen bottles. Two labourers sat waiting supper, in attitudes of extreme weariness; a plain-looking lass bustled about with a sleepy child of two; and the landlady began to derange the pots upon the stove, and set some beefsteak to grill.

'These gentlemen are pedlars?' she asked sharply. And that was all the conversation forthcoming. We began to think we might be pedlars after all. I never knew a population with so narrow a range of conjecture as the innkeepers of Pont-sur-Sambre.

R. L. STEVENSON, *An Inland Voyage,* 1908

*

WE WENT to *Aix* [Aix les Bains] to breakfast – that is to some raw hartichoaks stinking oil, salt and pepper – *a la poivreade.* We visited the famous hot baths here – the water of which seems to me much hotter than that at Bath in England. I drank 2 glasses of it to facilitate digestion of that nothing I had to eat etc. These baths I believe were built by the Emperor Gratian. There are several Roman inscriptions here, and many other antiquities; but nothing can have a more antique or *ruinous* appearance than the whole town, which however is in summer a good deal frequented on account of its waters, in dispight of every inconvenience of bad lodging, provisions, etc. The water is very offensive to the smell . . .

CHARLES BURNEY, *Men, Music, and Manners,* 1773

*

GOLDONI IS the most celebrated dramatic poet modern Italy has produced. He is called the Italian Moliere; but surely is very inferior. Low buffoonery you see naturally represented; but the elegant and easy manner of polite comedy, or the elevated sentiments of the Buskin, you cannot expect in a country where they have no longer any models for either. What think you of a Heroine who takes a flying leap out of a window, shewing at the same time to the spectators the most ignoble part of her body? – or of a poor Poet who catches his lice upon the stage, and throws them at the prompter? – or of Harlequin who eats pomatum, and drinks out of a chamber-pot? – Scenes which would not be tolerated at Bartholomew's Fair, are applauded here.

PETER BECKFORD, *Familiar Letters From Italy,* 1805

*

NAPLES, *March* 1766.

SIR,

Sermons are not the pursuit of the gentry in Catholick countries, and good preachers are therefore uncommon. I had rashly flattered myself I should have gathered much fruit from the pulpit, or at least, that I should have been entertained. At this season of the year, preachers of the most distinguished parts quit their convents, and spread themselves through the great cities of *Italy,* to instruct the people, and display their own talents. You may imagine such a capital as *Naples* invites some of the most eminent amongst them. These I have followed; but, as I have hinted, am disappointed and mortified. A foreigner cannot be too cautious in forming an opinion on the declamation, either of the stage or the pulpit: In every country, there is a different tone peculiar to that country, which it requires a man should be born there, to taste and to feel; so that what is sweetness to a native, is dissonance to a stranger. Making therefore an allowance for the chant of *Italian* eloquence; and supposing that their sing song manner of preaching be persuasive and masculine, I will endeavour to assign other reasons why I am mortified.

The picture of St *Paul* preaching at *Athens,* and the comparison (so common) of his attitude, with the action of the *Italian* preachers, had given me great prejudices in their favour : I had not conceived, till I was brought to the experiment, how dangerous it is to attempt much action, which, to be graceful, demands the nicest guidance. Some of the pulpits here, are a kind of gallery, which allow great scope for action : the injudicious preachers do not fail to take the advantage of it : very often in the heat of their discourse running from one end to the other; and it is this excess, this abuse of action, which I object to. It is the habit of this country to employ much action in the most trivial conversations : This habit infests the bar and the pulpit, and, from an indiscriminate application of it, on slight occasions, the force and effect of it is lost on great ones. We see upon the stage, where action is studied, how few know how to adapt it to the sentiment and degree of passion they are to express; no wonder, therefore, if the generality of preachers, men bred up in a monastery, far from the circle of the polite world, and perhaps, under the influence of a superstitious enthusiasm, should be deficient in an art of so delicate a nature. You see my opinion is, that, however powerful action may be, when restrained within the bounds of decorum and good sense, it becomes unpleasant and disgustful when it runs into boisterousness, as is too frequently the case in Italy.

But what gives me more offence still, is, a familiarity of stile which they have introduced into their compositions, when even God Almighty and our Saviour are the subject in question. I went the other day to hear the most celebrated preacher now in *Naples,* who, amongst other inelegancies, gave us a familiar dialogue, in a very familiar manner, betwixt God and *Jesus Christ,* in which our Saviour begg'd and pray'd him that he would not damn mankind; but God being inexorable, and deaf to all intreaty, our Saviour said, 'Why then if your justice must exceed your mercy, be so good to damn me and spare them.' This the preacher told us God was *so good* to comply with. I believe I have not mistaken him a jot, because another Gentleman, who was present, agreed with me in every particular, word for word, and I was so fearful of misrepresenting the truth, that I immediately committed it to paper. Now, if I do not abuse your confidence, and if this preacher be in the highest estimation, as I believe he is, in what a state of barbarism must the pulpit be at this juncture!

There has crept also into fashion, an idle custom of telling a story in their sermons, with which they sometimes finish their discourse, as our clergy do with a practical inference. It is true, the moral of their stories is meant to be a religious one, but their attempts to tell them in the character of a fine Gentleman, and a man of the world, you will readily imagine must often miscarry. A certain Catholick Lady informed me, that last year she was at church, when a celebrated Jesuit told the following story. – 'That Queen *Elizabeth,* so famous throughout the world for her heresy, made a compact with the Devil, that if he would indulge her in all she desired, and suffer her to reign so many years, she would surrender her soul at the conclusion of that term.' Accordingly, the day she died, there was a great black cloud ascended from the *Thames,* which drew the attention of an infinite number of spectators, who, at last, heard a voice from the cloud pronounce these words, *I am the soul of Queen* Elizabeth, *now going to the Devil for the sins I have committed.* There is one week in Lent, that most of the Ladies of distinction go to hear a sermon every day in the above-mentioned church, and it was on one of those days, the Jesuit told this story to the politest congregation in *Naples.*

The preachers here, have a crucifix, about two feet high, sticking close to their elbow, in the pulpit, but moveable at pleasure. The *Christ* upon it has, generally, a crown of thorns, and the streams of blood down his face and breast are painted with a lively red. At the conclusion of the sermon, or on any other apposite occasion, when the preacher is to set forth the sufferings and agonies of our Saviour, dying for the salvation of the world, he takes the crucifix in his hands, and displays the bleeding wounds of the image, when, if he have any pathetic powers, he never fails to extort from the audience such marks of contrition and horror, such knockings on the breast, such an effusion of tears, and, sometimes, amongst the women, such involuntary hysterical screams, as you Protestants have no idea of; so forcibly is the soul acted on when the eyes are the instruments by which it feels, and not the ears only. The adopting such a crucifix for that use in *England,* would be a dangerous experiment; but, were it practised, I would defy any of the audience to sleep, as they do now a days, in Protestant churches.

Powerful as the crucifix usually is, particularly in the hands of an eloquent priest, I am tempted to tell you a ludicrous story, bordering upon prophaneness, where its efficacy failed; it is one of those instances where a burning zeal, through a deplorable ignorance, furnishes matter of raillery to scoffers, and compassion to such who are truly religious. – At *Naples* there is a place called the *Largo del Castello,* not unlike our *Tower-Hill,* the resort of the idle populace. Here, every afternoon, Monks and Mountebanks, Pick-pockets and Conjurors, follow their several occupations. The Monk (for I never saw more than one at a time) holds forth, like our itinerant field-preachers, to what congregation he can collect; the Mountebank, by means of Punch, and his fellow comedians, endeavours to gather as great an audience as he can. It happened one day, that Punch succeeded marvellously, and the poor Monk preached to the air, for not a living creature was near him : Mortified and provoked that a puppet-shew, within thirty yards of him, should draw the attention of the people from the Gospel to such idle trash, with a mixture of rage and religion he held up the crucifix, and called aloud, *Ecco il vero Pulcinella:* '*Here is the true* Punchinello, – *come here,* – *come here!*' The story is so well known in *Naples* to be true, that the most devout people tell it; and, were it not for such a sanction, I should hardly have repeated it.

> *I am, Sir, &c.*
> Samuel Sharp, *Letters from Italy,* 1767

Afterthought

Then there were the abroad people. Naturally they had
viewpoints of their own, some of them not very charitable – and
scarcely any of them charitable enough to suppose that the English
would be charitable enough to allow them an afterthought, or
for that matter even a forethought. But so it is. Philip Guedalla,
who was English but had a foreign-sounding name, remarked
that the 'Englishman is a man who lives on an island in the North
Sea governed by Scotsmen'. But he also said, of Henry James,
who was foreign but had an English-sounding name, that 'his
work has always seemed divisible by a simple dynastic arrangement
into three reigns : James I, James II, and the Old
Pretender' – proving that he didn't discriminate when it came to
blowing darts. Home or abroad was his target.

Mine also. But a generous inclination not to discriminate
does not mean a generous attention to balance. Not here anyway.
However, the angel of generosity steps in where the fool of
principle fears to tread. The underdog is the Englishman's
favourite good cause, possibly because he keeps on shouting that
he will be underdog to none; and every underdog must have his
say.

So here are a few wry, disappointed, or bewildered comments
by the abroad people. It does no nation any harm to see themselves
as others see them : which might itself count as a comment by
an abroad person. One of the governing sort of course.

*   *   *

Afterthought

THE YEAR before I had been obliged to accept a new business manager, an Englishman who in his own country was the most upright, the most impeccable of men. But as soon as he crossed the Channel! What a change! Napoleon said the English were a nation of shopkeepers, and this was precisely why I could see a great future for this man as my manager. For a shopkeeper should be a business man first above all things! But once in France and Switzerland he became under the influence of something he supposed was Continental or Oriental. For his investments were never for me alone but for himself only. I had to meet more and more constant demands for money for the enterprises which he launched and which were not prosperous, quite the reverse in fact. Well! C'est la vie! C'est Anglais!

IGNACE JAN PADEREWSKI, *The Paderewski Memoirs,*
Vol. I, 1860–1914

*

A MOST extraordinary man, an Englishman, was brought to my studio by my pupil M. Lindsay Sloper. A nobleman, the title of him being the Earl of Falmouth. He is a great lover of music, a wealthy and *grand seigneur,* and of great courtesy, though he speaks haltingly in all languages, including his own. 'We get on famously,' he said to me, though surely it is I who have the fame? But his appearance! No elegance! One might give him a copper in the street, and M. Sloper says that in his London house he has a host of lackeys better dressed than himself.

FREDERICK CHOPIN in a letter to his publisher, May 1846

*

I WANT to thank you at once for the little book and to tell you that I am profoundly touched by many things you have found it possible in your heart and conscience to say about my work. The only thing that grieves me and makes me dance with rage is the cropping up of the legend set afloat by Hugh Clifford about my hesitation between French and English as a writing language. For it is absurd. When the Englishman travels abroad the greatest gift and contribution he takes with him is his language. You may take it from me that if I had not known English from the merciful spread of the language by the English traveller I wouldn't have written a line for print in my life.

JOSEPH CONRAD in a letter to Hugh Walpole, 1908

*

I ENCOUNTERED a small fat Englishman on my way here. Though I led him along paths of music, philosophy, art and history he diverged continually to the subject that pleased him most : that of food. How very extraordinary for a nation that seems to know nothing about the arts of the table except to produce vast quantities of roast beef and turtle soup, to be interested so exclusively in that of which they understand nothing. And the same with religion : they have sixty religions and no sauce.

PRINCE FRANCESCO CARACCIOLO in a dispatch to
King Ferdinand, 1797

*

NOT ONLY England but every Englishman is an island. He has all the qualities of a poker except its occasional warmth. On the other hand, his casualness is attractive. It is pleasant to see things done without fuss. It is engaging to meet an Englishman, as I once did in Hamburg, who will casually discuss Plato's *Republic* for an hour then indolently rise and announce, 'I must be off; my boat leaves for India in half an hour.'

KARL AUGUST VON HARDENBERG, *Fragmente*, 1800

*

THE LANDLORD of the hotel at Steenvoorde. He is quite a character, a Fleming, cautious, slow, heavy and stout, with round eyes, a round nose, and a round face, a man of forty-five perhaps; he does not welcome the arriving guest, but puts obstacles in the way of his taking a room or having dinner and has to be persuaded to provide him with what he wants; when he has overcome his instinctive dislike of the English traveller he is friendly. But he remains harsh about the English tourist. He quoted some Oriental as having said 'The good traveller knows not where he is going; the perfect traveller knows not where he has come from' – this to enable him to add misanthrophically, 'The Englishman always knows where he's come from and where he's going. He will travel thousands of miles to carve his name on the Pyramid or to stand against the Sphinx to be photographed. It is arrogance, nothing but arrogance.'

SOMERSET MAUGHAM, A Writer's Notebook, 1914

Notes on the Writers

Notes on the Writers

ADDISON, JOSEPH (1672–1719)
Literary partner of Richard Steele until they quarrelled over Addison's views of the Peerage Bill. He tried to purge the stage of immorality but quickly found what others have found since – that you cannot purge anything of immorality. Only three years before he died he married the Countess of Warwick and lived very grandly at Holland House, polishing the English language and detailing the exploits of Sir Roger de Coverley, whom Steele had invented as a sort of running gag in *The Spectator*. He brought a good deal of order to the business of literary criticism, which was very ragged at the edges before he hove into sight.

ANON.
He (also, surely, she) and Trad. are among the best-unknown contributors to music, letters, and dictionaries of quotations.

BAEDEKER, KARL (1801–1859)
Like John Murray, a publisher and the son of a publisher. His business was in Coblenz and he came to an arrangement with Murray to follow the example of the London man's Handbooks. He advanced the guide-book business a stage further by printing in German, English and French. To look at, he was Schubert to the life, though without the glasses, and he had music in him which emerged through a clarinet; but nothing like as much as the information he and his successors have compiled over the years for the benefit of the practically-minded tourist.

BATES, HENRY WALTER (1825–1892)
Self-taught naturalist who discovered 8,000 new species of insects, birds and mammals during his exploration of the Amazon and its tributaries between 1848 and 1859. Far from having the chunky construction one would expect in one so durable, he was pale, thin and ascetic. His formal education was completed by the time he was fourteen, but he taught himself Greek, Latin and French with the aid of primers in the local Mechanics' Institute, where he went to study at the end of each thirteen-hour work day in a Leicester hosiery warehouse. His first published article – in *The Zoologist* – was called 'Note on Coleopterous Insects frequenting damp places'.

BECKFORD, PETER (1740–1811)
A less interesting man than his Cousin William, who inherited money, collected art treasures, wrote *Vathek,* and built Fonthill Abbey; but a much more dedicated traveller. (William travelled mainly to escape the scandals brought about by his homosexuality.) He invented a machine for flattening the paunch. It was basically the same as the recent gimmicky 'slimming wheel'. There is no evidence that it flattened his paunch – or, indeed, that it was ever manufactured.

BENNETT, THOMAS (?–1929)
A travel agent who set up his own agency in rivalry to Cook and exploited the profitable notion of taking paid advertisements in his guide-books, offering in exchange the guarantee of a favourable plug in the text. Apart from this piece of chicanery he lived a Godly, righteous and sober life, much of it in the cool and Calvinistic countries of Scandinavia. Bennett was the man who inspired George Bernard Shaw with the virtues of Jaeger underwear.

BOSWELL, JAMES (1740–1795)
Scotch by birth, manic-depressive by nature. Macaulay called him 'a Bigot and a sot', which was typical. Boswell was much given to apostrophizing himself: 'Get on. Don't idle. Be straighfor-

ward.' Sometimes took his own advice. Told us most of what we know about Dr Johnson, the while he lived on a see-saw of hypochondria and joy. Primarily a lawyer, he was much better at being a literary chap.

BURNES, ALEXANDER (1805–1841)
'Bokhara' Burnes was a Scot who joined the East India Company at the age of sixteen. William IV used him as a messenger bearing a gift of five dray horses to the Sikh ruler of the Punjab, delivery of which meant navigating the Indus and the Chenab. During the year 1832 he travelled from Delhi to Persia and wrote about the journey in *Travels into Bokhara,* a classic of its day which brought him the lionization of London's ladies and gentlemen. His involvement in the Afghan War of 1841 resulted in his murder by an angry Afghan mob.

BURNEY, CHARLES (1726–1814)
Dr Johnson admired both the man and his histories of music, which remain read to this day. The material for his *General History of Music* was gathered during his journeys on the continent, which he made in 1770. His criticism can be criticized for its failure to appreciate Bach and Handel (unless, of course, you share that view), and his compositions are minor in other senses than that of key, for they imitated the vapid Italian scores of the day. But he was a tireless and mainly good-tempered traveller, an industrious writer, and a devoted father to his daughter Fanny, the novelist and diarist. The physicians despaired of his young life (he was said to be tubercular), which says little for their prognostications, for he lived eighty-eight years.

CARACCILO, PRINCE FRANCESCO (1752–1799)
Revolutionary sailor in the service of King Ferdinand I of Naples. His revolution was a small one and would not be thought much of nowadays, but it brought him to the yardarm of a Neapolitan frigate, from which he was hanged on Nelson's orders. An urbane and cultured man, he would have had no trouble with his

Neapolitan countrymen if he had not been so mercenary over his estates – which, they said, he valued more highly than his honour.

CHAMBERS, DR THOMAS (1809–1880)
Medical registers show him to have been a typical family doctor who had a minor appointment to the court of Queen Victoria. What the nature of the minor appointment was nobody seems to know. A family man himself (he had ten sons and four daughters), he did a fair amount of travelling – though not, apparently, far from his wife. He followed the current fashion of advising eating to keep the vapours at bay; and a patent medicine of the day, 'Appointment Wafers, for the relief of flatulence', bore his endorsement. One of his sons was a pioneer cyclist and became famous for hurtling round the Herne Hill track at astonishing speeds.

CHOPIN, FREDERICK (1810–1849)
His *oeuvre* of piano music is indestructible; but he, alas, was destroyed by tuberculosis, overwork, the weather in Majorca, and the overpowering attentions of Georges Sand.

CONRAD, JOSEPH (1857–1924)
Actually his name was Korzeniowski, but he dropped it and kept his two given names for the English literary market. He wrote elaborately and was much influenced by Henry James, whose involuted style he had better have left alone. He lacked money, good health, and confidence – the first because he was a hopeless manager, the second because he drove himself too hard, the third because he never really mastered English. All the same, his major works suffer from being translated into his native Polish.

COOK, THOMAS (1808–1892)
Has been well spoken of in the Introduction; but it might be added that before becoming a travel agent he was a carpenter and printer and after becoming one he transported the troops up the Nile for the relief of General Gordon.

244

DICKENS, CHARLES (1812–1870)

Dickens's travels in Europe and America had distinctly different results: Europe warmed and heartened him; the United States occasionally amused but more often horrified him with its brutal penitentiaries, racial segregation and slavery. His *American Notes* and the novel *Martin Chuzzlewit* expressed his horror in what American critics referred to as 'terms of insult ill becoming a writer so warmly welcomed'. Even when he returned twenty-five years later to give public readings from some of the novels that had made him famous the harshness of his criticism had not been forgotten. Nowadays his travel writing is cooped up with the *Sketches by Boz* and other minor works; but it is nonetheless perspicacious for all that.

DUMAS, ALEXANDRE (the *père*, not the *fils*) (1802–1870)

French of course; and in this anthology for the reason explained on p. 33. He stole other writers' plots, employed a team of hacks to stitch new stories together for him, and in his lifetime turned out some 300 volumes of fiction and drama – or, rather, melodrama. Aggrieved authors were always bringing actions against him for pilfering their tales, but there was no copyright as such and they always lost their cases. Dumas swashbuckled through life like his cardboard characters but left a colourful impression behind him which has not faded yet.

FORD, RICHARD (1796–1858)

Journalist, critic and traveller. Not much known about him except that he was thrice married (twice to titled ladies) and spent most of his working life writing guidance for travellers in Spain – with exemplary attention to detail, as is evidenced by the extracts in this anthology. A friend of John Murray the publisher, who commissioned him to write the Spanish *Handbooks,* and a detractor of Byron, whose *Childe Harold's Pilgrimage* he said showed 'evidence of profligacy'.

GALTON, FRANCIS (1822–1911)
A cousin of Charles Darwin. His *Art of Travel* was subtitled
'Shifts and Contrivances in Wild Countries'. He was an FRS
and Honorary Secretary of the Royal Geographical Society. He
started life as a medical student at King's College Hospital and in
his eagerness for experiment tried taking, each day, a dose of one of
the medicines in the dispensary, in alphabetical order. He stopped
at C, having taken croton oil with disastrous emetic effects; and
the only emetic he recommends in *The Art of Travel* is 'a glass of
gunpowder in warm water'. (The relief of constipation was one
of the obsessions of the Victorians.) He started travelling to relieve
the tensions of what he called 'a sprained brain' brought on by
the boredom of his student days at Cambridge.

HARDENBERG, KARL AUGUST VON (1750–1822)
Hanoverian statesman who began life life as a civil servant and
ended it, perhaps understandably, as a tetchy bureaucrat. He was
given the title of Prince to keep him out of other people's hair,
the same people having conveniently forgotten that his statesman-
ship at the Congress of Vienna had brought them miles of extra
territory in the Rhineland. Unlike that other German statesman,
Hitler, he was pro-Jewish and saw to it that the traditional re-
strictions on Jewish traders were removed.

HORREBOW, THOMAS (dates unknown)
The *Dictionary of National Biography* is as informative about
Horrebow as he is about owls in Iceland. (See p. 101.) He evidently
had a strong sense of humour or none at all.

HUNT, LEIGH (1784–1859)
Founder and Editor of the Sunday newspaper *The Examiner,* in
which his abuses of the Tory system brought him to jail for libel.
A remarkable editor, he discovered Shelley, Keats, Tennyson and
Browning. Voluminous outpourings in prose and verse, of which
little has survived except the *Rondeau* 'Jenny kissed me'. Went to
Italy in 1822 to found an English paper *The Liberal* with Shelley

and Byron; but Shelley inconveniently died and Byron uncongenially dissociated himself from the project. Hunt took a malicious swipe at him in *Lord Byron and his Contemporaries.* Quite right too; Byron was an uncongenial fellow.

JAMESON ANNA (1794–1860)
Daughter of a miniature-painter named Murphy, she was a Dubliner who would tolerate no blarney from her husband, the barrister Robert Jameson, who was appointed a judge in Dominica in 1829 but did not want to take her with him. She did not want to go anyway, and started out on a writing career – to find it much more profitable than being a judge's wife surrounded by West Indian sugar. A crossgrained woman, she was what today would be called a good hack professional. She wrote on a variety of subjects and always turned her MS in on time. Her *Legends of the Monastic Orders* was the big literary thrill of 1850, despite its being concerned with sacred iconography.

KÚKOL-YASNOPÓLSKY, MISS L. (dates unknown)
Of this transliterating lady, regretfully, nothing is known. Her task in transliterating the *Guide to the Great Siberian Railway* from Russian into English was almost as formidable as building the railway itself. Was she, one wonders, a little old lady like Constance Garnett (who translated all Dostoevsky, Chekhov, Tolstoy) or a sprightly young thing with a boy friend in the Cossacks? Her translation, though occasionally showing some amusing oddities, is on the whole remarkable.

LEAR, EDWARD (1812-1888)
Queen Victoria's drawing master. A near-sighted, slouching, ugly man who dressed sloppily and charmed everybody with his water-colours, whimsical verses and travel books. He enjoyed ill-health (in the positive sense of the phrase) because it made it necessary for him to live abroad, where he was constantly encountering new scenes to capture with his brush. 'I would have encountered the same newness in England,' he wrote, 'had I been

there and cast about me; but it is my lot to be pitched into the midst of the colourful corners of the five continents.'

MAUGHAM, WILLIAM SOMERSET (1874–1965)
The best-known, perhaps, of all twentieth-century authors, and the most fortunate. His riches were as vast as his fame. His great success was achieved through his powers as a story-teller, not because of his literary style, which was flat, dull and uninteresting. He hankered after physical immortality and went to no end of trouble to be injected with the elixir of life. In the end, though, he proved as destructible as the rest of us; and after his death his character was mercilessly dissected by numerous leapers onto the bandwagon of fame.

MONTAGU, LADY MARY WORTLEY (1689-1762)
Precocious daughter of the 5th Earl of Kingston who married the MP for Huntingdon and accompanied him on a special ambassadorial mission to Constantinople and there learned of the practice of vaccination against smallpox, which she introduced into England. She was a friend, and then an enemy, of Alexander Pope, who attacked her venomously without much effect, for she was well able to hold her own in the matter of malice. Despite her leadership of high society she was dirty, slovenly in her dress, and extremely avaricious. She was also one of the best letter writers of her day.

MURRAY, JOHN (1808–1892)
Son of Byron's publisher and himself the publisher of Darwin's *Origin of Species*. The Murray house at 50 Albemarle Street was, and to a considerable extent still is, a focal point for London literary goings-on; and after John II began publishing his 'Red Guides' it became literally the centre for Continental goings-on, for no one would have dreamed of going on the Continent without one of Mr Murray's 'stoutly bound and eminently sensible travel guides'. Or so said J. V. Desgrand, the patentee of elastic, in a booklet about the pleasures of the Pyrenees.

NUGENT, THOMAS (?–1772)

An Irishman who adopted London and was in turn adopted by Londoners, who thought his compilation of a French-English dictionary was extremely clever, which it was, and he was awarded a Fellowship of the Society of Arts and a Doctorate of Literature for it. A restless man, he was in many ways the ideal traveller, for he never stayed anywhere long enough to get under anybody's feet or in anybody's hair. He simply moved on, always hopefully. Between journeys he wrote his travel books and *Condilac's Essay on the Origin of Human Knowledge*, which was of course an essay on an essay, and very recondite too, and brought metaphysical purrings from the great Condilac himself.

PADEREWSKI, IGNACE JAN (1860–1941)

Prime Minister of Poland in 1919, concert pianist of world renown for the other years of his life. He wrote music too, had fiery red hair and an elegant figure, and is popularly supposed to have made women swoon with the romanticism of his presence. He irritated Bernard Shaw beyond measure and a great many other critics found his tampering with rhythmic measures unendurable; but the fact remains that he was the most famous and most sought-after pianist for at least five decades.

PUNCH (born 17 July 1841)

The first editor, Mark Lemon, was partly Jewish and was born behind what is now Peter Robinson's store in Oxford Street. Thackeray and Douglas Jerrold built the circulation up with their contributions and business ability. *Punch* was the first magazine to call a comic or satirical drawing a 'cartoon' – a description that is properly applied only to a sketch for a large work – e.g. the cartoons of Raphael and Michelangelo. Its famous cover, which lasted, with minor variations, for over 100 years, was the work of Richard Doyle, some of whose drawings illustrate this anthology.

ROBERTSON, GEORGE (dates unknown)

First Officer and later Master of the frigate *Dolphin* of George

III's navy, which was sent off by Their Lordships of the Admiralty under secret orders to discover what turned out to be Tahiti in 1766. He was probably about thirty-six at that time; and, as revealed by his Journal kept during the voyage, was a good navigator and a lively writer.

ROGERS, LT.-COL. ESAU (1842–1917)
A peppery old colonel of the type so often pictured as typical of peppery old colonels. He was not so old or so peppery, though, when he went to British Guiana in 1869. He wrote about his exploration endlessly, in one magazine after another, juggling the words and the advice a bit but never forgetting that having been to British Guiana he was not going to allow anybody else to forget it either. There was a demand for this sort of thing in Victorian days – as there still is, judging from the number of narratives that are published about circumnavigating the globe in everything from a teacup to a coracle. Rogers claimed to be the only man commissioned into the Queen's Royal Regiment of Foot with the name Esau, which statement no one ever challenged.

RUSSELL, SIR JOHN (1751–1836)
A Privy Councillor and a Judge. He judged in Bengal, retired from the Indian service in 1815 with a pension of £2,000 a year, and spent most of it, and his remaining years, seeing Europe 'and the remarkable people who inhabit it'.

SCOTT, ROBERT FALCON (1868–1912)
His journals of the weather-beaten expedition to the Antarctic are part of the nation's heritage, as are his ship *Discovery*, moored in the Thames below Temple Place, and the statue of him by his widow in Waterloo Place.

SHARP, SAMUEL (1700-1778)
A typical Grand Tourist and literary gent who was really gentlemanly rather than literary, though his letters are pleasingly full of what in jokier days would have been called '*Sharp* observations'.

(One can imagine Mr Pooter telling a cab driver this in italics and recording it in his diary with huge glee.) He was not the first to choose the obvious title for a book about the Grand Tour. 'One wonders', he wrote in one of his numerous letters, 'why a book-seller does not put into the world a pamphlet, or tract, describing what is to be seen and heard.' And of course one did.

SMOLLETT, TOBIAS (1721–1771)

A quick-tempered, quarrelsome man of uncertain aims who achieved fame as a picaresque novelist only after several attempts at becoming a doctor. With a number of collaborators he set up a literary word factory in Chelsea and turned out a lot of indifferent hack work; but his *Roderick Random, Humphrey Clinker* and *Peregrine Pickle* remain adventurers of whose literary merits all students of Eng. Lit. are, or should be, aware. His extensive travels abroad were made after the breakdown in his health brought about by the death of his only child in 1763.

STEVENSON, ROBERT LOUIS (1850–1894)

Had a congenital weakness of the lungs, married a divorcée, Mrs Fanny Osbourne (née Van de Grift), and wrote *Dr Jekyll and Mr Hyde* in Bournemouth, thus mildly disturbing the torpor of the residents. His voyage to America in an emigrant ship did his constitution no good at all; but *Treasure Island,* which was written for Mrs Osbourne's son, to some extent restored his health by way of the popularity it brought him. He died, not of tuberculosis but of apoplexy, while dictating a chapter of *The Weir of Her-miston* in Samoa – as strange a juxtaposition of location, *mise en scène* and circumstance as could have been imagined even by him.

THACKERAY, WILLIAM MAKEPEACE (1811–1863)

Considering that he wrote most of his novels in the Athenaeum Club they are remarkably lively. His connexion with *Punch* from 1842 to 1851 probably livened his mind to the extent that it was impervious to gloom. His wife's mind, unfortunately, became deranged after the birth of their daughter in 1840 and for all the fifty remaining years of her life she hovered on the brink of suicidal insanity. Thackeray's own physical health was no great shakes and he became hypersensitive and irascible, his irascibility building up into the great row between him and Dickens that shook literary London. He was born rich and died rich and celebrated; but between 1833 (when he lost some £20,000 in an ill-advised business investment) and 1847 (when *Vanity Fair* was published) he endured a spell of relative poverty as a competent but little-rewarded journalist.

YOUNG, ARTHUR (1741–1820)
An excellent farmer with revolutionary ideas in agriculture, an observer, statistician, surveyor, Fellow of the Royal Society, political reporter (for the *Observer*), author of a once-famous tract called *Political Arithmetic* which, astonishingly, was readable. He was also Britain's first Minister of Agriculture, though in those days Ag was a Board, not a Ministry, and he was called a Secretary. He farmed Bradfield Estate in Suffolk, which he inherited from his father, a parson.